CP 1st 15"

THE
PIKE
FAMILY

By

ROBERT PAGE LINCOLN

Illustrated by

FRED EVERETT

THE STACKPOLE COMPANY
HARRISBURG, PENNSYLVANIA

Printed in the U.S.A.

By

THE TELEGRAPH PRESS

Established 1831

Harrisburg, Pennsylvania

FOREWORD

This is the final work of one of the most inveterate anglers of this land and one who for four decades was a most prolific outdoor writer. His experiences were rich, his interest untiring and his influence widespread. His friend Gus Albright wrote as follows about the old master in the pages of *Outdoor Sportsman*.

Robert Page Lincoln has made his last river float and cast his last plug. News of his death will bring saddness to the hearts of many who cling close to the sport of fishing, for his personal acquaintances ran into the thousands throughout the whole of North America.

"Bob Lincoln, perhaps more than any other one person, did more to exploit the good and the bad in America's fishing waters; for to him fishing was of such personal interest that he devoted his life to the outdoors in pursuit of all available first hand knowledge obtainable on the subject. As a magazine writer, newspaper columnist and book author there was a note of sincerity in his writings that bespoke authority. He would spare no effort or personal feeling to impart his own findings to a vast reading audience.

"Bob 'took to writing' at the early age of fourteen and in those forty-seven years (61 at death) he has, without question, put into print more words on the subject of fishing in America than any person of his time. He was probably the first to bring to the attention of outdoor America a form of angling peculiarly adapted to the clear water streams of the Ozark region, now widely known as "float-fishing."

"Bob Lincoln was America's foremost authority on bass fishing. It was this king of fresh-water fish that presented an everlasting challenge to his many years of angling know-how, and it is a fitting climax to a life time of matching wits with these big and smallmouth scrappers that this summer brought the publication of his book, entitled *Black Bass Fishing*. This book will stand as a living memorial to Robert Page Lincoln's many fishermen friends.

"In his many columns of writing Bob Lincoln expressed himself as he saw it and lived it. He would pull no punches in his tirades against his dams, pollution and politics in conservation. His feelings were those of the every-day fisherman, the boat dock operator, the fishing guide, the little man and the next generation. He was forever blasting for pure, free water and, whether right or wrong in what he believed, no one could ever deny his sincere and honest approach backed by years of experience and travel.

"There was never a dull moment around Bob Lincoln. He could entertain for hours recalling his experiences in various parts of the country. Like his writings, his laughter was sincere and hearty. To know him was to like him; to like a man is to make a friend. Bob Lincoln was just that to millions of fishermen all over the world."

TABLE OF CONTENTS

PART I

*Northern Pike, Pickerel
and Wall-Eyed Pike*

IN THE BEGINNING

The one great big red letter day in any active boy's life is when he catches his first pickerel, or, if you will, his first great northern pike. The chances are that though many years have passed since the experience was realized, that day shines in memory now with the same brilliancy as it did then. The first pickerel you caught (and in those days the pike and the pickerel were joined as one) may not have weighed more than two or three pounds but, nevertheless, it was a monster in comparison to the fish you have caught up to date. An old fisherman told you that it was a "grass snake" but you were firm in your conviction that it was a pickerel.

"Yes," he said, "that's true enough; its a pickerel all right, but at the same time its a snake pickerel." You appealed to your father for help in properly classifying the fish you had taken, and you remarked with regard to what the old fisherman had said. Your father sniffed in disdain. He said: "The fish is a true pike as you will notice by the spots up and down its sides. Fishermen call small pike or pickerel snake pickerel probably because they are not very big around and they don't like them. They don't call a large pike or pickerel a snake pickerel, because when they get one they have more pounds of flesh. They have respect for a large fish but only contempt for a small one. That's why the old fisherman said yours was a "snake pickerel."

Your first pickerel may have been caught by means of a linen or cotton line of chalkline proportions to which was attached a large bass hook, and on the hook was transfixed a large frog that you had fallen foul of in a mud hole. The frog perhaps had jumped into the depression hoping that he was free from that greatest of all predators, Man. But a quivering, clutching, avaricious hand, with grimy fingers, had been thrust down and was presently withdrawn with the squirming victim. When you hooked on this protesting and terror-stricken creature and cast it out in the pads you had many hopes but never that such a finny monarch as a two pound pickerel would take it. But one did just the same and the next minute you were working the freshly cut hickory pole like all fury. You didn't stop to "play" him much though, for you threw the pole down, skidding it shoreward along the bottom and grabbed the line and ran and plunged for land with your mouth open and breathing hard. Finally the pickerel lay there on the ground flapping and opening his mouth.

Some of the expressions you used might be recorded. You said: "Gee whiz! Sufferin' cats! Jiminy—crickets! Will you look at that! Well—I'll—be—darned!"

Thus you gave way to your emotion and you were so nervous and awe-struck that you couldn't do anything but sit there staring at it. All the treasures of the Incas, the wonders of Aladdin and all other wonders lumped together as one could not have made such an impression on you as this adventure. You knew then that the world was, in reality, at your feet. You realized it as one realizes that there is a nail in the shoe. Fame was nudging you. Courtiers were come to welcome your presence in mighty courts. A serene feeling possessed you as your nervousness began to subside and you realized that the fish was really and truly safe in your hands. This you took pains to ascertain by judging accurately the distance between the lake and where the fish reposed. To make doubly sure, however, you carried him about ten feet farther inland and sat down to view him from another speculative angle. The feeling that stole comfortably over you was one that seemed to suggest, Now that I have gotten this far, anything is possible. When, after a long time, you decided that it was best to go home (being sure to walk around the pasture with the bull in it), you cut a stick with a stop or hook on it and slid the fish on, during which process you paused to look down in that pickerel's mouth. It was green inside, and you can remember the incident as vividly now as though it had happened only last week.

On your way home many people were met and they all paused to question, nod kindly to you and smile. You stopped to show your catch to old Bill, the carpenter, and he laid down his saw, adjusted his glasses and began:

"So you got him did you? At last you got him. I always said you would. Got that ol' pickerel over there by the broken-down cottonwood tree. Now that's what I call a *fish*. That's a mighty fine specimen I'd say. Course it ain't as large as it might be but I tell you son its sure a dandy. Come now, tell me all about it."

And you told, and you were going to say that you fought him hither and yon over the pool to the last ounce of his energy but somehow or other the baleful glare beneath Old Bill's (they called him "Windy" Bill, you remember) glasses, wormed the truth out of you. Later of course you had to bump into the Old Fisherman and he threw the wet blanket over the deed as previously recorded. When you came home your mother was waiting to chastise but remained to pray. Your father arrived home that night with four kinds of an appetite—the kind of an appetite that digests boards with unthinkable ease. The whole blessed pickerel had been rolled in cracker crumbs and had been fried deep in bacon grease to a golden brown. When your father opened the dish and looked in, his face broadened into a sunrise and he drank in the delicious arona of the offering with an unutterable feeling of reverence. He may not have eaten the fish, bones and all, but you were pleased to take note of the fact that when the ceremony was over there were comparatively few of the fish's structural apparatus knocking around.

But no method of fishing was equal to that of snaring pickerel which was done in the home creek later on. Snaring pickerel or any fish may not have any degree of sportsmanship

attached to it, but as a method of getting fish, you found it
had all the earmarks of success spelled with a capital S.
Snaring pickerel you found to your amazing happiness was a
most prolific method of getting pickerel to be found in this
world or in the next. It had all the delights and sensations of
catching fish in a net, which, the old-timer told you, was the
only way, after all, to fish for results.

Now in snaring pickerel a copper wire was used. You
simply made a six or eight inch noose on the wire, the main
wire being wound around the tip of the pole. It hung down
a matter of a foot. The manner in which this snaring process
was conducted was nothing if not simple and easy to fathom.
You walked along the bank, studying the waters below you
with an eagle eye. Sooner or later in the course of human
events you would see a pickerel sunning himself up on a bar
and your heart almost shot out of your throat from sheer
ecstasy and amazement. The fish probably looked as though
it were a scale-shattering three or four pounds. For a time
you could not get into action. Something held you back. You
felt like the time when old Brown caught you and the gang
in the orchard and gave chase. A paralysis made you inert and
you couldn't make time. Your feet and legs were working all
right but something, that indescribable something, filled your
shoes with lead. Seeing this fish made your hands shake as
though you had the ague. You fell twice and almost broke
your pole. But that pickerel lay there just the same as when
you first saw him, apparently inseparably and profoundly
oblivious to the world outside. He was no doubt speculating
upon the size and edible qualities of the marsh frog he had
just recently crammed down his gullet. There he lay, busily
fanning the water and a large and pleased epicurean smile
stretched figuratively from one of his ears to the other. After
two ages and a scridling of minutes you got the snare in the
water, submerged the tip of the pole, watched for the glint
on the wire to lead you right and then worked the noose
toward the fish. Your hands shook; your mouth was dry and
things jumped up and down crazily before your eyes. As I
say, you drew the snare toward the fish; you missed the snare
in the water; you couldn't rightly tell whether the snare was
above, below, around or in the fish. So you lifted on the
snare, or noose, and found that it was under his jaw. The

pickerel, far from taking fright, finned the water faster than ever and backed up just two and one half inches, got his bearings and lay as he had before, probably tickled no end by the wire noose that had slid over his opercles. The next time you strained your eyesight and took a new hold with your teeth on your tongue the snare passed over the head of the fish without touching it. Over the head it went, was drawn slowly backward until it got just forward of the back fin and then you jerked. The noose went tight and up came the fish out of the water like a sky-rocket and was flung out on dry land.

The next stage in pickerel fishing was the trolling method but not by means of rod and reel. That stunt was brought to your attention and use at a later date. The trolling you did was by means of that inevitable handline of past renown. There was the green linen or cotton line of heavy caliber to the end of which was attached a large spoon that was a family heirloom. You were allowed to use it but the stipulation and rule was laid down that should you lose it, it would be replaced by no other. You remember, don't you, that the spoon was a large one, possibly a Buel spoon. It had a treble hook at its business end that originally had had a glamorous vane of flamboyant feathers on it, but these had eventually worn themselves out and some turkey feathers had been added.

It was your good fortune to accompany the old timer and you were cheerfully accorded the honor of rowing the boat. But sometimes when in a kindly mood this same old timer would let you have the honor of holding the line. It was handlining pure and simple, without any frills or furbishes, and the sport of it was "pulling them in." Sometimes two lines were out, the spoonhook of one being closer to the boat than the other. Under these circumstances the old timer not too cheerfully rowed the boat and would hold his line in his teeth, while you held yours in your two hands. You always did marvel at the old timer holding that line in his teeth, between those tobacco-browned ivories. You would look at him searchingly when he wasn't looking at you, size up his face and would try to read his thoughts. Of what was he thinking? Was his a dream of greater and brighter fame wherein a fish of whalelike proportions would be his share? Was his the feeling of a martyr, realizing that perhaps such a large fish would strike the hook with enough energy to jerk out every tooth in his head; and rather than lose such a fish would he sacrifice his teeth? You didn't know.

You generally did get pickerel though. No doubt about it. The old timer held the key to the problem. In him was vested an immense knowledge of fishing.

"When the new moon hangs in the sky so that you can hang a powder-horn on it," he would say, wagging his head profoundly, "then the fish will bite, me lad. They always strike the best during the first and second quarter of the moon."

And he would go on to say that the fishing was always poor during the full moon, and that corn and trees planted during the full moon would not do nearly as well as those planted during the first quarters of the new moon. Or maybe it was the other way around, you don't remember. But you do remember what you did in those days and as your life adds up year after year, and childhood becomes further from you with each succeeding twelve months, you begin to appreciate more and more those days of long ago and recalling them, all you remember is the "pike" or the "pickerel," and nothing can take from you the memory of those events in the home brook and the home pond. Though you fish a thousand lakes and streams and travel untold thousands of miles, in the end you gravitate, in calm retrospection, to childhood—and the pickerel. Long may his shadow flicker over the golden sands of the home brook, a never-failing anchor for your dreams!

I

HISTORY AND RANGE
OF THE NORTHERN PIKE

One of the oddities with regard to the pike is the fact that its range instead of being restricted to the North American continent only, extends over Europe and Asia especially in the north temperate and arctic regions of their countries which naturally forms a band around the globe, in which band the pike is always more or less present, in greater or lesser numbers. It seems to thrive best in a cold climate and does not do too well in increasing its kind in parts of the world where snow and ice are virtually non-existant, although there have always been attempts made to increase the range of the fish in question into warmer climes. In Greenland and in the islands of the Arctic Ocean the species does not seem to exist, although rivers flowing north from Canada into the Arctic are often plentifully supplied with the fish. At the time

when I was fishing editor on the old *Rod and Gun in Canada,*
then published at Woodstock, Ontario, we printed the story
of a trip made by a gentleman which took him to Aklavik on
the Arctic shore. He had brought all manner of sturdy fishing
tackle along with him as he had been told that the fish in
these northern streams were immense and were able, apparently, to smash the most powerful fishing equipment and
snap the strongest of lines. The gentleman remarked how he
took all of this with a grain of salt. He found out however,
how true had been the statements made. Great northern pike
up to fifty, sixty and more pounds weight were common and
nothing that he had could hold them. Lines that he had
used successfully in sea fishing were snapped like threads
by these massive members of the species. The waters were
crowded with them, and they were voracious to a degree.
The natives speared these fish for winter use. The fisherman
told about finally loosing all of his lures so that in disgust,
he had to quit, unable to cope with these weighty members
of the *lucius* breed. It is interesting to state that the gentleman
remarked that he intended going back to those Arctic shores
for another try at the big ones. I do not know if he ever
made the trip. From his description of the voraciousness of
the mosquitoes in the region one would easily think twice
before making a return jaunt, even though there might be
one hundred pound pike possible in those waters as he
stated. I always think of this most unusual incident when I
think in terms of the pike and its range, and those who state
that the species is absent from Arctic waters or streams
flowing into them. Indeed they are probably found there in
greater numbers than anywhere in the world, and that would
apply also to the northern shores of Siberia which is virtually
a duplicate of North American conditions. While there is not,
to my knowledge, any record of fish species in the northern
Siberian region, it is possible that all of the streams flowing
north into the Kara and Laptevykh Seas such as the Ob, the
Yenisei, the Olenek, the Lena, the Yana, the Indigirka, the
Kolyma and smaller streams reaching up to Bering Sea must
be well populated with the pike. There is not the least doubt
but that the pike specie as found in North American waters
originally came from Siberia by way of the Bering crossing.
This may have occurred in the dim, remote past when there

was virtually a connection between the two continents. The pike is found in Alaska, especially in the Yukon, recorded years ago by Nelson and Townsend, and is surely found in the streams flowing north from the Brooks range of Alaska. Unfortunately, as yet, there has been no possibility of properly listing the fish species in northern Siberia or along our upper North American shore. That must wait for the future.

At one time there was a contention that the pike of North America differed essentially in structural characteristics and anatomical features from the European and Asian pike. Yet it is almost a century now since Cuvier and Richardson made exhaustive studies of the two. Cuvier compared specimens from Lake Huron with European examples, and Richardson compared like individuals with the pike found in England. Both the English pike and the continental European pike coincided flawlessly, in every feature, with those studied from overseas. This would, more than ever, point to the fact that racially the European-Asian pike and the North American pike came originally out of the self-same cradle.

The manner in which varieties of a species of fish evolve in the fish world is something that has always attracted the attention of scientists and ichthyologists. It generally causes no end of speculation and inquiry and usually ends by some scholar giving the fish its technical name and a Latin designation after which it is fairly well forgotten. Such was the case in Florida where, for years, a bass that was known as a smallmouth bass was accepted as such by *Field and Stream Magazine* in its annual fishing contest. Some of these Florida "smallmouths" that were taken ranged up to fourteen pounds in weight. As a result of this the smallmouth bass division was swamped with Florida bass and true smallmouths all over the country, that were really huge for the species, were considered "too small" to be entered. It should be mentioned in this respect that the world's record smallmouth bass measured 22½ inches in length, had a girth of 21½ inches and weighed 10 pounds, 8 ounces. Yet this was a minnow compared to the alleged smallmouth bass hauled out of Florida lakes and which even the learned Francesca La Monte stated freely were typical smallmouth bass. Later on, however, after a storm broke loose which denied the fact that these so-called Florida "smallmouths" were smallmouth bass at all,

an investigation was made by Dr. Carl Hubbs, who had
named many fish varieties before, in fact he was the man
who named the Kentucky or spotted bass *(Micropterus punc-
tulatus).* The "smallmouth bass" out of Florida was called
by Hubbs the Suwanee Bass and classified by him as *(Micropterus notius).* Hubbs dismissed the "Florida smallmouth bass"
by stating that there never has been evidence of the smallmouth bass species being found in Florida.

The case of the "Silver pike" of Minnesota is an instance
where a definite variety, that could be established as differing
from either the pike, the muskellunge and the pickerels, has
been disregarded and has found no one among the scientific
body to sponsor it.

It was some time in the late 1920s that a fishing companion
of mine of years standing, Elmer Welker, of Akeley, Minnesota told me about a fish he had taken that he said looked
as though it were a hybrid or cross between the muskellunge
and the great northern pike. After fishing with him and taking
some of these fish I had to agree that they looked very much
like a cross, as they seemed to have distinct pike characteristics.
The branchio-stegal or ray count in the gill covers coincided
and so did the scalation of the cheeks and gills covers of the
silver pike with the great northern pike. And yet for all of
this the fish seemed to look more like a muskellunge than a
pike. It did not occur to us then that this might have become
an established variety of the pike family and the matter was
dropped. Then five or six years ago and so continuing up into
the present, more and more of these pike (now known as the
Silver Pike) were taken. While the first ones were fairly small
in size, gradually the length and weight of the silvers stepped
up. It culminated in the taking of a 25 pound silver pike
through the ice in the Park Rapids region two years ago.
The proof was thus offered that not only was the pike in
question not a stunted hybrid type but a healthy, ambitious
true-spawning fish in its own right and it meant to establish
itself come what may, being not a great northern pike nor
a muskellunge. It was—and is—the nation's mystery fish as of
this date!

In Eddy's book "Northern Fishes," in which the fishes of
Minnesota are classified and described, the following information is vouchsafed:

"In recent years a distinct variation of the great northern pike has appeared in several places in northern Minnesota. This variant has the morphological characters of *Esox lucius* but lacks spots or other markings. The body is usually colored a dark silver or gray, sometimes flecked with gold. The fins are finely speckled with black. The opercle is scaled on the upper half only and the cheek is entirely scaled. Occasionally specimens with faint light spots on the caudal peduncle, identical with the caudal markings of *Esox lucius,* have been found. The total number of pores on both ventral surfaces of the mandible does not exceed 10 pounds. The writers of this book have never seen specimens weighing over 10 pounds.

"This fish," continues Eddy, "was first observed about 1930 in Lake Belle Taine, of the Mantrap chain of lakes, which is located near Nevis, Minnesota, where the fish is now rather common. The local fishermen report that it did not appear in their catches until about that year. It was named 'silver muskellunge' by the fishermen, though it is undoubtedly related to *Esox lucius,* the pike, rather than *Esox masquinongy,* the muskellunge. For several years this fish and the true muskellunge have been propagated in the Nevis Hatchery and planted in nearby lakes, and consequently it has become fairly widespread.

"A specimen of this fish has been collected from Detroit Lake, west of Park Rapids, Minnesota, where none have been planted. A report of its occurence in a Lake County lake has been received. Many specimens have been reared at the University of Minnesota, some up to three years of age. Apparently they breed true, for all the offspring are marked like the parents. When they are crossed with the northern pike the resulting hybrids have a peculiar black mottling on the body. *Undoubtedly, as proved by the experimental evidence, this type is breeding true to nature, for in the lakes where this fish occurs, pure silver-colored individuals of all ages, continue to appear and possible hybrid types are uncommon.* This fish is apparently a true-breeding mutant of *Esox lucius* and has definitely established itself in several lakes *where it breeds with others of its kind rather than with the accompanying great northern pike and muskellunge.* Properly, the common name for this fish should be 'silver pike' rather than 'silver muskellunge.'"

There were 29 entries of the silver pike in Earl Fuller's fishing contest conducted annually at Park Rapids, Minnesota, for the year 1952. The prize winner for the year was a silver pike weighing 11 pounds, 11 ounces, taken in Boulder Lake of the Park Rapids region. The second prize was taken in Blue Lake of the region, and weighed 9 pounds, 10 ounces. The third prize in this silver pike class came from Bad Axe Lake of the region, weighing 8 pounds, 5 ounces. The fact that specimens of the silver pike are turning up at various points, some far removed from the Park Rapids region, is interesting. Lake County, in the northeastern part of Minnesota for instance is several hundred miles from Park Rapids. As to whether these were brought from the Park Rapids region and planted is not known. Certainly the state did not transplant these pike at far distant points in the state, but it is altogether possible that catching the fish and transplanting it will become in the future nothing short of a well established practice. It is to be observed that at the time I wrote my essay on the silver pike for *Field and Stream Magazine* most of the letters I received asked how it would be possible to obtain specimens to insert in their home lakes and streams. That such inquiries came from a rather wide area is evidenced by the fact that I received one letter from Stockholm, another from Sweden and one from New Zealand. I do not have the slightest doubt but that in ten years the entire Great Lakes region, Minnesota, Wisconsin, Michigan and western Ontario will have the silver pike well represented among its game fish species. And this planting will not be done by game and fish departments but by fishermen themselves—and how they will stock the fish!

If my own opinion were asked regarding this fish I would say that, yes, it is breeding true; it mates and propagates with its own kind; and so is, let us say, an established variety. If it produces its kind as freely, and in as great a volume as does the great northern pike, it will not take long for it to make its presence felt. As an addition to the number of our game fishes it should prove extremely welcome and I say, may its kind reign evermore and lengthen its range into new and newer waters. It may fill a place in the fishing world that neither the muskellunge or the pike can command.

Yet another oddity or two are met with in a study of the

pike family, here and abroad. In Europe and Asia for instance the pike (the same great northern pike that is found in our waters) is the sole representative of the species found over that immense area. Yet in this country we have definite off-shoots from the pike, such as the muskellunge and the three members of the pickerel delegation, namely, the banded pick-erel, the little pickerel and the chain pickerel. To say the least, this is most thought-provoking and it is to be noticed that although fish authorities are here, there and everywhere prying into the past of our various finny species, not one, as yet, has ever attempted to track down the natal period of either the muskellunge or the pickerels. About all that has been accomplished is the promulgation of a belief that the birthplace of the muskellunge was in the upper St. Lawrence region or in an area in close proximity. But as to the birth-place of the three pickerels (unknown to the European-Asian scene), this is even more of a mystery and no one has even attempted an answer to it. There are no clues to go by and no leads to set one fairly right. At one time there was a state-ment to the effect that the muskellunge was present in some waters of Europe and Asia but the most exhaustive survey, check and re-check brought nothing to light. Waters where muskellunge were said to exist produced light-colored pike, no more, no less.

The pike never was native to the country west of the Mis-sissippi River and it is very doubtful if any have ever been planted in the streams and lakes of the west. The reason for this objection to the introduction of the pike has been the knowledge that it is a most voracious destroyer of other fish species, of which of course the various trout species are uppermost in the minds of all westerners and these, they feel, must be protected at all costs. It is certain that the pike would be harmful in killing trout, hence it would be like unto inviting disaster to place pike in such waters. A rather interesting observation might be made in this respect. In Lake Sherburne in Glacier National Park, Montana, which is lo-cated at Many Glacier, one has a body of water that originally had the pike to its credit, or discredit, whichever way you look at it. How the pike got into this lake is not hard to trace. The stream that flows from Sherburne wanders northward into Alberta and makes contact with streams well populated with the great northern pike. As a result there are annual spring runs of the fish into Sherburne. This, however, is a rather rare instance of a western water producing pike, the only reason, in this instance, being that it has contact with Canadian pike waters.

That the pike extends south into the southern states is fairly well known but its abundance is never very great anywhere below the line of demarkation between the north and south, indeed the taking of one in any southern stream or lake is a matter of surprise. The southern boundary of the range does not go much below Arkansas, Tennessee and North Carolina and through these states the line of southern terminus is very jagged and uncertain. Here, again, apparently no attempt has been made to introduce the species. Opposed to the scarcity of the pike in the South, the fair abundance of the chain pickerel is to be noted, more of which will be recorded in the portion of this book devoted to the pickerels. The greatest abundance of the great northern pike would lie through those states bordering Canada and the Great Lakes, with peak abundance in the states of Minnesota, Wisconsin and Michigan. The great northern pike is not as numerous in the state of New York, however, as many would suppose, in fact in some sections it is quite scarce, this in spite of the fact that the present record in this species was taken in Sacandaga Reservoir, N. Y., in 1940 which weighed 46 pounds, 2 ounces. It seems rather odd that with the whole pike region of Canada open to draw from, that specimens equal to, if not far superior to, this figure have not been taken. There is little doubt but that hundreds have been taken above this weight however they have not been recorded. In my own case I might mention that although I have fished for pike, intentionally or otherwise all my life, in some of the best Canadian and other waters, I still have failed to take a single specimen over twenty-five pounds in weight. It would seem to be merely proof that large pike are rather the exception to the rule and are not too commonly met with. As a representative over-all view of pike taken in Minnesota, which is a great pike state, one might consider the annual fishing contest carried on at Park Rapids, Minnesota. This is in the heart of a fishing region and the pike is found in the area in fairly unusual abundance. The contest for 1952 showed 623 entries of pike, 177 being over ten pounds in weight, the prize winner being a 19 pound, 13 ounce specimen. Of course there is an abundance of lakes in the Park Rapids region, and other sections of the state would not produce as well. However, in spite of this it would go to show the size of fish normally met with, not to forget that the chances of taking a ten pound specimen are a little better than one would suspect.

One might ask, how great do the pike get to be, here, and abroad? Izaak Walton has this to say in his *Compleat Angler* in the chapter devoted to the pike:

"Sir Francis Bacon, in his History of Life and Death, observes the pike to be the longest lived of any freshwater fish; and yet he computes it to be not usually above forty years; and others think it to be not above ten years; and yet Gesner mentions a pike taken in Swedeland, in the year 1449, with a ring about its neck, declaring he was put into that pond by Frederick the Second more than two hundred years before he was last taken, as by the inscription in that ring (being Greek) was interpreted by the (then) Bishop of Worms."

Commenting apparently on the same fish, this is what Al McClane says in his excellent book on spinning, in that portion of the volume devoted to spinning for pike:

"More lies have been concocted about pike than any other fish in the world. The bigger the lie—the more quickly it has been accepted. For the all-time record, we have the famous monster purported to have belonged to Emperor Frederick of Germany—which lived for two and sixty-seven years and measured nineteen feet in length. This 350-pound fish was caught at Halibran, Germany, in 1497. The captor found an iron ring fastened in its gill covers with the following inscription: 'I am the fish which was first of all put into this lake by the hands of the Governor of the Universe, Frederick 2nd, the 5th of October, 1230.' The fish was stuffed and sat for its portrait, and soon after both corpse and painting ended up in the Mannheim Museum. There are several other less popular versions of this story, but suffice to say, the 'pike' was eventually disclosed as a sectional reconstruction of many pike. The rubbery hand of the taxidermist had done a magnificent job, however, deluding a sufficient number of people to keep the legend alive for generations to come.

Actually, a pike nineteen feet long would weigh three thousand pounds, according to the normal lenght-weight relationship."

A New York review of the pike subject (1902) stated that on the continent of Europe the largest recorded specimen was taken at Bregenty in 1862, and was said to have weighed 145 pounds. In Scotland a pike measuring more than seven feet and weighing 72 pounds was reported. Berridge (England) reports:

"Pike grow to a large size and are believed to live to a great age. Ninety pounds appears to be the maximum weight attained by one of these fish caught in British waters, an individual from the Shannon having established that record."

Berridge brings out some further facts regarding the pike that are interesting. He states:

"In olden days pike were eaten in England, and we read that in the river Cam they were kept in cages and fattened for market. The flesh of the fish was highly esteemed during the reign of Henry I; it was considered to be superior to that of any other fish.

"The ancients," continues Berridge, "believed that the pike was associated in some mysterious manner with the Crucifixion, the fish showing in the formation of the bones of its head the shape of the cross, the sword, and the nails. According to tradition, when all living creatures fled and hid themselves at that most solemn time the pike raised its head out of the water and the sight that met its gaze was forever impressed upon its head."

That there are tremendous pike inhabiting our waters, larger than any one ever dreamed of, might be taken for granted. If this is true, one might ask, why are they not taken by hook and line? Larger muskellunge by far are taken than pike, the latter species, in a large size at least, apparently being the unknown quantity. There may be a solution to this in spite of the fact that one might also say, "If the pike grows old and dies, why are they not found floating up on shore?"

In spite of its apparently vicious and aggressive nature and a particularly dominant vim and pugnaciousness that makes him truly a "scaly assassin" the pike, in no way, is equal to the muskellunge either in long life or sustained energy, this in spite of alleged traditional pike that have lived to become a hundred years or more of age. As age comes on, the fish slows up. He no longer operates in the inshore waters. He becomes more and more a bottom feeder, pushes along on the bottom, feeding mostly on bottom fish, especially bullheads. All this is especially true if blindness assails the fish in which case his days are numbered. With lack of nourishment the fish grows feeble, pushes along into the thick weeds and is eventually covered over by the same. A like manner of death no doubt comes to the muskellunge, one reason why such large fish skeletons are always found when turning the bottoms of dried out lakes. It is obvious that there is only one way in which to take these large pike and that is to fish close to the bottom, possibly with suckers for bait. One might, in this way, also inveigle a large muskellunge to take the lure. As long as ninety-eight per cent of all fishing for the pike and the musky is done in comparatively shallow water one must abide by results, not to forget, however, that some of the largest muskies are taken in comparatively shallow water, inshore.

Mention with regard to the record pike taken from the River Shannon in Ireland recalls the fact that that country is noted for the size of the pike that are found there. I am indebted to Mr. E. H. McClister for information tendered me on these Irish pike. This gentleman was three years connected with the Pan-American Airways at Limerick, Ireland, and being an enthusiastic fisherman had many opportunities to try out the waters of that country both for trout and for pike. It seems that comparatively few persons ever fish for pike in Ireland. Most of the taking of pike is done by spearing and the use of shotguns when these great fish are on the spawning shoals and vegetation. According to my informant, pike up to 75 and 80 pounds are not uncommon. Much of his fishing was done in Lough Derg, a lake on the Shannon River. He fished for days at a spot above Killaloe on this stream in the attempt to take a pike that was said to go well over 80 pounds, but although he tried all manner of plug lures and live bait he was unable to interest the fish. Three lakes, besides Lough Derg, holding especially large pike, I was told, are: Lough Mask, Lough Corrib and Lough Conn. Having brought with him from this country about every lure that the Creek Chub Company makes (since this company pro-

duces the most killing of pike lures in their familiar Pikie
Minnows), he put them to work, being curious to see what
they would do in these waters across the sea. His companion
had never before seen a plug lure, nor had their guide, a
farmer who lived on the lake and with whom they lodged.
In fact the latter stated on looking at the lure that he (Mc-
Clister) might as well discard it for all the good it would do.
McClister claims that he was doubtful himself, but put on a
musky-size straight-backed Creek Chub Pikie and made his
initial cast. He had hardly reeled the lure five feet when he
was almost jarred off his feet by a prodigious strike. He set
the hook and the fish (a pike, of course), was finally reeled
in and taken. It proved to be a 42-pound pike. That amazement was registered by his companions can be taken for
granted. But that amazement was bettered when, on two
succeeding casts, one 35 and one 38 pound pike were taken,
in fact five pike taken in a short time in that immediate
neighborhood weighed 156 pounds. According to McClister
the Creek Chub plugs in the Pikie class are sheer murder on
these Irish pike. As stated, his preference is for the straight-
backed Pikie Minnow which he thinks is superior to the
hinged or broken plug which, while having a far better action,
still does not seem to produce as well as the straight-backed
number. No American plug lures, or lures of any kind, according to this gentleman, are found in Ireland.

In consideration of the large pike that are taken in Ireland, some of the pike recorded here as world records seem
rather puny in comparison. One wonders if some of our
energetic pike and musky fishermen were released on these
Irish lakes and streams what records would be forthcoming.
What records, indeed!

Peak abundance of the pike species is found in western
and northwestern Ontario in which region there are over
28,000 lakes, great and small, and all of them apparently
inhabited by the pike. Were it not for the fact that maps
made from aerial photos taken, district after district, throughout this lake region, one would have no way of ascertaining
the tremendous total of such waters. Yet these airplane maps,
accurate to a surprising degree, reveal a home for the great
northern pike that is second to none on earth. In the next
fifty years or more these waters will become the stamping

grounds of untold thousands of fishermen from the United States. Today a huge bulk of them are noted on the map as nameless, small lakes, medium-sized lakes, large lakes, long, narrow, riverlike lakes and some little more than pin-pricks on the map, yet when you come to the pin-prick you are likely to find it a lake two miles in length. For years it was our wont, when traversing this region by canoe to mark such and such a nameless lake on the map in close proximity of the water we were lodged on. Because of the flawless accuracy of the map-makers if you are camped on a certain island near the short of a lake or out on a point of land, that island and that point of land will be there on the map in the right place and right according to the compass. By the use of the compass such lakes (the nameless ones) are attained by crossing overland or by carrying the canoe and pack, often as not travelling light. Almost invariably. is the lake located just where your compass needle points. That all this is a credit to the Canadian map-makers is a compliment that is deserved and was certainly achieved at the cost of much labor and the observance of endless detail. Prospective visitors to this wilderness area of Ontario (western and northwestern Ontario) will find the airplane maps mentioned as little short of indispensable. These maps are obtainable through the Surveyor General, Hydrographic Service, Ottawa, Canada, each map detailing a given district. Five of these district maps covering this western Ontario region due north of Minnesota, taking in the Lake of the Woods region and east through the Quetico are as follows: Kenora District (Map No. 52 E); Dryden District (Map No. 52 F); Ignace District (Map No. 52 G); Rainy Lake District (Map No. 52 C); and Quetico Provincial Reserve area (Map No. 52 B). In an ordinary paper map type these sell for 25 cents; folder form, 35 cents and linen-backed, 50 cents. If the reader of this book has dreamed of the day when he will make that Canadian trip he should become the possessor of this list of maps. He will see displayed such a super-abundance of lakes that will leave him wondering if it can be possible. In surveying any one map detailing a district of this region it would seem that there is more water than land and in many places shown this is true.

This is the great "Canoe Country" of North America, and

it is also the great pike country. Yes, here the great northern pike, *Esox lucius,* holds out by the myriad thousands. If you are a canoeist traversing this vast expanse of lakes the pike will become as familiar to you day after day as land, and tree, and air. They are everywhere. In some places hardly a cast can be made without hooking into one of the species. Nor are they always four, five and six pounders. There are times when ten, twelve and fifteen pounders are hooked and you will have your hands full, no less, and it is then you will come by a realization that as a fighter the great northern pike is no set-up and has a bag of tricks all of his own to spring on you. To the canoeist-fisherman who has come from the states, where the taking of a six pound pike is something of an event, this sort of fishing is little short of a revelation. It becomes more and more fascinating day after day as one proceeds on one's trip. The fish taken are never wasted. They are carefully unhooked and released, for it is a fact that of all conservationists the canoeist in the wilderness is now the most law-abiding and sparing of all. Time was (yes, time was) when this was not true. But today few fish are wasted. This has been a rule brought into being by the guides in Canada who know conservation, have been taught it, and who exemplify its tenets all of their days in the woods. And what applies to great northern pike applies to other fish as well. There was a time when these pike were termed "snakes" and were flung up in the woods on shore in open disgust. But not now. Maybe the knowledge of fish scarcity has prompted a reversal of opinion as regards this fish, for it is becoming more and more manifest that fishing pressure will some day dictate that "thou shalt not waste." Too, with other game species of fish becoming less in numbers and some even rare, there is a natural disposition to accord increased prominence, even importance, to such species as are more or less flourishing. Possibly it is for this reason that the pike is now coming into its own even in the north. Certainly in the states the species has been numbered now as among the foremost of the game fish, brought about, as stated, by the lessening in numbers of other fish. When one considers that in some states in the country, carp are considered gamefish, and are so listed in the fish laws, and that in other states the channel catfish is considered a gamefish, one can easily see what transpires when fish species are killed off to a minimum or a close approximate.

So when on that canoe trip into the "Canoe Country" of Ontario and you take one pike after another, you do not fling them up into the brush and rocks, emitting a curse as you do so. The fish is removed from the hook and put back into the water with every consideration. All of which is as it should be.

Those who have fished for muskellunge in Lake of the Woods of western Ontario, in the earlier days as well as now in the present day, are aware of the fact that the pike has unconsciously been the savior of thousands of the muskellunge. Both species are fished for in the same waters, and those waters are the shore waters. Little trolling is done for muskies, all the fishing being by casting either with a large musky plug or spoon. The pattern is just about like this: You cast your lure and the chances are dollars to doughnuts that there will be a pike on hand who will seize the lure before any possible muskellunge on the scene has had a chance to sail into it to sink its fangs in it. So it is a case of day in and day out unhooking great northern pike and returning them to the water. Irate musky fishermen, in Lake of the Woods, years ago, invariably killed the pike they caught in this manner. Even today, with a lessening in pike numbers in Lake of the Woods due to the persistent commercial seiners, there are enough pike on hand to beat the musky to it in nailing a lure. But unlike years ago, today those pike are kept and are taken home to become the main feature in many a fish fry. A different kind of fisherman has arrived on the scene. Times have changed. And how they have changed!

II

PHYSICAL
CHARACTERISTICS

It is doubtful if nature has ever put into the waters a more voracious and savage a creature in scales and fins than the pike. If the fishes in the waters with him were ever oppressed by visions of murderers and assassins, then surely the pike could be classified as a choice example of hideousness and cruelty personified. Izaak Walton who called the pike "the tyrant of the rivers, or the fresh-water wolf" had some rather remarkable observations on the pike, some quaint superstitions believed to be the whole truth in the early centuries but some eminently accurate and known to be factual. That would especially apply to pike swallowing fish larger than themselves or equally as large. States Walton: "A pike will devour a fish of his own kind that shall be bigger than his belly or throat will receive, and swallow a part of him, and yet the other part remain in his mouth till the swallowed part be digested, and then swallow that other part that was in his mouth, and so put it over by degrees; which is not unlike the ox and some other beasts, taking their meat, not out of their mouth directly into their belly, but first into some place betwixt, and then chew it, or digest it by degrees after, which is called chewing the cud. And, doubtless, pikes will bite when they are not hungry; but, as some think, even for very anger, when a tempting bait comes near to them." He adds:

"And it is observed that the pike will eat venomous things (as some kinds of frogs are) and yet live without being harmed by them; for, as some say, he has in him a natural balsam, or antidote against all poison and he has a strange heat, that though it appears to us to be cold, can yet digest or put over any fish-flesh, by degrees, without being sick. And others observe that he never eats the venomous frog till he has first killed her, and then (as ducks are observed to do to frogs in spawning time, at which time some frogs are observed to be venomous) so thoroughly washed her, by tumbling her up and down in the water, that she may devour her without danger. And Gesner affirms that a Polonian gentleman did faithfully assure him, he had seen two young geese at one time in the belly of a pike. And doubtless a pike, in his height of hunger, will bite at and devour a dog that swims in a pond; and there have been examples of it, or the like; for, as I have told you, the belly has no ears when hunger comes upon it."

Berridge (previously quoted) also states about the pike:

"The pike is a notorious cannibal, and has been known to swallow fish larger than itself. On such occasions the diner can only dispose of its prey gradually, the part that has passed beyond the throat having to be digested before room can be found for the remainder. In addition to a diet of fish, the pike will also consume ducks, geese, voles and frogs, dragging the larger prey beneath the water and soon putting an end to its struggles. Needless to say, the fish has a very capacious mouth, and this is armed with a most formidable array of teeth. Even the roof of the mouth is provided with small teeth, and these point backward toward the throat, so that a victim that has been seized has little chance of freeing himself.

"Many accounts," continues Berridge, "have been given of the voracious appetite of the pike. It is recorded that an individual once swallowed the head of a live swan, but we are not told whether the victim succeeded in freeing itself from the grip of its attacker's jaws. According to report, the pike will also become so bold as to endeavor to rob the otter of fish that the otter has caught and an instance has been cited of a large specimen catching hold of the lips of a mule that had come down to the water to drink. Bathers have been attacked by pike, and Crouch tells us that a baby was once found in the stomach of one of these fish!"

So much for legend and otherwise. There is little doubt but that large pike are killers of all manner of waterfowl, ducks, goslings, grebes, coots, bittern, gulls, terns and shorebirds. As a killer of wild ducklings the pike has been held as a serious factor by the More Game Birds In America organization. There is no gainsaying that this is true, for throughout the whole northwest of Canada, in the so-called "duck factory" the predominance of the pike in water where the ducks breed is only too well known. What is to be done about it is a matter no one has yet been able to figure out, for pike were killing the young of waterfowl before the white man ever set foot on North American shores and will continue to do so from now on. Those who attempt to solve the cause of waterfowl depletion in North America would best look to the millions of well armed hunters that pour shot and shell into the down-coming waterfowl every hunting season. Yet these myriad of human predators are never held guilty of anything that could possibly have anything to do with a decrease in the waterfowl situation. One could vent a merry horse-laugh at the clownish attempts made to mask the real killers of the waterfowl of this nation and Canada.

" 'Tis not to be doubted," sayeth Izaak Walton, "but that they (the pikes) are bred, some by generation, and some not, as namely, of a weed called pickerel weed, unless learned Gesner be mistaken, for he says this weed and other glutinous matter, with the help of the sun's heat, in some particular months, and some ponds adapted for it by nature, do become pikes. But, doubtless, divers pikes are bred after this manner, or are brought into some ponds some such other ways as is past man's finding out, of which we have daily testimonies."

Having spoken ol' Izaak swigged him a becker of ale and called it a day. The immortal maestro always got tangled up in the figments of fancy and flights of imagination unconfined as perpetuated by Konrad von Gesner (1516-65). That erudite scholar may have excelled in bibliographies and histories of men and of languages, but as a naturalist he hardly made the first rung on the ladder. Although Walton was astonished at times by the deductions of Gesner, he held him in great respect and at no time doubted him in his most fantastic conclusions. When Gesner stated that pike were bred from pickerel weed, that was it, but still Walton had his suspicions. . . .

What no doubt led Gesner astray was the fact that pike spawn on grasses and weeds and it is possible that the great scholar had seen the eggs hatch and become pike on these weeds, although we have no knowledge as to what manner of vegetation is pickerel weed in England. Not being a nest-building fish the pike spawns over the weeds where the eggs are fertilized. In lakes where there is no stream up which the fish can go on their annual spawning run, the act of procreation is carried on in the lake itself. Where streams can be gotten into, the pike make long runs, at times ten or more miles from a home water, purposely to spawn in overflowed meadows and in watery marshes. In years past thousands of these fish—some very large—would be speared by the natives. In the present day a damper has been leveled against such indiscriminate killings and a degree of protection offered the species.

The spawning of the pike takes place in late winter and spring. The eggs are about one-eighth of an inch in diameter. Buckland found that a female weighing 32 pounds contained an aggregate of 595,000 eggs. In both the pike and the pickerel the spawning season is short, ranging not much over two weeks, although if the weather is adverse the hatch may not be completed for 30 days. Young pike are the possessors of unusually large yolk sacs and are able to care for themselves in a comparatively short time. Meehan claims that in pond culture the fry should not be placed in the same waters with mature specimens, but sorted as to length and kept in different ponds as would be done with any carnivorous species. "Growth in the pike," states Meehan, "is very rapid, and cannibalism, even among the young is strongly developed; hence desiring to rear their stock to maturity must expect heavy loss from this quarter."

At the age of one year the fish may reach a length of 12 inches, and if well supplied with food it will increase in weight from 2 to 3 pounds yearly. Normally the pike breeds at the age of three years. Like the bass, which, after caring for its young in a most dutiful and laudable manner, after the fish have been permitted to shift for themselves they seek their progeny to make food of the same in the manner of a cannibal that often confounds the fish culturist or the amateur in the field of fish propagation. Of course in the case of the pike, after the eggs are let and impregnated the fish has no more to do with them. It is highly possible that the large pike seek the young pike to make food of them just as do the bass. Possibly there is object in this sort of "madness" in that life in the waters is a survival of the fittest; only the strong, the alert, the swift win out in the race to survive. Possibly it is nature's way of cutting down on an over-production which otherwise would fill the waters to superabundance and so disturb the logical balance of nature. These small pike are slim and arrowy in proportion to their length and are no doubt great food killers; the pike is even more destructive than the pickerel, two specimens of which, measuring 5 inches in length, have been reported to eat more than 100 minnows in a day.

There is a reason why an imitation of the baby pike as exemplified by the Creek Chub Pikie Minnow is so popular. Bass attack these small pike in a most vicious manner, especially when they are guarding their nests from intruders. It might be mentioned that by the time the bass are spawning the young pike are on the move and it is possible that one of their choice places of call is the spawning grounds of the bass. Bass have actually been known, during the nesting period to kill pike up to a foot in length, which is not impossible since a pike of that length is hardly more than an inch in diameter and almost cylindrical. Too, the large pike being cannibalistic, there is another reason why they are so easily caught on the Pikie Minnow from the Creek Chub plant.

The confusion in calling these baby great northern pike, "pickerel" is met with at all times. Because these immature pike are narrow-bodied, slim and arrowy they are at once thought to be "pickerel" forgetful of the fact that the pike must at one time be small in size. For years it was contended that the true pickerel was found in the state of Minnesota and yet in a period of many years checking on specimens brought in, not one true pickerel appeared in the lot. They were all the young of great northern pike. The Game and Fish Department of Minnesota itself made a check on this subject as the result of which Thaddeus Sruber, head of fish propagation for the state, issued the decision that on the basis of investigations made, no true pickerel had ever been taken from Minnesota waters. To the best of my knowledge the same is just about true of the waters of the state of Wisconsin, for I believe that Bob Becker one time wrote me that he had been unable to find a true pickerel in the state. Yet year after year new and newer enlistments are made in the army of those who claim that these small pike are indeed pickerel. It is interesting that in England pickerel is considered the diminutive of pike, which is to say that a young pike can be called a pickerel. So far, so good. But in this country we actually have three varieties of actual fish related to the pike that we call pickerel which only adds to the confusion. Even more so since no member of the pike family is known to the waters of the British Isles save the true pike. In this country the young of the pike and the mature specimens as well are known as pike entirely, never pickerel in any manner that the name is juggled around.

I am quite sure that if it is always kept in mind that the pike has yellowish or lightish spots almost in rows up and down its sides, the same being fairly oval in character or bean-shaped, there is no need of confusing the fish with any pickerel that may be in the same waters with it. Of course there are variations. In some specimens the spots stand out perfect against a fairly darkish background coloration and the spots may be fairly yellow. In other specimens taken out of a lake or stream that has a light bottom the coloration is a light washed-out green and the spots up and down the sides, as detailed, are not vivid, in fact are very indistinct. Normally the background coloration of the pike ranges from a grayish tone to bluish or greenish gray. As stated, the coloration of the fish depends entirely upon the kind of water it is taken from. I have noticed that the darker the body color the more vividly outlined are the spots up and down the sides. All members of the pike family have the one dorsal (back) fin and this is set rather far back on the body near the tail, the forward part of the dorsal being in a line with the vent. The dorsal, anal and caudal fins are often very well spotted or reticulated, differing in various waters. It is supposed that the sliminess associated with the body of the pike, it being as slippery as the eel, has much to do with keeping it immune from fungus and various diseases. However, while on lamprey research on Lake Huron we took hundreds of pike, the major portion of them having the notorious sea lamprey attached to their bodies, proof that slippery as the body of the pike may be the lamprey does not seem to have much trouble appending to the body and eventually killing it. In fact should the sea lamprey work up into the waters of western and northwestern Ontario into the 28,000 lakes previously mentioned, it would surely contrive the doom of the millions of pike that are found in those northern waters. As yet, however, there has been no invasion of these border waters, although the lamprey has attained Lake Superior. Spawning runs of the creature are now found in ten or fifteen streams around that mighty inland water. Apparently they cannot get up above Pigeon Falls on the Pigeon River nor up the Nipigon River. Time will tell if this infiltration into the choicest waters on the continent will somehow or other be managed.

The pike is not what one would call a fish good to look at. One has a feeling that it is a mean rascal at best and even the most soft-hearted would have few qualms of conscience about rapping one of the breed on the head and making food of it. Says Hornaday:

"Look at any member of the pike family and tell me whether it does not make you think of a pirate. Observe that yawning sepulche of a mouth, that evil eye and low, flat forehead—all indicating a character replete with cunning and ferocity. Note the total absence of a dignified and respectable front dorsal fin, which nearly every fish of proper moral character possesses and displays with pride. Like scaly assassins, the pikes and pickerels lie in wait for their prey; and whenever one rushes like a green streak from under the lily-pads, and bolts a trolling spoon in one great, ill-mannered gulp, the angler feels a savage delight in thinking that it serves him right. These fishes are the most inordinate killers that inhabit our waters. The ambition is to devour every living creature that comes in sight. That they are found living with the bass, the perch and other fishes is generally due to the fact that it is impossible for them to devour all their neighbors."

There are two particularly outstanding periods in the twelve months around the calendar when the great northern pike can be considered at his "striking best," meaning when they will take the lure with the greatest show of savagery and insatiable greed. The first such period follows up the close of the spawning season, apparently during the time of preparing for the spawning and on actual spawning runs up streams, the pike does not take in much if any food. But with the termination of the spawning period, hunger returns and the viciousness with which a lure is taken is all too well known. The condition of feeding inactivity occurs during the month of August at which time the species is "in a bad way" due to a sore mouth and sore gums condition which, in the pike, is rather remarkable by reason of the puffed, swollen, inflamed conditions of the gums, something that is always a surprise to the fisherman and a mystery as well. The gums are often purplish and bleeding and in a human being would point to something gravely wrong. In the pike it would seem that it is an annual condition associated with the hot weather period, the dog-days stretch especially, although there are those who contend that a condition such as this occurs a number of times during the year. I doubt this, but would stand to be corrected only to state that as the result of my observations I have found no such condition prevalent save during the month of August.

In my study of the muskellunge I told of specimens of the jaws of this species being sent to the department of dental research at Harvard University. The result of the studies made of these specimens (which I quoted) were as follows:

"It was found that the looseness of the teeth was a normal anatomical condition, and the associated hyperemia was not a pathological lesion but the normal blood supply to the teeth. Further it was found that the teeth of this fish are of successive growth and attachment. They develop in the floor of the mouth, become hinged teeth and are finally attached to the jaw-bone by a bony union. The blood supply to the tooth is profuse, the reason for which is undetermined, especially when considering that the teeth of this fish are used for offensive purposes and not for mastication. When a tooth is shed, a boy base remains, and this is later removed by absorption, and a hollow results in the jawbone. In this hollow or depression a tooth, attached to a fibrous membrane, soon appears. This is known as the hinged tooth, the base of which is later attached to the jawbone by osseous union and so becomes ankylosed or a fixed tooth."

McClane says regarding the teeth of the pike: "A pike's mouth is a dental nightmare. The teeth point backward and the long, knifelike canine teeth in the paws can be depressed to allow entry of food but prevent withdrawal. There are rows of smaller teeth on the tongue and palate which are used for 'shucking' the scales off of hapless fish in the process of being swallowed." As to whether the pike loses its teeth and has new ones come on to replace the old is something no one seems to have concluded. One time we appealed to the U. S. Bureau of Fisheries for help on this question, hopeful that this body of fish experts would surely have the facts at their finger-tips? As a matter of fact, they wrote, not a line had been written on the subject and no investigation of any kind had ever been conducted. So much for acquainting the reader with the sacarcity of facts on the "sore mouth" condition in the pikes. I would say, after a lifetime of writing on fishing, that among questions coming in, that of telling the pike, muskellunge and pickerel, one from the other, and what causes the sore mouth condition in the pike family are two that persist year in and year out with never-failing certainty of being propounded.

There is another one that is a by-product of the question asking about that "sore mouth" condition. This question goes about as follows: "We have heard that one should not eat pike or pickerel when they have the sore mouth condition, as they are then unfit for food. Is this true?" It isn't true, and the pike, pickerel and muskellunge are as wholesome as food at this time of the year as any other. While it is true that during the summer flukes (popularly known as "grubs") are found in many of the panfish, particularly the rock bass, these grubs or flukes are rarely found in the pickerel, pike and muskellunge. By way of explanation, these flukes are those little white or yellowish "sacs" that you will see in the transparent flesh of the panfish you take, these being about a fourth of an inch long and a sixteenth of an inch in diameter. They can be picked out of the flesh with the tip of the knife. They are especially numerous in the thick flesh of the back. Some people refuse to eat fish in the summer because of this grubby or wormy condition, and yet after frying or otherwise preparing the fish for the table, no harm can possibly come from consuming the same. Popular legend has it that the tapeworm is ingested by the human being, these grubs being the tapeworm in its minute state. This is utterly untrue, having no basis whatsoever in fact. These grubs or flukes (the true name for them) come via the excrement of water birds in the water. They pass from this source to the fish and from the fish to the bird in a manner of cycle. The prevalence of this fluke condition is chiefly in the two months of July and August, although it may come on as early as the second week in June. As stated, to the best of our knowledge, various members of the pike family do not have these flukes, in other words they are not used as a host for the incubation of these transient visitors. In some weedy and fairly stagnated waters the pike will be found as possessing what is known as lice, told by the black spots, often very numerously distributed on the body. By steaking, i.e., filleting the fish, thus removing the skin, these "lice" are taken away with the skin. Normally the pike family is very nearly free from all manner of parasites, one reason why thousands of people call it choice food.

After the August seige of sore mouth the pike will be free of swellee and bleeding gums; in fact the gums will again be witish or flesh-colored and hard and firm around solid fangs. Around about the time the first frosts come on in the north during the September days the pike will again be in the pink of condition. If he has gone without his usual excess of food and has fasted much the same way as the muskellunge, this circumstance is now altered and to say that he feeds from daybreak to sunset is no exaggeration. If in the midst of these good stuffing transactions he spots the fisherman's lure he does not waste much time trying to canvass its nature; he simply backs and up rushes at it full tilt like an inflamed bull hastening to gore the matadore. Little wonder he ends his career in the frying pan for he probably, like as not, has the lure salted away down there in the gullet. From September then until ice covers the lake the fisherman can ply his line and lure with every reason of success. Nor does the pike cease his feeding during the winter months. Other fishes may be in a partial state of dormancy, but the pike is as wide awake as ever. Later on we shall tell about taking the pike with hook and line through the ice in the winter, a pastime that has much to commend it and certainly one that will enliven many a winter day with its possibilities of swift and tingling sport. To land a pike of size through the ice is something that demands no little skill. You need to know some rules to follow. In due course we shall tell you about them.

It might not be out-of-place in closing this chapter to mention how the pike gots its name. It is said that the origin of the name is involved in uncertainty; some trace it to the resemblance in shape of the snout to the pike or spear, while others believe it to refer to the darting motion of the fish when speeding through the water. The application of the term "Great Northern Pike" seems to be an old one. It is only known to the pike as it is found in America, yet even in the South one hears the name "Great Northern Pike" applied to the species. Jason Lucas comments of this name: "The name 'Northern Pike' is necessary, for there's but one pike. The name 'Great Northern Pike' is still worse— the Great Northern's a railroad, not a fish, but the confusion is so confounded that even the capitals are usually retained when the term is applied to *Esox lucius*."

There are those who actually believe that Jim Hill, founder the the Great Northern Railroad named the fish, but the fact of the matter is that it was named long before that time. To Henry William Herbert, our first great angling writer goes the honor, if so it be, of naming the fish. However, it was not Great Northern Pike then, but Great Northern Pickerel, but the fish so named was the pike that he found in Lake George, New York. There was a disposition at that time to call the pike a pickerel and Herbert (Frank Forester) apparently followed the line of least resistance and named the fish as most fishermen of the time knew it to be. Attempts have been made to shorten the name to "great pike" or "northern pike" but invariably the fish comes back into the fold as Great Northern Pike.

III
TROLLING FOR THE
GREAT NORTHERN PIKE

To state that the practice of trolling is one of the most popular ways of taking the great northern pike is of course repeating a truism. Next to still-fishing for pan-fish, trolling is the most doted on method of taking this fish. Just as there are fishermen who believe devoutly that you can catch fish only if you use live minnows, so are there others who not only believe religiously in trolling for the pike but cannot be budged into trying any other method. The average fisherman starts trolling about fifteen feet from "the dock." The line and lure is let out, the lure promptly sinking to the bottom and at once picks up a long weed as a trailer or a garnishing of coontail. After an hour engaged in pulling this around the man holding the rod suspects that something is wrong. He reels in, is pleased to know that he was right in his deductions, removes the weed and the trolling process again goes into effect. That there is a weed attached to the hook two-thirds of the time may be an exaggeration, but at least it is one of the established courses of trolling. It might be stated with all basis in fact that no fish ever hits a lure with a weed attached, even if it is one only six inches in length, in fact we made a trial one time to find out how certain was this deduction. Two spoon lures were trolled, one on either side of the boat. One was barren of weeds, the other had a six-inch-long weed attached to the hook. Six pike were taken on the weed-free hook while not one, not even a strike, was registerd on the spoon whose hook carried a weed attached. If you doubt the accuracy of this it would be a revelation to you to follow up the same process of deduction. It will rather surprise you, I am sure. The above emphasizes the first lesson you must learn in trolling, namely, that your lure must have no weed attached, even a small one. Obviously it is a credit to the eyesight of the fish that they see this unnatural appendage and are smart enough to avoid committing suicide by seizing the lure that is its host.

Some lakes cannot be trolled successfully, but nevertheless they are fished in this manner in spite of the beforementioned unfavorable conditions. It should be obvious that if the fish you seek by trolling are up in the weeds and pads around shore, or in the thick of this conglamoration of vegetation, you cannot possibly take them with a spoon lure sporting a treble hook capable to picking up every weed with which it comes in contact. This, however, does not deter the troller from hopefully dragging the spoon through the weeds, with much time utilized in removing them. The more the joke of it!

But presuming that you have weed-free water to troll in, right up close to the pads or weed beds, just what method should be followed to get the best results? You are successful or unsuccessful in proportion to the distance you troll from the pads and weed beds, reeds, rushes, etc. The belief of course is that the pike or, as the case may be, the muskellunge, may be cruising along the outer edge waiting for food to

come in from the lake into the weeds, or from the weeds
going out into the lake. It is good grounds; no doubt about
it. But that the spoon, as trolled, is the answer to the matter
of taking those fish is very doubtful—not as long as the
weeds are a barrier to fishing progress. Then consider the
spectacle of using an antedeluvian tub, ark, scow, flat-boat
or raft as a craft for trolling purposes. The fish no doubt
can hear such "boats" a mile off. The encumbrance eventually
passes the area marked X where that twenty-five pound
pike is waiting to give up his ghost in your behalf. Does he?
Not if the trolling is done as pictured. The boat passes with
much sound and much groaning and splashing of the oars.
About thirty feet behind the boat comes the spoon lure, all
too often fished out of the mud and slime in the bottom of
the boat, tarnished, drab, lack-lustre. Is it any wonder that
ninety-five per cent of all trolling, either for the musky or
the pike, as conducted in this manner, fails to take fish? I
mention the musky and pike here together in that where
lakes contain both of these members of the pike family you
are as likely to take one as the other, for as a rule they feed
through the same grounds.

I believe that the noisy approach by any manner of craft
cuts down on the number of fish you take to a most unusual
degree and yet it is the most common failing to be met with
in the whole fishing field. There have been those who have
stated that noise probably attracts the fish rather than
sends them swimming away from the area but my experience
has been that common sense would suggest the use of the
cautious approach. And that would especially apply to the
sizeable and older members of both the musky and pike
species who have, through experience, been taught to keep
a keen weather eye out for Man, their chief and foremost
enemy. Believing emphatically in the silent, noiseless method
of trolling I need hardly say that I consider the canoe to be
my pick of all craft for fishing purposes where a craft is
needed, especially, let us say, in the manner of trolling.
The canoe, either canvas-covered or aluminum, slides over
the water surface without the semblance of a sound, and
the fish lying along the outer edges of the weed patches, are
taken quite unawares. No boat operated by the use of oars
could match the soundless approach of the canoe with motive

power lodged in an expert paddle. But, strange as it may seem, fully ninety-five per cent of all trolling is done by boats, simply because boats are the universal craft for most all fishing and canoes are looked upon as dangerous by the average person unfamiliar with them. Yet those who know canoes and use them, find them an answer to their needs where a craft is concerned, second to none. It is an interesting commentary that most of the thousands of muskies that have been produced out of Lake of the Woods, in western Ontario, have been taken from canoes. Now that boats are used on this famous lake, the take of muskies has been almost negligent. One might ask, is there justification here that would fortify that belief? I think that there is.

If it is important that your approach be as soundless as possible by using the proper craft, it is also necessary that the amount of line you have out when trolling, be suitable. I called especial attention to this in my book *The Muskellunge*, published by the Stackpole Publishing Company, and I reiterate it here. You must troll with a long line out. If it were said that the more line you have out the greater are your chances of taking fish, then no exaggeration is meant. It is interesting to state that normally fully eighty-five per cent of all trolling is done with between thirty to fifty feet of line out, too limited an amount of line to say the very least. If conditions permit, I believe that most trolling as for pike and muskies should be done with no less than one hundred feet of line out and up to one hundred and fifty feet if circumstances permit. By "circumstances" here I mean first of all water that is practically weedless or nearly so which would assure passage of a spoon with a reasonable hope of not picking up a weed or a thatch of the same. Also there is needed a definite water depth ranging down to ten feet or more to prevent any possible contact with the bottom. It can be seen from this that not all lakes are suitable in which to exploit the possibilities of the long line. But where it can be done there are opportunities for taking fish that no short line ever could begin to equal.

The above, therefore, is a recommendation of the long line. No doubt one of the strong reasons for the lack of success with the short line is just that—the short line. Why should a long line be used? It is all very simple. In proportion to how heavily a lake is fished are the fish suspicious. That's only natural. If a boat passes, suspicion will be working full blast in the brain of the fish—such as it is. But as the sound of the boat begins diminishing, in proportion dies the suspicions. If the line you have out is long, the lure will appear just about the time the fears of the fish are quieted with the result that the chances of the finny one coming out to take the lures are greatly increased. Fish in the path of the boat are likely to move to right or left out of reach of it; few stay right in line with the course of the boat. You may have to interest fish ten to fifteen feet away from the lure. Can this be done? Among lures we have observed under water the regulation spoonhook, that is, the spoon that revolves on the shaft, has been foremost. To our eyes a spoon of this sort, well polished, throws a gleam of rays that we can more or less readily make out at ten to fifteen feet. It was definitely ascertained by underwater observation that the fluted spoon of the Skinner type threw more pronounced rays than did the spoon with a plain, uncrimped surface. Understand, this was looking at the spoon in movement through the water. If our human or "land-eyes" were able to make out this reflected light at the distance stated then it is reasonable to suppose that the fish, in his native element, would be able to make out this metallic gleam in the water far better. On the other hand we experimented with a dull, tarnished spoon such as is used by most fishermen and we could not see it. Obviously, therefore, if you would have luck: with a spoon lure it must be highly polished. It is the flash that gets the fish. A worn, lack-lustre spoon has not the slightest value, and yet half to two-thirds of all spoons trolled, lack a high polish, hence are useless.

In proportion to the amount of line you have out your lure is likely to sink in the water all the way from one foot to five or six feet. If you have a hundred feet of line out (or more), the amount of sinkage is really noticeable. To off-set this, use a light line, one, say, of about 12-pounds test, and preferably a line of this type that has had the stretch taken out of it in manufacture. There are such lines now to be had on the market. The value of a line with a minimum of stretch to it is needed in due proportion again to the amount of line you have out. If you have a hundred feet of line out (and that is not a great deal) there is far more stretch than there is in fifty feet, and, in one hundred and fifty feet, still more. In a pure silk line, as made from the product of the silkworm, a seventy-five yard line has from ten to twelve feet of stretch to it before breaking point is reached. While there is never any such stretch put into a line it nevertheless indicates that, according to the amount of line out, you have to set the hook forcefully if the power of that "setting" performance is to travel along the length of the line to the lure and be sufficient in driving impact to pierce through the jaws of the fish. Understand that a line "bellies" or hangs in a fairly well defined "sag" in the water and the heavier the line the greater the sag; the less the pounds-test of the line, that is, the less the weight or caliber of the line, the less it sinks. That is why a twelve-pound test line is more desirable than a twenty-four, thirty or thirty-five pound test line.

In scanning the above there would seem to be an objection to the use of a twelve pound test line by most fishermen, and that would surely be the case if one were fishing waters where large fish are to be met with. However, in most waters fished now the average size of pike is not too great and a twelve-pound test line will cope with any of them. For that matter a thirty to forty pound fish would find it hard to break a twelve pound test line, in spite of the misgivings of the ninety and nine.

Hooking a large fish and landing it are two quite differing propositions. If the fish is hooked close to the pads it is almost a certainty that he will attempt escape by diving into the thick of the weeds and pads where his chances of breaking the line are probably increased seventy-five per cent. Obviously, therefore, when a fish is hooked, the boat or canoe fished from, must be turned out into the lake so that the fish is drawn away from the obstructions. This is easily done if a canoe is used, but not quite so easily in a boat, depending of course upon the size of the boat and its maneuverability. A musky on being hooked is likely to go into action immediately; a pike is not always so inclined, in fact the trick of a large pike is to play possum and permit himself to be reeled in until he is near the boat. Once it has a glimpse of movement in the boat or when a premature attempt is made to land it, it will go into action in a manner that will leave no doubt as to its instinctive knowledge that it is held by an enemy and that it must get away as best it may by any power or cunning of which it is capable. All too often it does get away, especially if it is a very large fish, simply because attempts are made prematurely to make the capture. For that matter, most large fish are lost for this very reason. The rule to follow is the very simple one of rowing or paddling out into deep water, away from any possible weeds and obstructions and there stage the fight. A muskellunge will never go deep in the water when hooked but will stay a few feet to six feet or so below the surface. On the other hand a large pike will, most always, sound, that is, go down deep to fairly deep in the water. Both in the case of landing a musky and landing a pike it is a good idea, if possible, to beach the fish. This involves finding a sandy or gravelled beach and running the boat or canoe in on shore. The man with the rod gets out and backs away from the shore, inland, reeling and keeping a taut line as he does so. The guide or man at the paddle or oars gets out, lets the line slide through the fingers until the shaft or leader is seized. Holding at this point he then inserts the hand carefully in the gill cover from the back without getting his fingers in the gill rakers, and in one move brings the fish to shore. A pair of leather gloves are invaluable in protecting the hand. Most pike that are heavy, ranging twenty pounds or more in weight should be beached. The same of course applies to muskies. The use of hook gaffs, clincher gaffs and their like should never be countenanced and shooting a fish under the above circumstances is certainly frowned upon in all circles. If a fisherman by his and a companion's ingenuity cannot land a twenty pound fish without resorting to methods as above used then they should not go fishing.

One often hears it stated that the pike is able to cut a line with its fangs close to the hook or rather where the line is tied to the lure. Having taken thousands of great northern pike, large and small, I can truthfully state that in my lifetime I have not had a pike actually gash off a line with its fangs. Richard Daugherty writes about the pike that in landing it "the old hypocrite snaps the line with a convulsive shake of its grisly head." This I have never had happen to my knowl-

edge. It is possible that in striking the lure the fish may hit
from an angle and so contact the line but this would be the
only opportunity the fish would have of snapping off the
line. That it purposely backs up and grasps the line in its
jaws is about as far-fetched as imagination could take one
and would of course imply reasoning power in the fish, which
is not possible.

Mr. Daugherty, quoted above, has several excellent remarks regarding the landing of pike that would bear ob-
serving. He states:

"In landing this fish, I cannot stress too much the danger
that is always present. No matter how careful you may be,
a sudden twist of the muscular body of the fish may drive
the hooks of the plug or spoon into your flesh. Do not put
your fingers through the gills or allow them to get into the
terribly toothed mouth. Use a long-nosed pair of pliers for
removing the hooks. For smaller pike, grasp the fish firmly
with the thumb and forefinger, pressing tightly against
its gill covers; another grip is to press two fingers into the
eye-sockets. Both grips if sustained, seem to paralyze the
fish and makes it possible to extract the hooks. In landing
the larger fish, shooting is humane and safe, although objected to by many sportsmen. The clincher gaff is excellent.
When using the hooked gaff, let me remind you to be sure
that your fish is played out before attempting to gaff it. It is
good foresight to stun the fish with a sharp blow on the head.
But be sure to hit the fish on the head and not come down
on the line instead! Beaching the pike, is a good way of
landing it, but this puts a heavy strain on the line."

The above gives the usual recommendation of the various
gaffs and shooting the fish all of which we have objected to.
I am not against the use of a manner of blackjack for putting
the quietus to large pike, indeed while I have never used one,
I would imagine that the article used by the police would be
a mighty handy affair in both pike and musky fishing and
would obviate the need of a young baseball bat such as
the guides use to sock the daylights out of a mighty one.
One value of the more conservative blackjack is that with
it one can stun the fish but will not kill it. This surely is of
value should you want to release your fish.

Mr. Daugherty bring up an excellent point in stating that

you watch out when removing the hook or hooks from the jaws of a pike; a sudden violent, convulsive, wrenching movement on the part of the fish, occurring in the twinkling of an eye, may drive a hook into the hand. Never was this borne out more fully than in two instances, once when a hook was driven into my finger by a pike, and, second, that of a hook driven into the hand of a fisherman which I shall recount later.

In my own case it was one of the hooks of a treble on a Creek Chub Pikie Minnow. It entered the inside of the middle finger in the top joint or rather in the tough cartilage or sinew of the joint of the finger. It was driven in deep, so deep in fact that it was easily to be seen that ordinary methods would not serve to remove it. It was, in other words, a case for the doctor. We were able to remove the ganghook from the plug and in this manner, with the hook in my finger, I made my visit to the doctor.

Let me mention that the makers of Creek Chub plugs (and it is to their credit), place treble hooks on their baits that are the finest and strongest made. These are Mustad hooks, made in Norway. This is all right so far as hooks to hold fish are concerned, but if you are to have a hook driven into your finger, be sure that it is something softer than the Mustad ware or you are indeed in for a peck of trouble. In my own case the forcing of the hook point through the sinew of the joint was in itself an almost baffling project and it was doubtful if it would have been accomplished at all without cutting where the hook point was coming through. Eventually the point did come through. Next it became necessary to snip off the barb of the hook so that it could be turned back out the way it entered. The doctor promptly made a series of nicks on an elaborate snipping device he used and in turn was foiled in the use of several other devices. The Mustad steel defied all efforts to cut it. Being in a town in the farming country of Minnesota a farmer happened to be in the waiting room, learning about the efforts of the doctor to cut the hook, stated that he had a pair of barb-wire cutters down in his car. He brought them up and in one snip, the point was cut off. The bend of the hook was then coated time and again with full strength iodine after which it was turned out. The iodine served to cauterize the wound, an idea that might well be kept in mind by every fisherman. Also the method of removing the hook might be stressed. Just cut off the barb and turn it out the way it went in.

The second instance I previously mentioned, occurred up in a wild section of western Ontario. My guide and I were beginning a long canoe trip. We arrived at a certain lake on the canoe route about nine in the morning but a high wind having come up, which drove great waves against the shore, we decided to wait for the gale to abate so that we could go on without getting swamped.

While waiting at the edge of the lake a canoe was seen headed for the portage. There were three occupants. They were from a resort near which we had camped the previous night. As the canoe approached we noticed that the man in the bow of the canoe held out his hand as though to show us something. We didn't know what until the canoe was caught by the guide and myself at the shore. Then we saw. We noticed that the hand was swelled. Then we saw the reason. In the thick of the outer edge of the hand, between the base of the little finger and the wrist was imbedded a hook. Just the stem of it was sticking up. The rest of the hook, the bend and all was imbedded in the flesh. It was one of those utterly unpleasant things that we seem to have an instinctive dread for and which brings up all sorts of disasters that might happen as the result of the accident. On inquiry we found that the hook became lodged in the hand in the usual way; while a large pike was being unhooked in the boat it made a tremendous struggle and the hook was driven into the hand. Instead of hurrying back to camp they had spent many hours fishing during which fishing the hook was in the hand. The hand had started swelling and treatment was a necessity.

My guide, Clarence Bouffle had some practical knowledge of surgery by reason of a partial university course. He stated that the hook would have to be cut out and said that he could do it, having with him a razor and a first aid kit. Agreeable, the gentleman went through the ordeal which involved a deep cut into the sinew to remove the hook. It was accomplished successfully although at the time no one knew what the outcome would be as we were at the time a considerable distance from any doctor. Several days later two doctors came up the lake on the canoe route where we were camped. To our surprise they stated that they had come up to the resort where the injured fisherman had been lodged on the very day that he returned to camp. They had dressed the wound but stated that the operation had been every bit as good as they could have done it. Later we heard from the fisherman who had had the hook cut out of his hand. He stated that the wound healed successfully but felt that he might have lost his life had it not been for the amateur surgical skill of my guide.

I have written as freely as I have on this subject for the very reason that the pike is the one fish among our game fishes which should be handled with care. All too little by way of warning is devoted to the subject, which is a very grave omission. Not until you have had a hook cut out of your hand under circumstances as detailed in the above will you appreciate the need of care in handling the pike you take, and that certainly goes double for tussling with a pike of both girth and poundage. It might not be out-of-place to mention that there is a device that can be inserted within the upper and lower jaws of the pike which will stretch the jaws wide permitting one to remove the hook or hooks from the jaw of the fish without fear of the paws closing on the hand. Its a good precautionary measure but may not always be reliable. No attempt should be made to insert the fingers into the mouth to remove the hook. The removal should be made with a pointed pair of pliers.

But returning to the subject of trolling:

The size spoon you use in trolling has much to do with how fast and how deep it sinks in proportion to the amount of line which is out. Uusually the recommendation is that a No. 9 or 12 spoon be used and this size spoon admittedly will sink deeper than a small spoon of, say, the No. 5 size. This latter size works in perfectly with a 12 pound test line and is ideal for waters wherein the pike taken are hardly ever over eight pound and the average is far lower than that. Many years ago we trolled almost entirely with the No. 5 size Skinner spoon and took endless pike with it. In the present day this smaller regulation spoon seems only rarely to be used, the No. 9 and 12 being the selection of most fishermen. I believe that fishermen who like to troll would realize more success by far with this smaller spoon, in fact a few trials with it will prove convincing. Too, this makes an ideal spoon to cast, a method of fishing that we will call to attention in another chapter.

A method of trolling using a nylon leader is recommended to those who want so far as possible an invisible connection as between the line and the lure. The leader that answers perfectly for this fishing is the new (limp) monofilament Dupont leader which has none of the wiriness of the old nylon but is limp and flexible and as nearly invisible in the water as a leader can be. These limp leaders are to be had from a few pounds test up to sixty pounds test. Such of these limp monofilament leaders that test fifteen, eighteen and twenty pounds would be ideal for trolling purposes. One does not need more than fifteen feet of this leader at the end of the line to serve the purpose demanded of it.

As in muskellunge fishing, so in pike fishing, you need to take stock of the terminal point in your trolling outfit, in other words the connection between the lure and the line. The most common connection in this respect is the so-called gimp leader which is either made of braided brass wires or, in another type, a twisted wire affair. After being used a while they curl into loops and never stay straight. They are, without doubt, the poorest terminal connection equipment to be had, and yet one troller after another in endless procession come equipped with these gimp leaders. Usually they are six to ten inches in length and are installed for the express purpose of preventing the fish from gashing or biting off the line. If it is desired to protect the line as stated a better leader by far can be used. Obtain some No. 9 steel wire and make your leader six, eight or ten inches long as desired. Have a four to six bead Bead Chain ahead on which to attach the lure. A snap is utilized on the bead chain to make this connection. A small ring or eye is at the other end. Simply insert the steel wire end through the eye and with your pliers turn a loop on the wire thus holding the bead chain arrangement intact. On the other end of the short wire leader use a four to six bead swivel arrangement which differs from the first mentioned. Here there is a ring or eye at either end of this short chain. Insert the wire of the leader into one eye and with your pliers again twist the wire in a loop to the eye. To the eye on this bead chain in back you can attach your line either by tying it directly to the eye or if you have a snap on the end of the line the snap can be attached to the bead chain eye. The Bead Chain Company has a leaflet showing a great number of these arrangements. You can readily pick your terminal items, as above detailed, from this list.

One value of the bead chain, one at either end of the wire leader, is that the swiveling possibilities accruing through their use is of a most desirable type. No line can possibly kink when using them. Using the old single brass swivel type, kinking of the line is almost certain to afflict one. The bead chain fills a distinct trolling need!

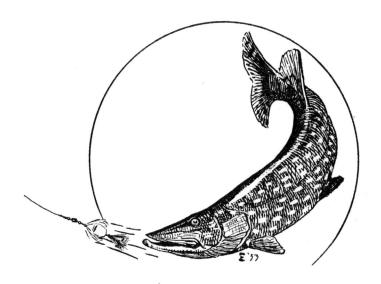

IV

SPOON LURES AND OTHER ATTRACTORS

If it is true that in some sections of the country (particularly the north) the great northern pike can be taken with great ease; the same certainly is not the case in areas where the pike is now far from numerous and one needs to use a little more skill in taking them than is evidenced in heavily pike-populated waters. It is a fact that pike running up to five pounds in weight are by far the size most commonly taken on the lure and those that are larger and heavier in weight come rather few and far between and really are the exception to the rule. As I have pointed out before, there is always a disposition to label these smaller pike, snakes, simply because they are small. But it is also to be noticed that as a pike increases in size it becomes unusually important according to weight recorded. The seeking of large

pike by fishermen all through the north has now reached
a new high and fishermen are going great distances to look
for twenty-five, thirty and possible forty-pounders. Indeed I
would go so far as to state that there are now fishermen
who are as interested in taking a huge pike as a muskellunge.
In fact in late years we have begun to notice more and more
large pike being mounted, something that one never saw in
the past, proof positive that the species are now, at last,
being held in increasingly high esteem. However, it is also
well known to all active fishermen that these large pike do
not come to net too often and the question is often asked,
what is the reason for this. Surely, it would seem to the fishermen, these larger specimens are (or should) be as attracted
to the same lures the smaller pike seize so savagely. Logically
it would seem so, but for the fact that in due proportion to
its size and the ease with which it is seen in the water, a
large pike instinctively keeps clear of the presence of his
chief enemy, Man, surely, at least so far as showing himself
is concerned.

That there are large pike in all the lakes known wherein
the species holds out is taken for granted. It is a natural
history fact that as pike grow old, they become increasingly
slow moving and eventually, as age come on, they become
decrepit and finally die. Most all really large pike eventually
become blind and as they do, they, like the large muskellunge, definitely become bottom feeders. I believe this is
one reason why many muskies are found on the flat rock
reefs in Lake of the Woods where bullheads are found in
numbers. In fact both large pike and large muskellunge are
bullhead consumers although I must admit that smaller
muskies also are partial to this sweet-fleshed diet. I recommended deep trolling for pike one time in one of my newspaper columns and as a result of this a fisherman, who followed up the idea, took no less than a 32-pound great northern
pike. Following upon this, other fishermen took the cue and
other large ones were located and hooked. It is merely proof
that if the larger members of the pike are not to be found
around the shores, you can almost be sure of finding them in
deep water. Of course deep trolling is always a problem
and that is especially true if the water fished has vegetation
in it. Normally, however, vegetation does not grow deeper

down than twenty-five feet as the sun does not seem to penetrate any deeper, and without the sunlight the vegetation does not develop. Best lakes, by far, for deep trolling (that is, close to the bottom) are those having sandy or gravelled bottoms but such trolling, in the north at least, is practically not gone about at all, although of course in lake trout lakes deep trolling is practiced. Naturally deep trolling for pike would follow the same procedure as lake trout trolling, and since the pike is partial to wobbling spoons just as is the lake trout, the lure and methods used for the one, answers for the other. Occasionally lake trout fishermen trolling deep will snag into a large pike at a depth no less than surprising. A companion of the writer took one in Lake of the Woods that weighed 26 pounds, which, while not a particularly large pike, nevertheless would belong in the heavyweight class which is so eagerly sought.

The method of deep-trolling for great northern pike brings up the matter of deep-trolling also in the manner gone about in the upper South where plug lures are used for bass. This is a method so new in the north and the upper eastern part of the country that if it is used at all it would be surprising.

Most of the deep-trolling for bass is done in reservoir lakes, which are sometimes quite deep, having shore waters that drop off deep down to six or eight feet less than fifteen feet from shore. In this deep-trolling a saltwater rod is used. The one that I have been using during a past summer measures 54 inches over-all, that is, from end of butt to tip-top guide. The one-piece tip or rod part is of typical glass composition, and measures 34 inches. The handle and reel-seat section is 20 inches, the handle being of hardwood shaped as is a surf casting rod. To this is attached a saltwater reel that will carry 300 yards of line. The Ocean City Reel Company carry excellent models in this type. But any maker of ocean or saltwater reels can supply the demand. It is, however, vastly desirable that the reel have a tension-regulating star-drag, as drag is a great value when employing a long line.

Oddly enough in this deep-trolling adventure in the TVA reservoirs and lakes in Arkansas generally and Tennessee especially regular nylon lines are not used. Rather nylon leader material is used, as much as five hundred feet often being had on the reel. This "line" is transparent and thus is not too easily seen in the water, at least not to the extent of a regulation line which is black. The new Dupont limp (flexible) monofilament leader material has proved ideal for such deep trolling, and does not have the tendency to spring up in coils as did the older nylon monofilament. In other words it "lays" better on the reel. The usual caliber of this nylon used is the fifteen or twenty pound test. It is an interesting observation that this limp Dupont monofilament up to fifteen pounds test is called "line" material, but from fifteen pounds on up to sixty pounds test it is called "leader" material. All this is rather odd in that one would think that the qualification would be vice versa. However, it is a fact that the monofilament from 2 pounds up to 15 is rather limp for leader purposes, but over 15 does well for both leaders and lines. I might mention that the Dupont Company had stated to the writer that this leader material should not be used as strictly line yet it is a fact that monofilament leader is now coming speedily into use and is "all the go" in the southern TVA lakes for line purposes. That it has given an excellent account of itself can be taken for granted. It would not however, be amiss to state that whereas this nylon leader material as line has a considerable "give" or stretch to it, one needs to give it many sharp, powerful jerks to properly set the hooks in the jaws of the fish. It should be remembered that with upwards of 400 or more feet of line out (and that "line" being Dupont limp monofilament leader material), the distance between the lure and the rod is quite great, hence the need of drastic, forceful jerks so that the impact of the same will travel the length of the line. The monofilament line comes in hanks or rolls up to 600 feet or more.

In deep-trolling for bass by the method detailed anywhere from 350 to 525 or 550 feet of line is used. The lures are plugs of the deep-trolling variety which are outfitted with an extensive flat metal bill in front the usefulness of which when the lure is trolled is that it takes the plug toward the bottom at an angle of between 40 and 50 degrees. Plug lures in this class are represented by such leading lures as the Bomber, the Whopper-Stopper, the Lizzard, the Heddon Go-Deeper and several others, not to forget the Woods plug with the long bill and the South Bend Fish-Oreno with the metal head. Because the plugs with the long bills go down of their own accord they will gain a desirable depth without need of line sinkers. However, by the use of fifty feet of monel wire or a leaded line of the same length in front aids materially in carrying the plug down to the required level as, while the weight of fifty feet of narrow gauge steel wire or a like amount of leaded line is not great, in combinatioin with a lure with a long bill required depths can be gotten. However, if no wire or leaded line is used and monofilament line alone is experimented with you may have to let out over 500 feet of that line to get the lure down to 40 feet. Opposed to this 350 feet of monofilament line, but with 50 feet either wire or leaded line in front will take the lure down the required depth. Trolling with a line length as given above, one figures to go down ten feet for every one hundred feet of line that is out.

During the fall of 1951 a number of tests were made with deep-running plugs in the states of Minnesota, Wisconsin, Michigan and in Lake Huron. The attempt was made to ascertain just what these deep-runners would accomplish in waters not normally deep-fished. The results were interesting, especially so since a very great number of pike were taken, and by this is meant the great northern pike. *While wall-eyed led, the great northern pike were a close second, which is saying something in that we have become so fixed in our belief that the pike is a shallow-water fish that we have excluded it almost entirely from a possible deep-water habi-tat.* It might be mentioned that while no outstanding great northern pike were taken, however most of them ran between eight and twenty-three pounds (as recorded). Small pike, which are universally taken in shallow water, did not seem to be taken at all with these deep-running lures. From the facts ascertained it is proof-positive that northern anglers and those generally in the upper half of the country, have passed up a good bet in failing to examine into the poten-tialities of the deep-roving plug with its progressive bill in sounding out the depths of their regional lakes. That such methods of deep-trolling have not been gone into is not strange. Fishermen in one part of the country are hard set in using only certain methods of fishing and frown at any other methods that are suggested or introduced from other sections. In this I would say is shown a degree of narrowness difficult to diagnose. No doubt actual visible examples of what can be done is all the difference between doubt and conviction. Of course there is always that bugaboo in northern lakes to contend with, namely, the universal condition of vegetated waters, often denying one the chance to troll deep without annexing these obstructions. However, there are lakes as previously stated possessing a gravelled or sandy, or rocky, bottom wherein such trolling can be carried on even more successfully and advantageously than in the reservoir lakes of the South, for some of these reservoirs have standing trees on their bottom and should the lure go deep enough it is almost certain to contact the branches with any but cheerful effect. But the knowledge can now be proclaimed for the first time that the way really to get more and larger, if not record-breaking pike, is to go deep for them in a manner of trolling as detailed.

Previously attention has been called to lines with a 50 foot wire or leaded line out front. Attention should be called to this leaded line for since it is highly possible that deep trolling for pike and other fish species may become the vogue in the future; leaded lines will sooner or later come into the picture.

Leaded lines have a lead core. That is to say the inner portion of the line is like a "wire" of soft, very flexible lead, and over this is woven the nylon covering, very strong, and impervious to breakage or "coming undone." So far as I know the Ashaway Line and Twine Company is the only one making these lines. The demand has never been too great. Now, with deep-trolling for bass coming into the picture, there is a greater demand for it. It is possible that the demands on lead by the war effort may have cut down greatly on releases of lead for fishing line purposes. Leaded line does much to aid a lure of the long billed variety in going down. Personally I would say that it is much more desirable than No. 9 steel wire or monel wire in that it lays better and does not flare up and kink as does steel wire. Both of these materials should be tried, using, as stated fifty feet, one or the other, on the front of the line to which the lure is attached.

Mention has been made regarding the South Bend Bait Company metal-headed Fish-Oreno. This lure has to be seen and used to be appreciated. The lure is built somewhat on the order of the famous Bass-Oreno, but does not have the chubby body of the latter, being, in fact, more tapering toward the tail. The head of the lure, however, is rather distinct in that it is of metal, solid metal in fact. Like the Bass-Oreno it has the same gouged head, but the gouge is in the metal. At first glimpse and without having tried it out one may well believe that it would be impossible to get the same sort of action out of it that is identified with the Bass-Oreno. However, trolling with it, assures one of definite wiggle and while this is no where near as perfect or seductive as that associated with the Bass-Oreno it is very attractive and is certainly killing—at least on some fish. What is of the greatest moment is the fact that it will sink to any depth desired in trolling and surely does away with the need of adding any possible sinkers on the line. Used with the special trolling outfits as for bass, it is peculiarly in its own and is a lure that must be seriously considered in trolling practice. It is said that this lure was put out to be used in deep trolling in the TVA lakes of Tennessee, but to the best of my knowledge it has made but little impression on the bass for which, presumably, it was produced. I may be wrong in this but it is a fact that one rarely sees it for sale in southern sporting goods stores in the deep-trolling region. If it ever did attain great prestige as a bass-getter that fame has largely disappeared, being crowded out by the long billed, deep-roving lures that have come on.

However, there was a happy circumstance that probably saved this lure from extinction. It was a lake trout lure that took toll of this species in a way that earned it no little renoun. In the last few years the South Bend Company have been discarding many lures they have been making in the past, but it is interesting to note that they still have the Fish-Oreno actively on their lists. When trolling with the Fish-Oreno has one outstanding qualification that is important: being heavy in front it virtually stands on its head as it were, as the result of which the head hits the rocks and the belly gang and the tail gang are thus protected from contact with the rocks. In this it proves rather invaluable in lakes with rocky bottoms. On the same type of bottom, spoon lures, both wobbling spoons and regulation spoons have a painful habit of lodging themselves in crevices and otherwise. Not so the Fish-Oreno. It hits the rocks and, as stated, bounces off. Used in combination with a fifteen or twenty pound test limp monofilament line, which assures an invisibility between line and lure connection, this is a lure to be considered seriously in lake trout fishing.

When I first trolled for lake trout with this lure something happened that gave me another clue as to its value. It did take large pike, in fact the result of my northern (Canadian) experiences got me to fishing in the states with it and there it proved a deep-trolling lure that deep-run pike would go for and would take even more eagerly than the wall-eyed pike, the latter also a deep-run rascal, going even deeper on occasion than the pike in the summer. Weedless, rocky-bottom lakes are ideal for deep-trolling with the Fish-Oreno and it is in such lakes that one often hooks into the largest great northern pike found in the region. Indeed, in the north, while trolling for lake trout with this Fish-Oreno, one often hooks into a large great northern pike. I have known of a thirty pounder taken on it in our Minnesota-Ontario border waters.

The question comes up that if one goes in for deep-trolling as outlined, isn't it possible to use a wobbling spoon as a lure as this certainly is a known lake trout spoon as well as one of the best lures for great northern pike. In fact to say that the pike fairly "eat it up" is no play upon the imagination.

If the wobbling spoon is only a lukewarm killer on muskies the same cannot be said for the pike. The musky may like the straight line progress of the regulation spoon, but for the pike the crazy, zig-zag gyrations of the typical wobbling spoon at once promotes the desire to kill. This is one reason why, when they seize the lure, it is likely to lodge deep down in the gullet. From the day that J. T. Buel founded the wobbling spoon up into the present day it has been a great hit as a lure. Buel saw a lake trout seized a tablespoon that had dropped from his hand into the lake, and as a result got the idea for the "spoon" hook and took trout on it. That same spoon today takes no end of lake trout. In fact if it were said that it is the first and foremost lure for this species, one would not be hitting wide of the mark. It is not only excellent as a trolling spoon but when cast with the bait rod it assures sports that is of a most notable order. So far as pike fishing is concerned, if one were to select one lure for the species and one lure only, then it must surely be the wobbling spoon. (By way of comment: Once in a while one hears this spoon referred to as a "wabbling" spoon, the wabbling to rhyme with bab-bling. The right pronunciation of the word is "wobbling" to rhyme with "gobbling." Not, however, that it makes any difference.)

There was a time when wobbling spoons were made only with a silver or nickel finish. In the last twenty or thirty years all manner of finishes have been exploited, such as gold, bronze, copper, aluminum, mother-of-pearl, shell, and enameled spoons of all kinds. There is little doubt but that the striped enameled spoons, either white with black stripes or white with red stripes have been the most popular, indeed are so popular that it is possible they out-sell all other finishes of wobbling spoons two or three to one. I do not know who first produced the striped enamel spoons but am willing to accord the honor to Lou Eppinger. The Eppinger "Daredevil" spoons have long held sway in the market and no doubt millions of them have been sold. There are imitations on the market that are almost exact copies of the Eppinger "Dare-devil" but when used a while the enamel comes off and the spoon is ruined. The Eppinger spoon has its paint baked on by a special process and is immune apparently to abuse. We one time bought an enameled spoon, a copy of the Epping-er product, being unable to obtain the latter. In casting with it the spoon happened to hit a rock on its edge, that is, the edge of the spoon. Imagine our surprise to see almost the en-tire paint job on the spoon come off in one great flake. The fact that you can buy striped wobbling spoons, imitations of the Eppinger original, five cents each is interesting, but if you knew how worthless they are you would leave them right where they are. It is a great pleasure indeed to recommend the Eppinger spoons knowing their full value and worthwhile manufacture.

An unusual spoon that came out at least thirty-five years ago was what the maker called the "Red-Eyed Wiggler." It was (and is) made by the Hofschneider Corporation, Roch-ester, New York. There are at least two imitations of this spoon, although, strangely enough, the original is covered with patents. Interesting is the fact that this lure has taken a number of prize-winners in the national Field and Stream contest. A great attraction in this spoon is its two flashing eyes which must, in some way or other, be seen and appreciated by the fish. So far as pike are concerned they seem to fall all over themselves in paying it court. This is an absolute recommendation along with the Eppinger Daredevil!

The "Doctor" spoon, made by the Brainerd Bait Company, is a wobbling spoon possessing unusual action and sheer murder on pike. They just do not seem to resist it. There are two sizes.

The famous "K-B" spoon, made in Superior, Wisconsin has a long record of usefulness in the lure field and while pike will take it more or less freely it is at its best as a lake trout lure. When trolling deep, however, as previously detailed, it becomes a large pike lure of serious import.

A lure that is made by the Horricks-Ibbotson Company, Utica, New York, called the "Old Lobb" is a small wobbler but has been selling freely through New York state and the east generally for over forty years. It casts nicely, in fact we like it better as a caster than for trolling.

These, above-named, are just some of the wobbling spoons that you will find most useful in pike fishing, and, if you want, lake trout fishing. There are many others, mostly imitations, since there does not seem to be any patent that applies to wobbling spoons other than that those with, let us say, red bead eyes, may thus be protected. One of the rules I have found in selecting wobbling spoons is that if such a spoon is trolled, it can be larger in size than if it is cast on the surface. Some such spoons five inches in length and two to two and one half inches in width are sometimes used, but chiefly in lake trout trolling. For normal trolling fairly close to the surface your spoon need be only two and one half to three inches in length and for casting, a two inch spoon will take as many pike as a larger spoon, possibly far more readily. The reason obviously for a large spoon as used deep down is that it is more readily seen than a smaller spoon and that, of course, would go for large pike as well as lake trout. I have mentioned that fishermen do not appreciate how deep down a pike will go. In Whitefish Bay of Lake of the Woods I took a sixteen pound great northern pike at a depth of 80 feet below the surface. I would never have believed this had I not seen this happen.

A recommendation of the striped enameled spoons has been made in this survey of the wobbling spoon. These I must admit I am very partial to. But for all-round use one would be poorly fitted out if some nickel or silver-plated wobbling spoons were not included. If you have a plating company, plate your spoons, you will find that a very high grade nickel plating will be every bit as lasting and bright as real silver plating. One objection to silver plating is that it must be carefully polished frequently or it will tarnish. For that matter, after use, all spoons should be rubbed down, covered with some white vaseline and then wrapped around with cleansing tissue, some of which can always be carried in the tackle box. One operates on the belief that a spoon is as good as it will gleam and throw rays through the water. The tarnished or discolored spoon will not do this, indeed many times fifty per cent of its effectiveness is lost by actual reason of dimness of the finish. Hence, an obvious reason for keeping the brightness of the spoon at high gloss. Enameled spoons of course do not need this care.

Whatever may be said for trolling for pike it is doubtful if it can equal that of casting a lure for the species, whether it be a spoon or a plug. As stated, for casting purposes the choice lies between a two inch to a two and one half to three inch spoon. This of course would apply to either the enamelled spoons or the plated ones. While some of these wobbling spoons have two gangs or trebles of hooks, one in front and one at the tail end, the forward hook, it would seem, rather impedes the action of the lure. I do not believe in more than a trailer hook on a wobbling spoon. There is something to be said for the use of a pork rind strip of the commercially bottled type attached to the hook. Usually the fisherman hooks the rind strip on one of the three hooks of the treble. While this is all right in its way, it would be much better if the rind were located centrally in the treble hook as the result of which the rind would not impair the action of the spoon. To accomplish this, solder a snap into the center of the crotch of the gang where the three hooks curve out. It is very simply done. When the rind strip is now hooked on, it will be found to operate centrally to the best possible effect.

While many fishermen use a gimp wire leader, braided or twisted, on the end of their line, the same being six, eight or ten inches in length I positively feel that the inclusion of the same is without actual benefit and that it positively destroys the action of the lure. The use of these gimp wire leaders of course is to prevent the pike from over-striking onto the line and so gashing it off. This has always been a bugaboo with fishermen without actual basis in fact. Having caught thousands of pike in my day I must confess that I have done this entirely without the aid of any gimp leader. As I have said before, a six inch steel wire leader, made from No. 9 guage steel wire, would do far better, inasmuch as these braided and twisted brass wire leaders curl and double up on themselves and never seem to be straight as they should be. Just twist on a snap on one end of this six inch wire and an eye-twist on the other to which the line is attached. That's all there is to it. But should you pass up both the wire and gimp type leader be sure to attach to the end of the line a four to six bead swivel rig with a snap on one end of it and an eye or small ring on the other to which the line is tied. These are made by the Bead Chain Company and are to be had in most well supplied sporting goods stores or can be obtained from the Ashaway Line and Twine Company, Ashaway, Rhode Island. In this type of terminal arrangement each bead acts as a swivel and does not, in any way, interfere with the action of the lure.

Usually there is a split ring at the tip of the wobbling spoon to which the snap it attached. I particularly call attention to this, and that it should be seen to that this snap is a strong one because when playing a large fish it is likely to snap or break in two. This may seem impossible. However, I shall recount as experience I had with a large pike, possibly the largest I have ever hooked that was caught on a small wobbling spoon which had a very thin and inferior split ring. I should have examined this ring closely before fishing with the lure but it was just one of those things you forget about.

It was on a certain October day up in Minnesota. We were fishing down a lake shore, taking a nice pike now and then, until finally I had occasion to drop the spoon up in a deep indentation in the pads. I had hardly reeled the lure more than two feet when something took it, what, I did not know. At first I thought I had hooked into a log and then I realized that it was moving, though very slowly. The fish made no wild dashes, just doggedly held on and kept himself under the surface. I directed my companion who was rowing the boat, to move out into deep water which he did. As we moved out the fish came with us, my rod, which was a solid steel True Temper, being at a perfect arc, the strain on the lure of course being very great. I slowly forced the fish toward the surface wanting to get a good look at it and to see if possible if it really was a pike. More strain on the rod. Gradually the fish, by main force, was impelled to the surface. For one moment I had a glimpse of the head of the fish, one of the largest great northern pike I have ever looked upon. Generally we land great northern pike by reaching down and spanning the top of the head with the hand, and then pressing down with the thumb on one side of one gill cover and the other fingers on the other. This momentarily paralyzes the fish and it can be lifted out without any action whatever on the part of the fish. It was when I saw the top of the head of the fish that I realized I could never land the fish by the skull-spanning method, in fact with my hand spread out the length from thumb tip to the tip of the little finger still didn't reach the edges of the top of the head on either side. I then realized for the first time that I had hooked one of the largest pike in my varied career, one that would go between 35 and 40 pounds in weight. The length of the fish I figured would be well over 50 inches.

While I was deliberating what to do, and with the rod bent even more than ever, the something happened. The split ring holding the ganghook snapped in two and the spoon shot up, and coming at me on its edge, hit me on the bridge of the nose. Fortunately it did not break the bone. If it had landed either one half inch to the right or the left I would, I can assure you, have been minus one eye in the deal. That indentation and spot on the bridge of my nose was the result of the wobbling spoon that flew up at me and left its trademark. Take note of it the next time you see me. I later wrote the company making this lure and what I said to them regarding the cheap split rings they put on their wobbling spoons was what you would call a roast to a turn. Later they sent me spoons with split rings on them that a marlin or a tuna could not straighten!

To say the least it is an actual pleasure to cast using a wobbling spoon. The lure cuts through the air like a bullet and makes it possible to contrive accuracy casts that surely are not possible with typical plugs or regulation spoons. It is for this reason that I like casting with this lure. With accuracy, one can sneak in casts in between the pads and up in the heart of them where one sees a clear avenues or streak of water through which one can reel the lure. As to whether a spoon with red stripes on white or black stripes on white is the better is difficult to say. They are both good, and both have been qualified killers of undoubted merit.

While it is true that I have given the palm to the striped enameled spoon as a casting lure, this is not to forget my first love in this casting department for pike. I am refering here to the smaller models of the regulation spoon of the Skinner type, preferably the No. 5 size. While this seems rather small compared to the No. 9 and 12 sizes, it still has attractions and possibilities in number. The Skinner type spoon has a treble trailer gang that is marked in a three-cornered vane of feathers, the objective of which vane is to keep the lure from turning in the water which it does to a rather remarkable degree. You can also solder a snap in the crotch of the treble and attach a tail of pork rind thus adding about 50% to the seductiveness of the lure. It is cast into very much the same spot as the wobbling spoon is directed, and with, I believe, about the same, if not better, results. The caster who cannot take a small two and one half to three inch striped wobbling spoon and a No. 5 regulation Skinner spoon with a fluted blade and with a pork rind strip as detailed and take pike in numbers—and large ones—is still far from being a good casting exponent. These lures, or several of them to make up for possible losses, should be in every pike fisherman's tackle box. Pike lures certainly begin with these two types of lures. Should your selections end there, you still would have about the cream of the crop!

V
FURTHER NOTES ON PIKE FISHING

While it is true that the spoonhook, either in the regulation variety or as a wobbling spoon, it is the nemesis of many a stalwart pike, it is not to be forgotten that the species is also prone to fall upon plug lures with a murderous glint in the eye that forebodes no good for these animated wooden or plastic attractors. If one were to take one plug in special, Creek Chub Pikie Minnow, I am sure it can be said of it that it has contrived, in its day, the doom of such an aggregation of great northern pike as would defy the comprehension to compute. I am reminded years ago of a Pikie Minnow that I always carried along with me. It was scarred by teeth innumerable and finally it got so ground down by pike teeth that I had to discard it. I had painted and re-painted it but finally these re-conditionings failed to help. It had definitely died in service—and how. The only reason I kept using it was that it never failed to take fish, sometime bass, but mostly great northerns. It seemed that the battered and chewed-up condition of the lure only served to add to its effectiveness. There is something in this that I have never been able to solve, *i.e.*, why old, worn baits will take fish when new baits, glossy and right out of the cardboard box, will do but half as well!

Yes, I am sure that any lure that has the coloration of a small pike minnow, bars and all, is one of the best plugs that you can use. The reason for this is interesting, simply being that the pike is an inveterate cannibal and would rather eat the young of his own kind than any other food. So when a pike-colored plug comes along, it falls upon the same with a merry gusto and that's that. I might also state that the pike-colored plug is always good on bass, because the young pike pester the bass during spawning and are known to kill the small bass, hence the adult bass lose no time in striking back. But here is a very singular thing as regards the pike. In its adult state it apparently never does feed upon or kill the bass. At the time I was a column writer on a northern paper we made a special investigation into this matter, as the result of which thousands of stomachs of pike were opened to ascertain the kind of contents therein, while all manner of rough fish young and panfish were found, no one found a pike stomach that contained a bass. Having, on my own initiative, studied stomach contents of fish all my life, during which time I, also, have examined thousands of pike stomachs, I have never found a bass in one. It would seem from this that the adult pike at least do not kill bass quite apart from what the baby pike do in pestering the spawning bass. Probably they consume the spawn rather than the fry. From the above it would seem that pike and bass get along quite well in the water, some sort of natural dispensation of things of which we have little knowledge.

I don't know if Henry Dills, who was, I believe, the founder of the Creek Chub Company that makes the Pikie Minnow, originated this minnow, but I feel sure that he was the instigator of the jointed minnow, that is, a plug minnow that comes in two pieces, the same joined together by a hinge or wire loop. When reeled the swimming action of this lure is profoundly natural, assuring the most lifelike movement through the water of any lure I know. It is an interesting observation that not only is this jointed plug in the large, or musky size a killer on muskellunge but for large pike it is almost the best. This might be an answer to the question that is bobbing up right and left these days, which goes about as follows: "It seems that I can do pretty well in taking moderate sized pike but how am I going to get those really large pike to strike, and what lure would you suggest as best for them?" To this I would say that the musky size jointed minnow, pikie coloration, is right out there in front as one of the best that can be selected.

In relation to the above circumstances, let us look at the matter as to why more large pike are not taken. How many ever cast with musky plugs for great northern pike? Save only now and then are these large plugs employed in pike fishing, and then mostly in the north where the plugs are used in musky fishing during which trial numbers of great northern pike are likely to be taken. But in pike fishing, within the states, only very rarely are large plugs used. This is definitely an omission since it has left one of the most truly killing lures on the market untried. Understand that should large plugs be used and should they prove an incentive of a devastating character for the pike to strike, they must be natural enough in the eyes of the fish to impel the fish to action. In casting large plugs you will need to use a stiff-backed rod of the True Temper solid steel type or the Gep rod, also solid steel plus 24-pound test lines. The singular backbone of these rods make it possible to toss a plug of this musky type quite a distance. After a little experimentation it will be found that one can become quite accurate in such casting.

The times of the year when the large plug is best used, and the manner in which it is used, must be abided by. For actual casting of the plug in inshore waters it will be found that in the spring, as early as the law allows, is one of the best times. Again it will be found that the fall is an excellent season, starting in about the tenth or fifteenth of September, after the pike have overcome the sore mouth condition that inflicts itself upon the species during the latter part of August and early September. During these days of fasting, *i. e.*, taking in very little food, the pike become well nigh starved. Following after the close of this siege of jaw trouble, the pike really go into action and from the middle of September on to freeze-up (and through the winter for that matter), they are on the prowl, hunting food, busy around the clock stowing away vittles for fat, looking forward to the inclement season. October is probably one of the best of the fall months, although early November, should there be the blessing of Indian Summer weather, can also be a propitious period. During this fall interval the big pike cruise around inshore and sometimes project themselves very close to shore. It is, therefore, an ideal time for large plug casting.

As in casting any type of plug lure it should be remembered that it has bare treble hooks and they will hook into obstructions. That being the case one must conduct his casting by a careful study of the surroundings, aiming to put the lure in weed-free and pad-free waters and to lead the lure so far as possible through spots where the plug will not hang up. In a way it is a sort of picking your spots and not over-fishing or, if you will, over-casting. One makes comparatively few casts but aims to make each one count. There is a distinct advantage in having one of these musky plugs light enough to float when it is not reeled; both the Creek Chub Company and the Heddon Company have such large plugs. Such plugs, as usual, have metal collars in front to aid in taking them under. One distinct advantage of having a lure of this sort that floats is that by very slowly reeling it, it will move along on the surface in a distinct swimming action, especially if it is a jointed plug such as previously mentioned.

The best time to look for large pike in the inshore areas of a lake, is in the summer, mostly during the very early morning from around daybreak to about five or six o'clock. The same of course is true of the muskellunge, in fact both pike and muskies are early morning feeders. Again, large pike are likely to be found inshore from four in the afternoon until close on dusk. While some pike do feed after twilight it is a fact that the pike is not a night feeder, although the musky will feed up until dark. As to the reason for such early morning and evening fishing is uncertain. Possibly the inner waters are then more crowded with minnows and food in general, or maybe the lack of man's presence around a lake in the morning and evening is a clue to the movement of these fish. That would certainly be the case so far as lakes close to, or within the confines of civilization, are concerned. It seems to be instinctive with truly large pike that they are cautious often to the extreme—certainly so in much fished water. For this reason I would much prefer the use of a canoe in working over pike grounds. For one thing a canoe is a more maneuverable craft and one can get in and out of places with a minimum of propelling power, whereas shifting a boat from pointing in toward shore and then out is not too easily accomplished, especially if the boat is a heavy one. If a boat is used there is one way of managing it to "get underway" in a hurry when a fish is hooked and that is to keep the boat backed in toward the weeds, reeds, pads or general obstructions. The man at the oars can then row straight out into deep water without turning the boat. I think that if more fishermen would operate in this manner in all kinds of casting for pike, muskies and bass they would lose far less fish because of trouble in getting the boat organized for a quick departure.

In the previous chapter attention has been called to trolling with plugs that go fairly deep down such as the Bomber, the Whopper-Stopper and the Heddon Go-Deeper River Runt. One can of course govern the depth at which these long-billed plugs operate by the amount of line used. Aside from the use of these deep-running plugs we come upon another way of deep fishing with a different kind of plug. I am referring here to the six inch long jonted musky plugs described above that are used successfully both in casting for muskies and pike. Trolled as it is without any weight attached, it will go down at the most only about two feet or so. It is obvious, therefore, that a sinker must be placed up ahead of the plug to bring it down in the water. There is a failure recognized here in that placing a sinker on a line does much toward curbing or hampering the action of the plug, since it is obvious that unless the plug has the swimming motion it assures in the upper water its attraction is cut down fully fifty percent in deeper water.

It is a good idea to use the leaded line told about, whether thirty-five of fifty feet depends upon the depth at which one wishes to troll. Good trolling grounds lie off of points of land, in deep water arjacent to islands, between islands,

in fact anywhere the water drops off sharply. It is a fact that
large pike are in the habit of cruising along these slants in
from ten to fifteen or twenty feet of water and obviously
the only way you reach down that many feet is by trolling
deep either with the long-billed lures or with the regulation
casting plug of the jointed type. One failure of course with
the trolling spoons is that they do not go down deep enough
to get to the attention of the pike. In Lake Nipigon in Ontario
above Lake Superior the depth was fished was from ten to
fifteen feet and this was sufficient to contact large pike, in
fact some up to twenty-five pounds, although plugs of the
jointed type that have been trolled deep as outlined have
accounted for some Nipigon great northerns that have gone
to thirty and thirty-five pounds. If Lake Nipigon has had a
great reputation in the past as the home of brook trout, it
has been increased in the past few years by the great northern pike fishermen. In fact there is now almost as much interest attached to taking pike out of Nipigon as brook trout.
Here is another instance where the pike cannot be considered
an enemy of the trout, for the two seem to live side by side
without the pike making food of the latter.

Slow-trolling, using the jointed musky plug, with thirty-five
to fifty feet of leaded line "out front" will assure you a trolling depth for this plug of eight feet per every one hundred
feet of line. As to whether monofilament line should be used
some might consider open to question. I would rather suggest the use of 24-pound test regular line to which to tie the
forward leaded line. You might have a bead chain arrangement at the end of the leaded line to facilitate smooth swivel-
ling. All waters of a rocky, sandy or gravelled nature afford
excellent trolling grounds off of sloping shores and are more
or less ideal for a jointed plug run deep with proper weight
to carry it down. If a leaded line is not used a sinker can be
placed about three feet ahead of the lure, but never closer to
the lure or the action is lost.

Trolling down to twelve or fifteen feet can successfully be
conducted in the spring, summer and fall, for pike keep
themselves at about this depth much of the time.

Live bait fishing for pike belongs approximately in the
same school of endeavor as that of live lure fishing for muskies,
indeed the two may be classed in the same category. One

might say that when you fish for muskies with live bait you are as likely as not to meet up with a large great northern as well. Live bait fishing for great northern pike has never been told about outside of a few scattered paragraphs of dubious origin and by writers who have been uncertain in dealing with the subject. Too, I do not think that too many fishermen actually fish for either pike or muskies with large lures so it is a method that might well be listed with the known but unpracticed.

There is an interesting observation with regard to taking pike on a live lure that might be called to attention. Have you ever been fishing for panfish either with worms or minnows, during which period it is possible the fish were striking like mad? Fish everywhere all around, you might say. Then, suddenly, for no apparent reason whatsoever the striking has stopped and the fish seem to have flown on finny wings. You ask yourself, what was the reason for vanishing? Something must have frightened them away. But what? The chances are strong that this sudden retreat was caused by the arrival of none other than a large pike, and the larger the pike the more conclusive the withdrawal of the panfish. Having noticed all the excitement on this certain spot the pike has wandered in to see "what goes on around here." It is then if you have a large live lure ready in a minnow bucket, proper hook and line, you can let it down with every reason in the world of attracting the intruder below there to strike. I recall many instances where this has taken place. It is almost a sure-fire method of taking a big one. The lure should be fished at exactly the same depth you were fishing for the panfish so that you will be on the right level. Use a sizeable bobber, even though the lure takes it under. Bobber resistance on the line by the way does not scare a pike—not when there is a healthy active fish on the hook awaiting his pleasure. I might mention that in all live lure fishing there should be at least a ten inch wire leader on the end of the line with a swivel in one end to tie the line to and a snap on the other end. In writing on muskellunge fishing I have told about and recommended a special snap known as the Caldwell Safety Snap, which same has a locking pin device that makes it quite impossible for the snap to come undone. These are to be had with braided wire leaders and they obviously are a recommendation for live lure fishing for pike. However, I never recommend any such leaders without the statement that few of them are worth using. For one thing they coil and loop up on themselves and never stay straight, a terrible fault by the way. If you are willing to get hold of some No. 9 steel wire (which is silvery) you can make your own leaders, twisting a loop on one end that will hold the snap while the other end has a loop or turned ring that will hold a two ringed swivel. This is all you need, very simple, very efficient. And it will not loop up and kink on itself. A ten-inch length is sufficient.

If you were to ask me what live lure in the fish aggregation I consider the best of the lot for pike I would certainly say that a one foot long dogfish rather rivals comparison, although a sucker of the same length might be considered as eligible for second place.

The dogfish, *Amia calva,* which is also known as the mudfish, the grindle and the lawyer is without doubt the toughest fish that ever swam wet water—well, fresh water anyhow. A pike will take this lure in preference almost to any other. Its use for bait, however, is frowned upon by the authorities who do not want it distributed, for sometimes no doubt specimens used as bait will come off of the hook and will live to bring forth their young in the lake that is being fished. However, the fact that most all lakes and streams are inhabited by the dogfish, anyhow, makes this admonition rather inconclusive.

During my youth I can remember a fisherman who was constantly on a still-hunt for youthful dogfish. As lads we were encouraged to raid the brooks for them and for each of the right bait length that we took we would receive the sum of twenty-five cents. This fisherman stated that for every dogfish a foot long he used he was sure to get a large pike, and I believe that he was never failing. He apparently knew of a hundred and one Minnesota lakes where large pike were to be found and he knew just exactly where to go for them. One of his choice places in any lake was off of points of land, where the water dropped off deep. He used a large bobber. Sometimes he took no pike but more often he did, because he had the patience to stick it out. When a pike took the lure he would let the fish have line and sometimes permitted it to have the lure a half hour before setting the hook. Invariably he would take his fish because by that time the pike would have swallowed the dogfish deep down into its vitals. The long wire leader he used was protection against any teeth the pike might slash over it.

The secret in properly hooking a pike that has taken a live lure must be known, otherwise misses will be numerous. In taking a foot-long dogfish or other fish lure the pike seizes the lure across the center and swims away with it. He does not, however, immediately swallow the lure but keeps moving about, holding it secure in his jaws. How long this process continues is difficult to say. Eventually, if not disturbed (during which you feed out line) the pike will work the lure around, possibly with some difficulty, until it is in position to swallow, the swallowing being done with the lure passing down head first. There is a reason of course why the fisherman I told about allowed the pike a half hour before setting the hook. It can't exactly be too easy to masticate a one foot bait!

There is a question which involves the size of hook to be used, and whether that hook should be a single hook or a treble, that is, three hooks in one. It is certain that there is greater hooking possibility in a treble gang than in a single hook. If a treble hook is used each hook in the three should have a width across of a half inch, though even larger would be worth considering. But whether trebles or singles they should be European made, a suggestion being the Mustad bronzed steel. These are among the best made, nor do we have anything in this country that is an equal. One hook of the treble is seated in the tough muscle around the roots of the back fin which will hold the hook secure against all efforts to remove it. The hook should be impaled toward the back of the fin, not in the center of it or in front. So placed, the lure will have little difficulty in swimming around, as it should. If a treble is used then this will leave two hooks doing duty and that of course should be sufficient. These hooks should be kept needle sharp, which is possible on the Mustad hook by reason of its superior tempering. A single hook on the other hand has to be impaled to hold the lure and do duty at the same time in hooking the fish. This is not always so easy. I would say that a treble hook would by far be the most acceptable and is the surer hooker of the two.

There is a method of using two ganghooks as told about

in my coverage of the muskellunge and fishing for it. Select a Bead Chain that is three inches in length which has a snap on one end and a small ring at the other. Through this ring pass a very fine steel wire many times and then lodge the ring in the center of the crotch where the three hooks of the treble turn out. Now wrap the wire around and around where the hooks branch out and around the lower stem of the hooks, passing the fine wire now and then through the ring on the Bead Chain. Now solder the connection smooth and you have a double-treble arrangement that will give you the best possible hooking set-up. The back treble is seated at the roots of the back fin of the lure as stated, while the forward treble, hooks just under the skin along the rounded top of the back in front. This is almost a surefire proposition. Of course the snap on the Bead Chain holds the front treble hook.

While the dogfish is an excellent lure, as stated the common sucker takes second place, with redhorse or blackhorse suckers about as good. While hard to obtain in a small size, buffalo fish ten inches to a foot in length have possibilities. Regular minnows, such as chubs and shiners have little use inasmuch as they do not have the stamina and toughness of the lures stated. Bullheads up to a foot in length, with the spines in the fins clipped out, are likely to produce some very excellent results, although I am prone to state that the liver-colored operator is a better muskellunge bait than pike bait. Muskellunge, it would seem, make consuming bullheads something of a habit. One thing is certain in using the bullhead as a lure on the hook, the tough, leathery skin makes it possible to insert the hook in it without its breaking free. I am very skeptical with regard to the use of yellow perch as a live lure and while yellow perch, it has been echoed for years, are leading foods of the pike, still I doubt that this is the case, although I may be wrong. We have taken great northern pike in small lakes with a far-too-numerous perch population and while some of these pike have shown up with perch in their stomachs, the greater portion of their diet has been other fishes. We found this especially true in in the Upper Peninsula of Michigan. From this and other like observations I would say that while the pike do take perch (and yellow perch are here considered), they would far rather seize other food if it is available. If perch are used for live lures the suggestion would be that they should be at least eight inches in length.

There is a method of "jugging" for great northern pike that I have seen used a number of times—and very successfully. This involves putting a line with lure on it down into good water where pike are known to pass and re-pass, as pike make regular rounds over certain areas. Instead of a jug being used as in catfish fishing, however, a gallon can of the syrup variety, with cover pressed down tight will serve the purpose, and very well. The line is tied to the bale or handle. This floats and holds the lure at any depth desired. When the fish takes the lure he cannot sooner or later help but become hooked, and it will usually be deep down, for there is nothing to prevent its swallowing the lure. This is one reason why it is a good idea to use a twelve or fifteen inch long wire leader when thus fishing. The pike cannot pull the can under as a result of which all you have to do is locate the floater bobbing on the surface and you'll like as not have baked pike that night. It is an interesting observation that this method of fishing for the pike may be unlawful in some states, the possible stipulation being that the line must be attached to a rod and reel, or pole. In other words, the can with line attached cannot float free. While making a provision of this sort at the same time a state will permit those assassins with spears to sit in the dark of a fish house and virtually rid a whole lake of its pike population during the course of the winter. This merely points to the utter lack of knowledge or discrimination manifest in many game and fish departments which are usually dominated by groups that control the reins of state government, if not national. Knowing the above it would be well to check with your game and fish department as to your right to fish in the manner outlined, that is, with a can to hold the lure, and with no connection of the line with rod and reel.

One difficulty manifest in thus floating a bobber-can is that in a wind it will float up on shore or at least close to shore or probably across a lake. One good fisherman I knew took sixteen great northern pike one autumn in the manner stated, all of size, fished off of a point of land where the water dropped off deep. After the line with the bait on it and its floating can had been placed in position off of the point another line from the handle of the can to shore was fastened to some object. Then at least forty feet away from the can, out in the lake, a stone or some other heavy object with a wire to it was let down to the bottom. This wire came up to the surface and was tied to another floater. By having a line running up to shore from the bait line floater and then out to the floater in the lake it was quite impossible for the arrangement, with the lure on it, to float away, even in a wind. I have mentioned that pike of size are usually taken in this manner and there is of course a reason for this in that the lure used is generally too large for a small pike to handle, although the fisherman I mentioned told about a small pike that had come to its death trying to swallow a live fish lure that was almost as large as he was. The fish had virtually choked to death as, while it had scissored the lure around to swallow it head first, it had gotten the head down in its gullet and had died or choked to death in this fashion without ever contacting the hook which would have been an impossibility.

There is little doubt but that the last ten days of September, all of October and in early November (if the weather is agreeable), is the best time for inshore fishing for all sizes of great northern pike. The can method of fishing, as described, is then also at its deadliest. It would seem that the great northern pike does not go into any dramatic action in the summer, August certainly being a month that leaves it sick or ailing. While, during the so-called "dog-day" season, normally the last two weeks in August, it is troubled no end with shedding teeth and a sore gum condition; this disappears in the month of September. While it is true that the pike sheds some teeth in August it should be remembered that it loses teeth at various times all through the year, but there are constantly new ones coming on. True as this may be it will be found that in the autumn and through the winter the jaws and the teeth of the pike are in perfect condition, proof that cool to cold weather has everything to do with this singular sore mouth or sore jaw condition.

The blustering winds and stormy condition generally in autumn do not seem to be much of a hindrance to the pike as regards its moving about, and feeding. Other fish may slow up and move into deeper water, but not so the pike. It seems to like this wild condition of wind and wave and that some of the largest of the pike are now taken is an assured fact. If, during the summer, these pike have been much in solitary hiding, moving about like shadows in the deep places, keeping out of all possible sight of man, feeding in the early morning and in the late afternoon to twilight, in the autumn they feel a strange urge to move about and to project themselves into the inshore places in quest of an almost endless and continued meal. Later on, in the winter, it may take them four or five days to digest a one foot long fish, but starting in the autumn and lasting until winter seals the lakes, the pike feeds well and does not seem to have any lengthy trouble in digesting its food.

There are times in the month of October when the great northern pike seem to go upon some sort of a feeding spree the reason for which is difficult to diagnose. Just when this strange activity will occur is hard to say. Whether John Alden Knight with his Solunar theory, or Grady Coble with his "blacker the fish the better the fishing" could find a reason for it is problematical and not apparently answerable by any conclusions man may have concocted. Only if you should fish every day in October and fish the inshore waters in a lake known to have plenty of pike in it you will be treated to an exposition of the feeding spree I have told about.

Let me take one case in special regarding this excessive feeding condition of the pike. It was one October day, some years ago in Minnesota, when we fished a certain lake. This lake at that time had a considerable population of pike to its credit and some very large ones, though not larger than other lakes in the same category and in the same region

As I remember it, the morning of this October day had been stormy, and somewhat chilly, at around noon the wind went down, the sun came out and the day was one of those that certainly exemplifies October at its best. In fishing this lake we usually started in at a point where some birches grew on shore, as at this spot the water deepened somewhat and lily-pads appeared. I was casting with a red and white Eppinger Daredevil wobbling spoon three inches in length. This spoon casts remarkably well, is not deterred by wind resistance, in fact it is one spoon which permits rather fine accuracy.

It was possibly on the second or third cast that I took my first pike, one of five or six pounds. If you start out good you'll end up bad I thought. But two more casts brought in another pike and so in quick succession as we worked down the shore they came trooping in, one following another for all the world as though they had never seen a spoon before. It was after the tenth or twelfth one was landed that we (my companion and myself) came to the conclusion that this was a most unusual condition, one that we could not account for. In the meantime two boys on the shore across from us were also having a Roman holiday with pike as they were using a canepole and frogs for lures. The shouting finally resolved itself into a plea that we come over and fish on their shore as there were pike everywhere. That we did not come to their rescue was because we had enough to contend with in our own division.

In a length of shore water not over eight hundred feet from where we started and where we left off we took, as I remember, thirty-eight pike, the largest a twelve pounder. Most of all these were returned save some that we took home. Since that time I have regretted that we did not continue further down the lake as there were some choice spots we knew of where large pike were always a possibility. But after hooking and releasing most of thirty-eight pike we quit fishing. However, on going over to the other side where the boys were jumping up and down and shouting to us still to "come on" we found the pike even more numerous, in fact here it was a case of virtually one every cast and, if anything (save the twelve pounder), they were larger.

What was the reason for this feeding spree? We never did find out even by examining the insides of the fish to see what, if anything, they had been feeding on. Fact of the matter is we found most of the stomachs virtually empty!

That this condition of pike being found almost to their entire population in the inshore stretches of the lake striking like mad, became all the more a puzzle when, the next day we arrived on the scene for another bout with old *Esox*. True to our usual procedure we started in at the birches and prepared for the onslaught. The day was almost an exact counterpart of the previous day. Fifteen or twenty casts went into effect; then eighteen and thirty-six casts; then forty and sixty-two casts and not a pike nor the sign of any fish. After covering almost the entire lake we did not take a pike nor see scale or fin of one. Try to explain away that one.

VI

PIKE THROUGH THE ICE

There are many who will not like this chapter and because of it are liable to condemn the entire book. Or, should we say, those who will be up in arms against it are those who like to sit in a well-warmed house (of sorts) over a hole in the ice from the seclusion of which, like an assassin in the dark, operate a minnowlike lure luring the pike up to the hole when a spear is driven down with telling effect. If there is any sport in this sort of killing of the great northern pike I fail to see it. Yet you will hear the spear-devotee get excited no end over this manner of taking old *Esox*, in fact will exhibit the same enthusiasm evidenced by the dry-fly fisherman in telling about a dazzling bivisible floating the water like a lambent breath of thistledown.

It is hard to comprehend that any human being can wax enthusiastic over killing anything with a spear. True, back in the cave-days there was a reason for the spear but in this advanced day, when we are supposed to be head and shoulders over the muck at least, one can see not the slightest justification for the murder of the pike as it is carried on the length and breadth of the snow-belt of the north by means of the ghastly times. That form of killing is one whit better than that of sneaking up on an innocent person in an alley and driving a knife into his back or killing mother birds on the nest. It is something so reprehensible and repugnant to awaken ones deepest disgust. That state game and fish commissions do not do something about stopping this practice is merely proof that the state law-makers are prevented from outlawing the practice because of small main-street cliques of doctors, lawers, grocerymen, etc., who find it a pleasure to have a fish house on the ice and sit there through the cold winter days spearing fish that should be taken only by fishermen with hook and line as they should be taken, whether in the winter or during any other time of the year.

Some years ago when I had a daily outdoor column on a large Minnesota newspaper I came out strongly against spearing through the ice and I pointed out that unless the practice were brought to a close the time would come when our Minnesota lakes would be barren of the pike and the state would have to go about propagating the species to plant in waters that had been denuded. For this telling of a grave shortcoming I was figuratively pillored and held up to ridicule, and such a storm of protest came from a lot of two-bit shyster lawyers, second rate pill doctors, and third rate grocerymen and their ilk in the small main-street towns and villages that the powers that be higher up on the paper dictated caution in writing any further on the subject. Too anonymous threats came in, if I showed up at this or that lake I would summarily be taken care of. It was not until the adventure in telling the truth about winter spearing of the pike that I realized fully what a tremendous interest there was in spearing through the ice, quite regardless what fascination it might have at all. Too, there were little snivelling groups having game associations of sorts who had speakers who also condemned me for writing against spearing through the ice, contending that unless the pike were kept in check, most terrible things would happen to the other fish species in a lake. These speakers were generally well applauded and that I was not tarred and feathered as a result of my defense of the great northern pike was not because there were not sufficient numbers who would like to do the tarring and feathering but rather they did not know how to proceed about putting the act across. Just what the Minnesota Game and Fish Commission at the time thought of the matter I do not know, but it was to be noted that they did not voice their opinion one way or the other. This was merely proof that the nit-wit worms in the small towns and villages had had their way.

Then at long last, what happened? After years of uncontrolled and wholly indiscriminate spearing not only in the fish houses on the ice but in the streams in the spring, Minnesota came to realize, by profound example, that you cannot decimate the pike without suffering a grave disarrangement of nature's system of balance and proportion. And this, certainly, was, and is, the case with the pike. So at the present time the state is engaged in rearing pike to release in the lakes that the ice-spearing gentry wiped out, doing just exactly what I said would some day have to be done if this spearing through the ice practice was continued. It is strange that the course we take in game and fish endeavors has to be learned the hard way just as Minnesota had to learn the hard way that you cannot kill off the pike and have them, too. The oddity about this winter spearing has been that persons in the resort and fishing areas are the ones that have been the strongest for spearing through the ice. Jason Lucas states:

"Practically all winter spearing is done by residents of resort districts, men who are mainly dependent for their living upon money spent by sportsmen in their region in the summer. So in running the sport for the summer visitors, these year-'round residents are neatly and effectively cutting their own throats, sending sportsmen elsewhere. Shakespeare had the word for it—'What fools these mortals be!'"

There are lakes in the states of Minnesota, Wisconsin and Michigan that at one time had teeming numbers of pike which are now in the extremely doubtful column, due of course, to the fact that excessive spearing has been permitted to the extent that the pike have all but been wiped out. In some of these lakes where twelve and fifteen pound pike were fairly common, now the taking of a six pounder is considered something to crow about. Then the wonder is openly expressed: Where are our pike going ? Such moronic reasoning you'll come across all over the north even in those regions and lakes were pike that have been speared have been piled up like cordwood outside of fish-houses, something that happened one time on Tenth Lake of the Crow Wing Chain in Minnesota. Then they wonder what has happened to the pike. If this isn't enough to throw one's risibility into a spasm I would not know what could have a more profound effect. As to whether the facts of the case have properly infiltrated into the heads of these winter spearing groups and the law-makers, that the pike are necessary in numbers in our lakes, is uncertain, but it is gradually beginning to dawn upon the upper crust in fish conservation in the north that the pike has at last come into its own. It is not now classified as a killer only and a prime nuisance but a fish worthy of anyone's tackle and that to continue its kind in the waters is, in the sense of things, something constructive and vitally necessary.

For many years I have looked upon the great northern pike as the controller of the fish in a lake. Indeed I have gone so far as to state that without the pike a lake must eventually be over-run with all manner of common species and varieties of fish, the keeping in check of which could belong to the pike and the pike only. In other words the pike controls in part at least, the increase of the commonfish which, otherwise would increase out of all sense of proportion and so act to keep the balance of nature preserved. This opposes the belief of some biologists who contend that balance in nature is a myth, a figment of the fancy. Yet we can show you lakes where, at one time, there was no predominating over-population of common fish but which are now utterly over-run with these species due expressly to the removal of the pike from the water by the man with the spear—and the man with the spear understand not only spearing through the ice but spearing in the streams in the spring.

Previously I have called attention to the efforts I made to find whether the pike was a killer of the bass, something, I might mention, that was brought up in my arguments against spearing through the ice, the contention of the proponents being that the pike was a destroyer of the bass, obviously for food. Hundreds of replies came in on this and the sum total was that no one had found a bass of any size in the stomach of a pike but that baby pike had been found in the stomachs of bass. This proved to be such an alarming trend in upholding the objectivity of the case that a silence as of the grave fell upon the subject. The opponents of the pike as destroyers of the game fish, entirely had the bass in mind. If there were any other game fish that might be considered as prey of the pike then it would be the presistent wall-eye and here again no one has risen to state that the pike is a killer of this greater member of the perch family. As a bass destroyer therefore the pike cannot be considered in the light of a menace to the black bass population so that if there is a diminishing supply of the black bass in a lake the charge of cutting it down to a positive minimum can be laid at the doors of man, for man will kill bass by any manner known and still will wonder why the species is decreasing. For instance, the habit fishermen have of fishing on the spawning beds of the bass. This practice may be tolerated in the south but in the north conditions are different. If a backward season comes along and finds the water under 55° F. the bass may not spawn. They will be on the nests, yes, but they will wait there till the water is the right temperature for spawning. Yet the season for fishing is open. So the fishermen as one move in on the spawning beds and are able to take about all the fish on the beds—before they have spawned. Yet no one has said anything against this obvious indiscrimination on the part of man. It is far more easy to charge the pike with the deed.

I do believe that pike feed to a certain extent on panfish but these are normally numerous in most northern lakes, in fact too many of them, so what "harm" the pike does in taking some of these for food is positively negligent. The fear that the pike would increase to the extent that they would prove a threat to the lives of other game fish is answered by the fact that with the present heavy fishing conducted and the usual eagerness and viciousness with which pike strike a lure this would mean a positive curb to any such over-production for they would help kill themselves down.

At the time I criticised spearing through the ice, I did not come out against fishing pike through the ice, out in the open. This, in itself, raised a bombastic howl and a succession of main-street whines. If it were to be unlawful to spear through the ice, then it should likewise be unlawful to fish through the ice. This in spite of the fact that for every possible ten fish the man would spear in a house on the ice, the man out in the open, without shelter, fishing with hook and line would take one. As a conservation measure, of the two I would say that fishing through the ice for pike is every bit a howling success. While the man fishing through the ice has no shelter—in fact can have no shelter by law—the man with the spear can sit in comfort, in pleasant warmth and need not take pneumonia or otherwise lay himself open to the miseries. All this while he is planning to murder a fish by stabbing it in the back. Most of the time he can't hit with accuracy—one reason why so many fish are injured and get away.

So far as fishing through the ice for pike is concerned I doubt if it can be called a very successful method of pike fishing. Understand, this isn't because pike can't be taken through the ice but that most fishermen do not have the patience to "stick it out" and do not know the methods involved in fishing for pike. Like fishing through the ice for the panfish, taking pike under the same circumstances means a long wait and a very cold one—usually.

There are some fishermen who are wizards at taking pike through the ice but they, too, have been able to muster a lot of patience and hours on the ice waiting for the *something* to happen. But just patience doesn't count for anything unless you know where to fish. You might go out in the middle of a bay and fish there until you are blue in the face—from cold—and you might not make connections. Therefore, knowing where to fish calls for more or less a knowledge of the lake you are fishing, where the deep places off shore are found, good spots out from mouths of streams flowing into lakes, the deep water off of either end of a channel connecting two lakes, deep sloping water off of points of land and deep water between islands, all those places where pike like to pass and re-pass during the day. To say that the pike frequent just about the same places they tarry in during the summer is not hitting far a-miss of the mark. We have proven this time and again to our entire satisfaction. The only thing that differs so far as the winter pike is concerned is that it takes but a minimum amount of fuel bodily to keep it in good condition, the reason for this being that food is digested by fish in the winter at a comparatively slow rate as compared with summer when a steady procession of finny provender is ingested by the pike and still the creature will be looking around for more. Winter pike will be found in a most excellent condition physically, due to the heavy intake of food during the fall when fat is accumulated in preparation for the inclement season when food may be scarce. While the pike may be moving about—in fact he is always on the move in the fall and winter— he does not take as much food as one might suspect, one reason why winter taken pike may be quite barren as to stomach contents. If this is through disinclination or need to feed or an inability to find forage fish on the move is something I have never been sure. We do know that the pike will follow a decoy minnow up almost to the hole in the fish house where it is speared. The pike is always inordinately curious with regard to anything that moves in an unusual way in the water and this certainly goes for the species in the winter as well as in the summer, possibly more so.

The "tools" used by the ice fisherman do not differ much from those used by the fisherman who concentrates all his efforts in the taking of panfish, *i.e.*, crappies, sunfish, perch, etc.,

One very necessary item is the ice chisel, without which one might have to use an axe, and an axe is the least recommendable of all instruments one could use in cutting down to water. An axe is dangerous in the extreme as, without warning, it may skid or glance with deadly effect. We remember one instance where an axe slid out of a fisherman's hands and shot across the ice lodging in the foot of a companion. One should be warned at all times not to use an axe in cutting through the ice.

The best method is to make an ice chisel. This can very easily and effectively done. A carpenter's' 2½ inch wide worn-out wood chisel can be welded to a one inch diameter pipe of the common water-pipe type. When the chisel is welded on the overall length of the arrangement it will be four feet long. This is inclusive of the chisel. To make this a take-apart affair the pipe can be cut in the center after which the ends can be threaded and a sleeve-coupling turned on. It takes but a minute to screw together and the sections can easily be carried in a canvas bag made for the purpose of holding them. To add heft to the chisel end of the affair, melted lead can be poured into this part of the handle giving it sufficient weight to sink into the ice with a minimum of bodily drive. The top end of the pipe, where the hand must go, should also be threaded and a T-coupling about 3½ inches in length turned on. This will give a secure grip. Through it a strap or rawhide loop can be affixed, the same passing around the wrist to hold it secure against slipping out out of one's grasp.

While tip-ups are more or less effective in pickerel fishing through the ice, these are of little value in pike fishing as the pike you are likely to take, at the smallest, will be far larger than any of the three pickerel varieties known to our waters. In pike fishing the best method of using a line is to have 150 or more feet laid out on the ice and when the fish make its run, this line is fed out and is retrieved in accordance with the actions of the fish. Rarely are these runs very extensive, although at times a fish will flash away like an arrow when it finds itself hooked.

For pike fishing through the ice I much prefer a 38-pound cuttyhunk linen line, or even heavier than that. This is not needed because of its actual pounds test, believing that a pike will break a lighter line, but simply that a heavier line is easier to hold in the hands without slipping to easily. One's grasp can hold it secure. Some ice fishermen make a series of knots on the line for about fifty feet back from the twenty feet used actually in the water. These are spaced a foot apart. The knots assure a better grip on the line. There is reason to believe this is true but we have never made use of the idea.

The same double-hook arrangement elsewhere recommended in live lure fishing for pike in spring, summer and fall (that is, two treble hooks), works just as effectively in the winter as in the summer. Thus one of the trebles is seated in the thick muscle at the base of the dorsal (back) fin while the forward hook (which is connected with a bead chain to the back hook) is seated just under the skin of the back, forward of the dorsal fin. This makes almost a never failing combination. Again the suggestion is made that, if possible, treble hooks of the bronzed Mustad type be selected, as they are not only exceedingly strong but one can maintain a sharp point on them with but a few passes of a small file or a hook hone. It is of the greatest demand that hooks used should be needle keen.

It may be relatively simple to obtain minnows and small fish in the summer for pike fishing but not quite so easy in the winter. Marshes and swamps connecting with lakes often have fairly considerable ponds of water in them. By opening up a hole in the same, dogfish and other common fish can be attracted. A hoop net of fine mesh can be let down to the bottom, the wire hoop having four cords spaced equidistant around it, reaching up to a central point where the four cords are tied to a main cord. This main cord can be attached to a sapling. One can stand away from the hole in this manner and lift the net without frightening the fish, over the same. The bait can be bread, chopped up spaghetti, in fact most any scraps. There are times in marshes where aeration is at a minimum when thousands of these minnows large and small, including bullheads, will be attracted to the hole by air alone. It might be mentioned that the mud minnow is commonly found in such muddy locations and are used more or less freely in panfish fishing, though it is too small for pike. While it is dark colored and is not too good as a bait minnow by reason of its hue, still it qualifies as very useful in that it is tenacious and will move around carrying the hook for hours at end.

Suckers often school up in pools in the rivers. If the water of the stream is clear, one can cut through the ice and by throwing a canvas over one so that the hole is also covered and looking down one can ascertain just what is the fish populations in the pool. Sometimes great numbers of common suckers, redhouse, blackhorse, buffalofish and other hob-nob together in these pools. They can be seined by running a net along through a series of holes cut in the ice across the lower pool and then in holes cut about the seine, poles can be inserted in the water to create a disturbance that will drive the fish down into the net. This is a method that will often net you a great number of suckers large enough to use for pike bait. It should be mentioned that winter-taken suckers have far more vitality than those taken in warmish weather, even spring weather. They do better than any other lure on the hook save the dogfish.

Usually minnow dealers in a region where much fishing through the ice is done will have large minnows and fish up to a foot in length for use. In fact this has solved the problem for many a winter fisherman. As a rule the fish kept for bait use are the ones that the pike will take. It is possible to take large numbers of perch (yellow perch) in the winter by fishing through the ice. As I have stated before, while the pike do not seem to make a habit of feeding on yellow perch if they can obtain other food, it nevertheless is conceded by many that the perch is a typical pike food. Unfortunately, most perch are small in size. If it is possible to obtain this species eight inches in length, a desirable lure is had. We are not considering panfish (sunfish and crappies, particularly) as live lures for pike, for while they take the same there is a law that usually protects these panfish from us as bait. For that matter I do not think panfish are too desirable as lures.

Of course if you are using a lure ten inches to a foot in length the two treble hook arrangement is recommendable but should the lures be down to eight inches in length the size of the hooks must conform in size to the lure. Hook sizes for each hook in the treble therefore could be No. 1/0 or 2/0 for size, and a single treble hook can be used instead of two as suggested for the foot long lure. A small lure of course can be turned by the fish and swallowed far more easily than a foot long lure and the single hook may, in many cases, be more effective in actual hooking potentialities than the two treble-hook arrangement. Usually the one advantage of the large lure is that it inspires the fish, without uncertainty, to strike. One rather believes that the pike sees in the large lure a remarkable example of a four-cornered meal all in one gulp so he loses no time in taking it. On the other hand he may fool around with a small lure and finally leave it.

In fishing for pickerel of all three varieties in the winter, as previously stated, tip-ups of several varietes are used. The line on these is fixed to go from the tip-up to the fish, hardly more than twenty feet or so. You cannot fish pike in this manner. The line must be so arranged, as outlined, to lie on the ice and to be taken out by the pike in accordance with his runs. Most pike fishermen, however, do use a bobber up to three or three and one half inches in length and two inches in diameter to hold the lure at a given depth. So far as the pike is concerned it has no exquisite niceties of perception and a bobber on the line, offering an unnatural resistance on it, does not awaken suspicion and debate—if a pike can debate with himself. The lure in swimming around may take the bobber under now and then but it will bob back on the surface at intervals. Therefore the use of a bobber is a suggestion and if the larger size you can obtain and if it is red and white, that's what you want.

Thus the simple equipment and arrangement for taking large pike through the ice. Making a hole to fish through that is just right is something that is a positive demand. If you make the hole in the shape of a V you will have a generous diameter at the top and a tapering or narrowed diameter at the bottom which is all wrong. The best hole to cut is one like a V upside down, wide at the bottom and narrowed at the top although even at the top the hole should be no less than 12 inches across; 15 inches would be far better, and the bottom edges of the hole 20 inches or so in diameter. You may doubt the need of this, but never forget that taking a small fish from the hole and one that might range all the way up to a possible 30 pounds are different matters. The aperture in the ice must be roomy. Leave no jagged edges around the bottom of the hole against which the line can be gashed. It is strange how lines can be cut on sharp ice!

One of the largest winter pike I have ever seen taken weighed exactly 24 pounds. That's quite a fish; in fact it is one of those sizes that fishermen are now going all out to acquire and which many concede as equal to a muskellunge any day. Just to show you how things have changed!

My fisherman friend Bill took me on this trip. Just as there are anglers who cannot wait until the trout season opens so they can wet a line and work a fly in the water, so are there fishermen who are likely to quietly scorn summer and generally fine-weather fishing, but who cannot wait till the lakes freeze over so they can start cutting through and dropping lures down to the mighty. These rugged individuals, with iron constitutions, absolutely immune to cold feet, would rather take one good fish through the ice than scorch for a month on the lakes in the summer. Bill once told me as much. Too, Bill was a big pike specialist and it was from him that I took my first lessons at fishing for *Esox* through the ice. The accent here of course would be on *large* pike. During the summer it seemed Bill was busy finding lakes where the pike were large and would be ideal specimens to work on in the winter. He didn't generally fail in picking the right ones, although I'll swear we sometimes went fully two hundred miles from home to make connections.

It was the winter the snow was so deep in Minnesota. I always have that to go by. This time the lake he had concentrated on was no more than fifty miles from home, which was one consolation at least. Secretly I had hoped to get out of this deal but found no reasonable way of worming clear of the act. Too, Bill had laid it on thick. The lake, he said, was a natural. Evidently spring-fed, water clear as crystal, was well back on a farmer's land and few people ever went there. At one end of the lake a stream came in, just a small rivulet type, also evidently coming from springs. Best of all, said Bill, as he almost broke my shoulder with a slap, was that he had seen a pike over near this drop-off at the incoming stream that would go (so he claimed) no less than thirty pounds in weight. He had fished the spot thoroughly hoping to take the big fellow, but all that happen was that once as he was reeling his spoon in the fish followed it almost up to the boat. It was then that he got a close look at it and it was his belief that it was the largest pike he had ever seen.

We had driven in Bill's truck to the farm-house on whose land the lake was located. We had a toboggan, a canvas for making a shelter, and a wash boiler in which two or three kinds of lures were kept, chief among them being three or four suckers. This wash-boiler had been wrapped around with blankets to prevent ice forming inside, all of which was more necessary later on than while we were en route in the car.

It was fully a half mile from the house to the lake and the farmer on whose land we were to fish shook his head. He thought he would rather stay indoors than be out there fishing. "Better," he said, "that we should come there and fish in the summer and then we could get us some bullheads." But now, he said, it was crazy to think of fishing. No fish would strike at this time of the year. After we got half way to our destination I very nearly agreed with him. If weather conditions had anything to do with it we had surely picked a day that might end in a blizzard or its close approximate. The further we got from the farmhouse the more certain I was that this was Bill's wildest of wild goose chases.

As luck would have it the lake lay virtually in a large hollow with hills rising around its shore. Luckily, too, where we were to fish was close to shore and trees were thick enough to form a protection from the north wind, the trees being young oaks that had retained their dry leaves.

Bill was not long in finding where the little stream came in, or where it came in during weather more propitious than that at present. The snow was cleared away with a shovel and the hole installed about where Bill was certain the drop off was. He made the hole large, in fact larger than any I had, up to this time, seen fashioned. He said that you needed them big if you were to take out large pike, and especially a pike that might go 30 pounds in weight. When he said that I looked at Bill and Bill looked back. He added: "He'll not go an ounce under that!"

It was about ten in the morning when we each had a hole cut in the ice and were ready for pike of both length and girth. Bill's optimism, I might add, was quite contageous and it was not long before I was leaning comfortably toward the belief that this was it. The old mossback pike of Hilly Lake was about to give up his ghost. But as the hours crept on past noon and not the sign of a fish hitting at either of our lures I began to have my doubts. Hot water, powdered coffee and sandwiches at noon and a good fire helped restore whatever faith in the fishing that we may have lost. I say "we" but that is stretching it a point for Bill never to my knowledge ever was discouraged in any of his ice fishing anywhere, anytime.

"Its like this," Bill offered by way of explanation. "Pike do their circulating around in the morning, sometimes very early, even in winter. Then they lay quiet. Anywhere from two o'clock on to dark they are on the prowl again. That's when we'll have results."

Between one o'clock and two if I remember correctly, something happened. It happened on my line. I was using an eight inch long perch that I had selected out of the wash boiler, chiefly because I had heard that pike do feed on perch and that if you use one see that it long enough. The strike came suddenly, to the extent that the big oval red and white bobber went under like a shot. I rushed to do something about the line but Bill hollered: "Pick up the line, that's okay. But let the line feed out. Don't jerk it or its all off. Just let him have it. Maybe you hit the jack-pot. Aren't you the lucky one!"

I had visions of a thirty pound pike, a larger pike than I had ever taken; my largest at that time being no more than twenty-five pounds.

I said: "Suppose I give him about twenty minutes with the lure. He ought to have it turned to swallow by that time."

Bill shook his head. "Better give him not less than a half hour. He'll never give up the perch. He'll hold onto it till hell freezes over!"

That was a long time to wait. Occasionally the fish moved around, pulling that bobber with him. I fed out line. When the half hour or so had passed I got a jerk motion of the hand from Bill and I set the hook. The fish was on and hooked beyond all question and for the next few minutes I was busy paying out line. Then he came in willingly, only to make another spurt for freedom. After about fifteen or twenty minutes of this he began to come in in a rather docile fashion. Bill, standing by, said: "Its a good pike; but its not the old mossback." Well, it wasn't the thirty pounder, but when I landed it and it lay there flopping on the snow, a gleaming jewel of a fish, I was quite satisfied. Bill said: "Good enough. He'll go fifteen pounds or better." He fetched out his scales and sure enough the fish went to sixteen and a half pounds.

The above happened at about two o'clock. Not a thing had happened at Bill's location but he was not disappointed. One hour passed; two hours. It was now getting onto four o'clock and early dark would settle on the land by five o'clock. And it was getting colder right along. I heaped wood on the fire to keep warm but Bill stood there by the hole in the ice no doubt secretly hoping and wishing at the same time. His eyes apparently did not leave the cork.

On one of my trips from the fire to the hole in the ice that I presided over I noticed my bobber go down out of sight and my heart leaped up at sight of the action. Another one was trying my lure. This, I thought, must be the big one! But while standing there with the line in hand listening to Bill's admonitions not to be hasty, up came the bobber and rested where it had been before. But something had tried my minnow. There was no doubt of it.

Then something else happened. Bill at his spot, bent low with the line, galvanized into concentration plus. I slipped over and took a look. The bobber was out of sight, no where to be seen: a fish had it, that was certain. We neither of us spoke, but both of us were watching the line at the point where it pierced the water. Some time transpired before anything happened. Bill said in a half-tone: "He's got it, the blame brute. The sucker is quite big for him to handle. I'll have to give him at least three quarters of an hour but if its a big one—if it is that thirty pounder, he'll be able to get it turned very shortly."

Some five minutes later the line suddenly shot down and Bill was busy feeding out the reserve. I pulled the line up where it had frozen to the snow and held it lightly in my hand. The run that the pike made was a fairly short one. This was followed by another pause. Still Bill did nothing about it. It was obvious that he was taking no chances.

I am sure that I was fully as excited over the event as was Bill and was impatient to see the hooks set solid in the jaws of the big one. I said: "Any indication as to how big he is?" Bill answered: "Can't tell. But we will soon know. The next run he makes will be a long one probably and if so it will mean that he has swallowed the bait or has it going down his gullet. Then when he pauses again I'll set the hook."

True enough the line once more shot out and this time we fed out twenty or thirty feet of line, not the slightest resistance being put on it by our hands. The pause came and I knew that this is what Bill had waited for. He breathed: "Here goes!"

Men may have set hooks in a fish more powerfully than Bill did in this instance but I doubt it. Having set the hook for the first time Bill was certain how big the fish was. He said: "Its a big one. I can just budge him and that is all."

If I say that much of three quarters of an hour slipped by before we even got him to the hole I am not exaggerating. By that time the big fellow was pretty well tuckered out but might be playing the usual 'possum trick they have in letting you believe they are done for, only to flash into action at your very hands. I crept down by the hole and told Bill to keep pulling him in till his head was near the hole and I would slip my hand down and catch him under the gill cover. Bill said: "If you do for heaven's sake don't miss and get into his jaws or you're a dead duck!"

It was odd that the pike did nothing as he came up into the hole. Probably it was because it was getting dark fast. Anyhow the head was about to clear water. . . . But before it came out into the open I had slipped my hand down and under the spread gill cover. Then in a grip as hard as I could manage it was up and away and heave ho! The pike was out of the water just as I slipped and fell full length over him, plunging my face deep into a heap of snow. And that was that.

About that time the big fellow came into action and the way he threshed around was something words could hardly tell about. In due course we had him on the scales and were weighing him. I said: "He'll go at least thirty pounds." Bill with a twinkle in his eyes said: "No. Not thirty. Twenty-four. He's not the old moss-back. The two we have taken may be his brother and sister but the old cuss himself is still at large. Now we'll have to come back and get him some other day!"

See what I mean about fishing for big pike through the ice?

VII

THE NORTH AMERICAN PICKERELS

In his classic work "Walden, or, Life in the Woods" Henry David Thoreau has this to say with regard to the pickerel found in his immortal pond:

"Ah, the pickerel of Walden! when I see them lying on the ice, or in the well which the fishermen cuts in the ice, making a little hole to admit the water, I am always surprised by their rare beauty, as if they were fabulous fishes, foreign as Arabia to our Concord life. They possess a quite dazzling and transcendent beauty, which separates them by a wide interval from the cadaverous cod and haddock whose fame is trumpeted in our streets. They are not green like the pines, nor grey like the stones, nor blue like the sky; but they have, to my eyes, if possible, yet rarer colours, like flowers and precious stones, as if they were the pearls, the animalised *nuclei* of crystals of the Walden water. They, of course, are Walden all over and all through; are themselves small Waldens in the animal kingdom, Waldenses. It is surprising that they are caught here—that in this deep and capacious spring, far beneath the rattling teams and chaises and tinkling sleighs that travel the Walden road, this great gold and emerald fish swims. I never chanced to see its kind in any market; it would be the cynosure of all eyes there. Easily, with a few convulsive quirks, they give up their watery ghosts, like a mortal translated before his time to the thin air of heaven!"

He continues elsewhere:

"There have been caught in Walden, pickerel, one weighing seven pounds, to say nothing of another which carried off a reel with great velocity, which the fisherman safely set down at eight pounds. . . . I have seen at one time, lying on the ice, pickerel of at least three different kinds: a long and shallow one, steel-coloured, most like those caught in the river; a bright golden kind, with greenish reflections and remarkably deep, which is the most common here; and another golden-coloured, and shaped like the last, but peppered on the sides with small dark brown or black spots, intermixed with a few faint blood-red ones, very much like a trout. The specific name *reticulatus* would not apply to this; it should be *guttatus* rather. These are all very firm fish, and weigh more than their sizes promise."

It is obvious from Thoreau's description that these three pickerels that inhabited Walden were the three pickerel varieties known to the North American continent, namely, the Banded Pickerel *(Esox americanus)*, the Little Pickerel, also known as the Trout pickerel *(Esox vermiculatus)*, and the Chain Pickerel or Eastern Pickerel *(Esox niger)*. While the first named is found apparently only east of the Alleghanies, the last two are found not only through the east but west of the Alleghanies as well, in fact the latter two range as far southwest as Louisiana and Texas, strange as it may seem but true nevertheless; and these are there of their own natural accord and were not transplantings from the east. So when Thoreau stated that there were three different pickerel species found in Walden Pond, near Boston, Massachusetts he probably was entirely correct. The pickerel he states was "a long and shallow one" was undoubtedly the banded pickerel; the one that was "remarkably deep" (that is, of body in proportion to length), was no doubt the little pickerel, or trout pickerel, while the last named was unquestionably the chain pickerel. It would seem that Thoreau was not too observant in his description of these three pickerels, and most particularly the chain pickerel which he stated should have been designated as *guttatus* rather than *reticulatus*. The reticulations or chainlike markings on the chain pickerel are usually very distinct, and they should have been perfectly distinct on this Walden chain pickerel, but this apparently slipped by Thoreau's attention. It would seem that Thoreau, though generally very accurate in descriptions of birds and animals, failed in describing fish. Not long ago I took a chain pickerel in Narrows Lake, a reservoir lake on the Little Missouri River in Arkansas that had a vivid metallic molten yellow background coloration with the "chain links" or markings standing out vividly against this golden background. I do not know if the chain pickerel of Walden Pond were like this specimen in coloration and markings but if so Thoreau certainly would have taken note of the "reticulations" which McClane has stated look like "the links of a tire chain." This is about as close as one can get to telling what these markings on the chain pickerel look like. LeSueur (1818) first named the chain pickerel *Lucius reticulatus;* Mitchell (1825) classified it *Esox tridecemlineatus;* while Jordan & Gilbert (1883) named it *Esox reticulatus*. The modern designation for the chain pickerel, *Esox niger,* is comparatively recent. It has been stated that the chain pickerel got its name from the chain armor of the knights of old and that William Henry Herbert *(Frank Forester)* applied this name to the pickerel of Lake Champlain.

"In appearance," states Al McClane in his excellent book 'Spinning For Fresh and Saltwater Fish of North America,' "the chain pickerel is much like other members of the genus *Esox*—slim, long-jawed and camouflaged to perfection. After capture, you have little difficulty in distinguishing *niger* from the rest of his relatives; the overall bronze-green back and flanks differ from the bluish or greenish-gray of the northern pike *(Esox lucius)* or the dark-brown to silver-brown of the musky *(Esox masquinongy)*. Too, if you are color-blind, the chain pickerel has very distinct markings along the

sides which give the impression of links of a tire chain—
whereas both pike and musky are spotted. One form of
musky, native to the Ohio drainage system, has cross bar
markings which widen out into diffused blotches—but there
is no chance of mistaking a musky for a pickerel. The pickerel's stomach varies from a snow white to a creamy yellow,
and the fins are without markings. Both northern pike and
muskellunge generally have marked fins. Pickerel range from
a pound to three pounds in weight. Although four and five-
pounders are uncommon, the pickerel is capable of greater
growth, probably up to ten or twelve pounds. In general,
river pickerel average larger than pickerel taken from lakes
and ponds, probably because most eastern rivers have an
abundance of forage fishes such as chubs, suckers and young
game fish. The largest pickerel I have knowledge of was
taken in the tidal section of the Peconic River, on Long
Island. Apparently this species can adapt itself to salt or
brackish water.

"The chain pickerel," continues McClane, "is found along
the Atlantic coast, as far southwest as Texas and as far north
as Maine. The major distribution occurs in the Eastern states,
becoming progressively scattered southward. The pickerel
are hardy fish, getting along under biological conditions in
which the blue-blooded trout would perish. Given enough
water to swim in, a bed of weeds to hide in, and a plentiful
food supply (which consists of anything that will fit into its
mouth), they will propagate rapidly. Their spawning habits
are rather hap-hazard, the eggs being deposited in long
masses among submerged brush and weeds during April
and May, the exact time depending on the locality. After
being deposited, the eggs are quite forgotten by the parent.
In many ponds where two insignificant forms, beside chain
pickerel, occur—the mud pickerel and barred pickerel—all
three frequently hybirdize. The mud, barred, and the hybrids
are of no angling interest, however, as they are dwarf species
of the family."

In a later chapter on the range of the pickerels in this
country and Canada it will be found that the chain pickerel
has a far wider range than generally suspected, and these
were creatures of natural distribution and not through plantings made by man. Tarleton Bean (1902) stated with regard

THE NORTH AMERICAN PICKERELS 101

to the chain pickerel that: "It does not occur west of the
Alleghenies, but is found from Maine to Florida and Alabama east of this range of mountains." It is now known
west or southwest as far as Texas. Bean states (1902): "It
(the chain pickerel) has been introduced by fishermen into
many waters in which it is not native and has greatly multi-
plied. In the Potomac, the Connecticut, the Delaware and
other large eastern rivers the pickerel abounds."

As to what aid has been granted nature in the distribution
of various fish species is of course uncertain but it might be
suspected that fishermen have been making plantings of
pickerel from the earliest times. Like Johnny Appleseed
who carried apple seeds from the cider mills of Pennsylvania
and planted them all along the frontier of Ohio and north,
so there are no doubt self-appointed distributors of all
sorts of species of fish. No doubt this may have served to increase the range of both *niger* and *vermiculatus*. As a rule I
believe you will find that little distribution of any of the
pickerel varieties has been done by the states themselves.
The reason for this has no doubt been the belief that the
pickerels would be detrimental to the life of other fish
species in the water. However, it is rather strange to note
that most fish biologists and fisheries authorities seem to be
of the opinion that the pickerels are in no wise the killer of
other fish that has been suspected (not charged, understand!)
and that it has even been proved that pickerel live in the same
streams with trout and do not act to kill them (the trout) as
food. Of course positive proof of this could only come through
the examination of hundreds of stomachs of pickerel that
are actually found in trout streams, and I doubt whether this
has been done. Indeed I do not know that the pickerel
subject has been considered worthy of this trouble, that is,
examining stomach contents of the species to determine on
what it feeds. Bean states: "Pickerel are to be found in large
numbers lying in wait among the river grasses or in ponds
under the shade of leafy water plants for the minnows which
it consumes in enormous numbers, or some unlucky insect,
frog or snake which attracts its voracious appetite."

If it can be proved by exhaustive study of the food habits
of the pickerel, especially the chain pickerel, that it is not
an inordinate killer of game fish then it would seem that

there is reason for propagating the species and introducing it in waters where the fish is fading out or where it never before has been present. In making a statement of this nature one naturally comes up against the question as to whether the pickerel group is important enough to deserve extension by distribution into desirable waters. I am now convinced that it is, and I believe that there are untold thousands who would welcome the chance at taking this fish, and would surely enjoy its presence along with other game species. This naturally opens up avenues for investigation that may lead to something definite in the future. In a letter I have from Charles K. Fox he stated in regard to the position of the pickerel in the eyes of certain Pennsylvania fishermen:

"Some fishermen are very nearly fanatical about fishing for pickerel and even travel around quite a bit to get to choice places."

And, in a letter I am to quote in my chapter on the range of the pickerels in this country (reports from every state and province having one, two or three of the established pickerel varieties), here are some excerpts by A. Heaton Underhill, Director of the Department of Conservation of the State of New Jersey. He remarks:

"New Jersey has the chain pickerel (*Esox niger*) pretty universally distributed over the whole state. On the basis of numbers, availability and actual fishing efforts, it is probably our most important fresh water game fish."

Like reports coming from all quarters attest to the position of the pickerel as a game fish so far as the fisherman is concerned as differing, let us say, from what game fish officials and their versions of the matter may be, although it is to be noted that many of these are disposed to grant the pickerel serious consideration as a legitimate game fish of no mean order.

Obviously the chain pickerel (*Esox niger*) is the most important of the three pickerel. In the list of freshwater fishes the largest chain pickerel recorded was taken in Green Pond, New Jersey, on January 5, 1948, by Russell Kimble. It weighed 9 pounds, was 30 inches long and had a girth of 15 inches. Normally in fishing even the choice waters it will be found that a four or five pound chain pickerel is an unusually good sized one and it will give a good account of itself.

The fighting ability of the chain pickerel in North Carolina is told about by Rupert West, in his chapter on the eastern or chain pickerel in the book "Angling Success" edited by our good friend, Mortimer Norton. He writes:

"Probably no game fish has caused such difference of opinion as the Eastern Pickerel (*Esox niger*). Chain pickerel to some; green pickerel to others; and just plain pike to many. The reason for this difference of opinion is that the fish themselves are so different, not only in their habits but also even in their comformation, depending on the locality in which they are caught. There is this about the Eastern or chain pickerel, however, on which most fishermen will agree, *and that is that he is a game fish—second, I think, only to the black bass.* Whether hooked in the murky waters of a feeder creek, the clear waters of a running stream, or the placid waters of a mill pond, once this duck-billed specimen of the finny tribe is hooked with light tackle, there is something to tell about even though he does snap the tip off of your favorite fly rod or break your best bait casting line.

"There are some sportsmen who have a very poor opinion of the Eastern pickerel," continues West. "They look down on him as being something that children fish for with bent pins and angleworms. In making this assertion, I am reminded of a friend of mine who had somehow gotten this impression of the Eastern pickerel. He was a bass fisherman; bait caster of some fame. We were fishing in a river noted for its largemouth bass in the eastern part of North Carolina. We had fished much territory that morning without having any luck."

So the writer (West) made the suggestion that they quit bass fishing and go up one of the creeks in the region and try for pickerel. It took some urging to get his friend to go but finally he agreed.

"Knowing that chain pickerel are individualists at times, I decided to try out a lure that I had so far been unable to get a bass to strike at, much less take. It was combination of lures—a small wooden minnow to which I had attached a narrow strip of pork rind. The minnow floated of course and the pork strip just fluttered along behind. I was fishing from the bow of the boat; my friend from the middle seat. We were both casting, and as the creek was narrow our casts were not

more than twenty feet. Just ahead of the boat I spied the end
of a partly submerged log, which had been there for years.
There was not more than 18 inches of water in the creek at
this point, but I knew that shallow water and a submerged log
was a likely combination for pickerel. I made a cast, and my
lure struck the water within six inches of the end of that log.
I retrieved the lure very leisurely, even allowing it to come
to a complete stop at times. When it was near the boat I
lifted it from the water preparatory to making the next cast.
As the lure left the surface of the water, I saw a swirl near
the end of the log. At this moment my friend using a like pork
rind lure, dropped his bait at precisely the same spot where
mine had landed just a few seconds before. His lure had
hardly touched the water when there was a mighty splash,
and I saw his light rod whip into an arc. The next moment the
shimmering form of a chain pickerel shot from the water
only to disappear again.

"Our guide," concludes West, "familiar with the submerged
snags and underwater stakes at this particular point in the
creek, began working the boat slowly off shore until it was
almost in mid-stream. By this time the pickerel had taken
two-thirds of the line off of the reel and had broken water for
the second time. I shall never forget the expression on my
friend's face. It was some time before he took the fight out
of that pickerel and got him to where I could slip a landing
net under him. It was not the largest pickerel I had seen
caught in that creek, but it was the most perfectly formed
fish I have seen taken anywhere. The markings, too, were
perfect. Its lines were graceful, and its fins and tail were as
clear as glass. It weighed a fraction less than four pounds.

"It's the gamest fish I have ever hooked," exclaimed my
friend, he who had scoffed at fishing for pickerel. He is just
one of many who have found out that the Eastern pickerel is
truly a great game fish!"

Many years ago I did my first extensive chain pickerel
fishing in the state of New York and I believe that it was in
Lake Piseco in the southern Adirondacks that I got my first
introduction to the species. It happened in this way. I had
advertised one spring in a New York City paper asking for
someone to accompany me on a summer trip on the upper
reaches of the Mississippi River. One of those who answered

my inquiry was Frank Rix, still of Ilion, New York. Most of his fishing had been done in the Adirondacks and he was thoroughly familiar with the fish in that region. But he had never taken any great northern pike, and when we made contact with hundreds of these northerns he was no little impressed, especially since we did all our fishing with fly-rods and flies and spinners in combination. That is to say the No. 1/0 bass flies were attached to a spinner shaft, the spinner being a No. 2. We generally removed the wing feathers from this fly and used it only with the inch-long hackles at the head. The fish that we took that summer on these lures might indeed be considered as surprising in number, mostly great northern pike but some smallmouth bass.

Frank was interested greatly in the pike. It was a fish he had never, to my knowledge, taken. The fact that they rarely leaped out of water rivited his attention. He stated: "Our pickerel back home come out of water three or four times, like bass, when you hook them. They are more gamey than these pike." I heard that remark all summer. When I came to the Adirondacks the next year one of the things I had in mind was to check on the gamey nature of the chain pickerel, and the way it had of leaping out of water. If I had ever doubted the matter I was soon to find out one way or the other.

In Frank's cabin on Lake Piseco there is some writing I believe telling about my taking some of the first smallmouth bass in Lake Piseco, which, right or not, I do not know. These were taken the same way we took smallmouths up in Minnesota, on the fly and spinner combination. My favorite fly, as always, being the Yellow Sally, or it is sometimes known, the Yellow May.

I had taken my chain pickerel and had found out about their degree of gaminess when, one evening, just about sundown, we discovered a spot on the north shore (I believe it was off of a small island) that really proved one of those unusual places to which the pickerel seemed to come—and kept on coming as they were taken out. I say that "we" discovered a spot of the sort. My companion at the time was a famous outdoor writer, the late Raymond S. Spears. He wrote up our fishing later on in a story.

The sport we had taking those chain pickerel in a small narrows by the island has never slipped my memory. In fact,

remembering always the great sport we had with those
fish I have never lost my respect for this member of the pike
family, to the extent that if I were offered smallmouth bass
fishing or chain pickerel fishing, both to be taken on the
fly-rod, I would without hesitation select the latter. True to
what Frank Rix had said, those pickerel came out of water
time and again, fighting with a stamina that aroused our
admiration. Spears, a ruddy, hearty and big man roared
his approval every time one was hooked, and roared again
every time one went out of water. It is a vivid picture in my
mind, something that might have inspired those artists of the
past to some lively outdoor sketches. I am referring to the
three late artists of the out-of-doors, Phillip R. Goodwin, Oliver
Kemp and Hy Watson. When Frank asked me later what I
thought of the chain pickerel I said, with feeling, much as
the companion of West in his incident recounted previous:

"The chain pickerel is every bit a game fish and I think
that it deserves a place alongside of the smallmouth bass
and the trout. It's a better game fish than the great northern
pike ever was, regardless of size!"

I believe that the largest chain pickerel I have ever taken
weighed five pounds, and that, lest you are unacquainted with
the species, is quite some chain pickerel, considering, let us
not forget, that the world's record is nine pounds. However,
let this, too, never be forgotten, that taking this fish on
fly-rod tackle suitable for trout, and taking the same fish on
heavy bait casting tackle or by trolling are a different
proposition, the light tackle only giving the fish a chance to
assure one a scrap that is worthy of the name. Yet, taking
these smaller fish on tackle suitable for landing a fifty pound
musky, one often hears fishermen state that: "The damn
snakes haven't got a good wiggle in them!" There is such a
thing as sportsmanship but there certainly are thousands
who do not know the meaning of it in the very least. As view
the tuna tackle they use on our inland fishes!

It is not strange that so far as the pickerel are concerned
almost the entire show is stolen by the chain pickerel. There
is at least something to the chain pickerel they will tell you,
whereas the barred pickerel and the little pickerel, the two
other varieties, are small and unimportant, and have little to
recommend them. Yet there are those who fish for the little

fellows and what outdoor boy is there who has lived and grown up within ranges of the pickerels who discounts the charm there is in fishing even for these two minor members of the pickerel factions.

There is a method of telling the three pickerels from the great northern pike and from the muskellunge by the scalation or positions of the scales on the cheeks and opercles (gill covers) of these varieties. In the muskellunge it will be found that scales occur on the upper portion of the cheeks and the upper part of the gill covers only. The lower half of the cheeks and the lower half of the gill covers are barren of scales. In the great northern pike the cheeks are covered with scales but the upper half only of its gill covers have scales; the lower half of the gill covers are free of scales. Opposed to this the three pickerels have both the cheeks and the gill covers entirely scaled over. These scales may be small in size if the fish as small, as in the case of the banded or barred pickerel and the little pickerel, but a reading glass will show the scales completely covering gill covers and cheeks. It is an unfailing method of differentiation. Memorize the scalation applicable to each species or variety belonging to the pike family, as set down in the above, as there may be many times when you will be called upon to pass on this subject, for if there is one thing that has more fishermen befuddled than any other question in the fishing world it is the telling apart the members of the pike family.

The Banded or Barred Pickerel (*Esox americanus*), which is also known as the Redfin Pickerel and Bulldog Pickerel is no doubt the smallest of the pickerels and in the northern part of its range, which is definitely eastern, in fact east of the Alleghanies, ranging from the St. Lawrence River east of the Alleghanies down to Florida, it will reach a length of a foot and will weigh a half pound to a possible pound. Bean states: "In Pennsylvania it is limited to waters in the eastern part of the state, and the same is true in New York. This pickerel is too small to have much importance as a food fish. It resembles in general appearance and habits the Little Pickerel (*Esox vermiculatus*) which is found west of the Alleghanies. The Banded Pickerel frequents clear, cold and rapid brooks *and will associate with the Brook Trout without injury to the latter.*" The reader's attention is called to the last remark in this assertion, *i.e.*, that the Banded Pickerel is not inimical to the welfare of trout in the same stream with which it lives.

While it is true that in the northern part of its range the Barred or Banded Pickerel does have a minor length and weight, in the South, particularly in the Carolinas, Georgia and Florida it assumes a more respectable length and weight. Several years ago a fisherman told me of taking what he termed a "pickerel" in Okeefenokee Swamp in Georgia which he stated did not have the markings of a chain pickerel, which he was familiar with, but rather had darkish bands or stripes up and down on its sides. No one, he stated, had been able to tell him what sort of a pickerel it was, so that he took it for granted it was a freak. At once it came to my mind that it was a Banded Pickerel. I asked him what length and weight the fish was and he said he thought it would be about eighteen inches in length, with a weight of between three and four pounds. This *was* a surprise as it might be reckoned an unheard of weight for the Banded Pickerel. Since that time I have found that in the southeastern part of its range it does attain to a better weight and length than that found in northern representatives of the variety.

While the Chain Pickerel and the Little Pickerel have fins that are clear, with no marks whatever on them, the Barred or Banded Pickerel has sometimes reddish fins. The Chain Pickerel has, often, fins that are clear as glass. Thus both of these pickerel varieties can be told from the Barred or Banded Pickerel, the pike and the muskellunge, with which latter two the pickerels are often confused, that is, if some should believe they are the young of the pike and the muskellunge.

The Barred Pickerel has dark bars on its body, the same alternating with lighter bars in between. Sometimes, depending upon the water it is taken in, these bars are very dark and zebralike, but normally they are only medium-dark. In the Barred Pickerel (*americanus*) there is a black bar below the eye that leans obliquely back and then down. Raney contends there is only the one bar below the eye, while Daugherty states that (*americanus*) "has a black bar below the eye and another running from gill covers to snout." In (*vermiculatus*) are found two dark bars, one downward from the eye and one forward, but not through it. I believe that the Banded or Barred Pickerel was first named out of Murderer's Creek, New York by Mitchill in 1818 who called it (*Esox scromerius*). In 1842 DeKay named it (*Esox fasciatus*), as collected in the streams and ponds of Long Island. Tarleton Bean named it (*Esox americanus*), in 1893, and the name so remains today.

The Little Pickerel (*Esox vermiculatus*) also known as the Trout Pickerel, Mud Pickerel and Grass Pickerel is found chiefly west of the Alleghenies ranging from southern Wisconsin through the lower Great Lakes to the St. Lawrence River and Lake Champlain, thence southward into western Pennsylvania and so south to Alabama, west to Texas, north through Arkansas and Missouri and so back to southern Wisconsin. It is said to inhabit the upper Mississippi Valley but this is quite untrue as will be called attention to in the chapter on the up-to-date range of the pickerels as known to the country today. Just how great are the numbers of this pickerel within its range at the present time is very largely open to question, but it can be said with every degree of truth that it is not as numerous as is the chain pickerel which is found within the same range with it, that is, west of the Alleghenies. Because of the fact that the pickerels have never been considered game fishes of note and of special worth, there has been an almost universal disposition on the part of game and fish departments to disregard it entirely. As a result there has been but little set down with relation to the number of these found in a state and where varieties intermix and over-lap. For instance there seems to be no exact knowledge as to whether (*americanus*) is not found west of the Alleghenies, and if (*vermiculatus*) is not found east of the Alleghenies. Of course we have to state, not knowing otherwise, that (*vermiculatus*) ranges only west of the Alleghenies to avoid official criticism.

There is no reason whatsoever why the fisherman should confuse the chain pickerel with the other two pickerels. Remember always the metallic yellow background coloration of the chain pickerel on which are those chainlike black markings, the lines of which are narrow and give the impression of tire chains. It is easier to tell the chain pickerel at a glance than the other two, that is, the Barred Pickerel and the Little Pickerel. The Little Pickerel might, however, be mistaken for the Barred Pickerel. The former also has oblique bars on the sides of its body but these are more diffused and indistinct, never so sharply and clearly defined as on the Barred Pickerel. The background coloration is fairly light but the lines are more like streaks than bars, and even these streaks seem to be joined in a blotched effect. Like the Chain Pickerel the Little Pickerel has clear colored fins, never reticulated or blotched. Those of the Barred Pickerel are reddish or overcast. In the Little Pickerel (*Esox vermiculatus*), the eyes are smaller than in the other two pickerels and the snout is shorter.

It is one of those oddities that like some other fishes, the varieties of the pickerel meet and mingle as the result of which there are cross-breeds, just as there are cross-breeds among some of the sunfishes. However, that such meeting, mingling and cross-breeding is a common thing is not true nor are hybrids as common as some would believe. Normally it can be said that each variety sticks pretty closely with its own. If this were not so the varieties would be in a mix-up from which one could not be distinguished from the other and this is definitely not true.

It is generally considered that the pickerels are very easy to propagate but there has not been the slightest disposition apparently to increase the kind through any state hatchery operations. The reason explained for this is that there is a general fear that the pickerels will decimate the young of other species which may or may not have its basis in fact.

Regarding propagation of the pickerel, Meehan states:

"Eggs of the pickerel may be pressed from the female without any trouble whatever; the eggs, however, are glutinous and have to be thoroughly rubbed and cleaned after fertilizing, and before being placed in the hatchery jars where the treatment should be the same as that for whitefish or shad. It is possible to gather eggs of the pickerel naturally desposited, but it is better to keep the fish in captivity and take the eggs from them by expression. A pond of three-fourths of an acre or an acre will contain many hundreds of pickerel in good health and condition if they are liberally fed with live food, for the pickerel will take only a moving, lifelike object.

"Spawning," continues Meehan, "begins very early in the

year, soon after the ice disappears; but the spawning season is very short and the hatching period is about two weeks. As the pickerel is strongly a carnivorous fish, it is important that the fry should not be placed in the same ponds with mature specimens, but kept in smaller ponds as would be done with any other carnivorous species. Growth is very rapid and cannibalism, even among the young, is strongly developed, hence persons desiring to rear their stock to maturity must expect heavy loss from this quarter. The culture of pickerel presents no difficulties when the eggs can be obtained from wild fish. There is no difficulty in retaining the brood-fish in hatching ponds where they will live safely for an indefinite period provided the ponds are large and deep enough."

An observation might be made that is not carried in Meehan's observation and that is regarding the need of sorting these pickerel young as to size otherwise there will be noticed a tendency of the larger of the young to fall upon those lesser in size to make food of them. I do not think, however, that this degree or cannibalism is anywhere near as distressingly pronounced as in the wall-eyed pike which is by far the worst cannibal among our freshwater fishes. By careful selection, watching the growth of individuals carefully, one can practice selection and obtain specimens for planting that are not only the healthiest to be had but also the fastest growing and largest. There is little doubt but that over a period of years a race of pickerel in each variety could be obtained that are larger than wild-run specimens. It would be possible to practice with the larger specimens of these varieties.

There are hundreds of individuals who possess large land holdings, estates, etc., with ponds and even small lakes on their domains who seek to find fish to plant in the same who might like to experiment with chain pickerel or the other two varieties. Surely, on the whole, few fish could be easier propagated than these nor could any stockings of any fish prove as successful in the sum total than would accrue through using the pickerel for the purpose. Because bass and sunfish can be planted with them the results should prove entirely successful and worthy of serious consideration. What fish culturists would say about this, however, is open to question.

VIII

PICKEREL
FISHING METHODS

It is obvious of course when one mentions pickerel fishing
the chain pickerel is immediately thought of in this connection. With many fishermen, this sort of fishing begins and ends
with *Esox niger*, for it is not only the largest of the pickerel
tribe but there are more of them to fish for and they are found
in more varied waters. That most of the methods used in
taking the pickerel have been rather crude might be generally
admitted in spite of the fact that some of these methods will
take fish, and many of them. But that there are hundreds of
anglers who are using light bait casting tackle and lightweight lures in such fishing, and, for that matter, fly-rod
tackle and flies, or flies in combination with spinners, is well
known. Indeed, more and more anglers are using fly-rods,

which is a hopeful sign and points to a day that is emerging which will see lighter lures used in all fishing and a greater degree of accuracy and naturalness of lure presentation exerted in taking fish. I am sure that when such tactics in taking the pickerel come into common use more appreciation will be voiced in this sport of fishing than ever before. It is then, and only then, when this so-called "lesser member" of the pike tribe will be able to give a good account of himself. It is strange that up into the present day there has existed such crude tactics as trolling for pickerel with a chalkline and a large hook with a too-large minnow on it. Yet so often have we come across these sort of fishing methods leveled against the pickerel that the conviction grows on one that here surely there is room for vast improvement and the introduction of more commendable and up-to-date methods.

Here is a typical letter that lies by my typewriter here on the table. It is from a fisherman who always used a cane-pole in fishing for pickerel but he "has seen the light" and now wants to take this fish with bait casting tackle. Let me quote:

"I am what you would call a dyed-in-the-wool pickerel fishing enthusiast and I suppose there must be thousands of others like me. I live in a region where we have good fishing for the chain pickerel, which I know is the kind because I checked with the game warden on it. Most of my fishing has been done with a cane-pole and if I do say so I have taken some mighty fine fish on it, and was fortunate one year in taking a whopping big one that weighed close to five pounds.

"A year ago a fisherman came to our stream fishing and he carried a bait casting outfit that I thought was very light, certainly lighter than any I had ever seen. I heard that he was quite good at taking pickerel so I asked him if I could go along with him one day as I knew some good places where I thought he could take some good ones.

"I want to tell you that I really got the surprise of my life. That fellow cast to perfection and there wasn't a place six inches across it would seem that he couldn't put his lure in. I believe he took fifteen pickerel that day, returning all except five of them to the water. The largest of these was a four pounder according to his de-liar scales.

"Ever since that time I have been thinking in terms of a

bait casting outfit and had meant to find out what his was but I didn't see this fellow again since I was away for three days. When I came back his trailer was gone."

So this fisherman wants me to pick out for him a light-weight bait-casting outfit, rod, line, reel, lures, just like that. And apparently he has never cast with a bait casting outfit before in his life. In other words this fellow will practically have to start from scratch and learn bait casting from the bottom up. I have written him that it would take a book to tell all about bait casting; and heaved a sigh of relief when I thought of my own book that I have recommended to him, namely: "Black Bass Fishing" published by the Stackpole Publishing Company, the producers of the present volume on the pike family. If this does not solve the problem of selecting an outfit which will go well for pickerel fishing as well as bass fishing then I will have to do better next time. Or if you would like to obtain a treatise on the subject by an advanced master in the art of the use of lightweight tackle get the excellent book by Charles K. Fox entitled "Advanced Bait Casting" published by the G. P. Putnam Company, New York City. This is one of the best books to be had in the selection of light-weight outfits for bass, and naturally the same outfits would do as well in pickerel fishing too.

The introduction of the glass fiber rod in the bait casting rod field has opened up possibilities that definitely puts it in the forefront of recommendable materials in the lightweight class. Since these rods are to be had in light, medium and heavy types, the pick should obviously be a light rod with a length of say, five feet six inches which would be an excellent selection. This light rod needs to have an agreeable amount of backbone but must not be whippy; it can be flexible, but able to flick a light bait a distance of thirty feet with a turn of the wrist. Under no circumstances should a rod of the sort be picked without a reel attached. For that matter this is a good suggestion in picking any rod, for without the proper reel attached the sense of balance will not be appreciated, and that is all-important.

For a light bait casting rod the demand surely is for a light reel and for pickerel fishing I surely am thinking in terms of a tournament type reel. A reel of this sort will weigh about 5½ ounces, will have a spool diameter of 1½ inches and pillar

length of 1⅜ inches and will match in with a 5 foot, 2 inch or a
5 foot, 6 inch glass rod. A reel of this sort will have a capacity
of 50 yards of 10 to 12 pound test line or about 100 yards of
4½ to 6 pound test line. These types of very light reels are
actually used in tournament work but also in actual fishing.
They have either cork or balsa wood arbors and are meant
expressly for casting light lures in the ⅜-ounce to ½-ounce
class. Such is the ease with which they cast that one can
operate the same hours on end without the slightest wrist
ache. With a glass fiber rod to accompany a reel of the sort
an almost ideal outfit is obtained. Three reels in this lightweight tournament class might be listed to advantage in the
interest of doing away with endless correspondence on the
subject. Two of these reels are made by the Shakespeare Company, being their No. 1740 free-spool tournament reel and
their No. 1973 Sportcast reel. Now it should be remembered
that the No. 1740 is a tournament reel, in fact the makers
state for it that "there is little doubt that more records have
been made in tournament casting with the Shakespeare No.
1740 than any reel ever made!" This reel, while ostensibly for
accuracy tournament casting is one of the best reels for "the
very sportiest light line fishing." It is a free-spool, that is to
say, the handle stands still when casting, but when you start
to reel the handle engages with the spool and the line is
taken in in the natural manner of reeling. If one were to
say that this is the *ne plus ultra* in lightweight reels there
could be no possible objection, for it measures up flawlessly
to standards set.

The Sportscast reel, No. 1973, weight 5½ ounces, has a
lightning fast lightweight spool with cork arbor, spool diameter 1½ inches and pillar length, as in the recommendation
previously given in telling about lightweight reels, of 1⅜
inches. The company states for this Sportcast reel that:
"Several U. S. and world records for accuracy casting have
been set by champion casters using the Shakespeare Sportcast reel." Those who are doubtful of the free-spool feature
in a reel would do well to select a reel such as this. In the
present day the free-spool reel is not common, whereas, years
ago, it was considerably in use. One would actually need to
cast with a free-spool reel to understand it.

The Shakespeare Company also put out their Classic reel

which I have used, off and on, in its various models, for a number of years. It, too, possesses an extremely light spool which is suitable for tournament casting, but aside from that it is a reel that will take the abuse of heavy fishing in spite of its tournament qualifications. The Classic has a capacity of 100 yards of 15 pound test line, but with the cork arbor will take about 50 yards of such line or commensurately less in proportion to the lightness of line of lesser pounds test. The weight of this reel is 6.4 ounces, its spool diameter is 1½ inches, with a pillar length of 1²³⁄₃₂ inches.

Another tournament type reel which I have used off and on for several years is the Langley Lurecast reel, built on the same tournament style of the first two named Shakespeare reels above. It has the same spool diameter and pillar length and has a casting ability that is of a most unusual order. I find that I can cast day in and day out with this little Langley reel and know not the semblance of wrist fatigue. It answers well to the use of light lines, 6 to 9 pounds test and is a perfect reel for use with a light glass fiber rod.

One thing should be remembered with regard to this selection of a lightweight bait casting outfit for pickerel fishing. Do not think for a moment that any such light outfit, as suggested, would be applicable and suitable for pickerel fishing only, indeed it will prove to be an ideal outfit for bass fishing as well, so that indirectly it can be used for all-around fishing where of course the fish do not run to especially large weights, as, for instance, should you hook into an unusually large great northern pike while you are pickerel or bass fishing. In some waters this is a distinct possibility. Yet, barring obstructions, one should be able to land even a large pike on this tackle although it must be kept in mind that you will have to play a large fish, giving and taking in line as the actions of the fish dictate. This can be accomplished only where obstructions are at a minimum and clear water affords unhampered action.

One of the fears fishermen have as regards the use of lightweight tackle and light lines is the belief that the fish will snap the line or the fish will break the rod. There is little doubt but that in the hands of some fishermen a lightweight outfit, including a line of minor pounds test, might prove inadequate and the line at least might be broken but this is rather an exception than the rule. In a lifetime of fishing for muskellunge, pike and pickerel I must state that the number of lines I have had broken have been at a positive minimum. I believe it is mostly in how calmly, coolly and deliberately you play your fish (without hurrying him, understand!) that this line-breaking can easily be cut down to nothing. Unfortunately, too many fishermen cannot get the fish into the boat or to hand fast enough and therein lies disaster. This is especially true of the meat-getting fisherman who would be heart broken if he lost a fish!

Obviously you could not break a glass fiber rod in playing a fish, and certainly the reel does not bear any of the brunt of the abuse levelled against an outfit; so it follows that it is the line that is the only doubtful item in the outfit.

If you use a regulation bait casting reel, not in the tournament class, you can of course use lines in pounds-test up to 24 or more pounds. But, if using the lighter or tournament type reels, this calls for light lines. If these lines are soft lines of the Ashaway type the best possible results will be had in casting. When "soft lines" are mentioned this would mean the Ashaway Squidding line which is braided of Dupont nylon and is extremely soft and flexible and works to absolute perfection on the lightweight type of tournament reel or its stepped-up relative the Classic reel. While this type of squidding line is much used in saltwater, its usefulness in fresh water can hardly be minimized, in fact it is a perfect line for light lure casting. This line is heat-treated to remove stretch and is waterproofed by an exclusive Ashaway formula to resist wear and to make casting easier. It will not waterlog, needs no drying and will not rot or mildew. It is of semi-flat construction which prevents too tight packing on the reel and lessens the risk of spreading reel flanges. Several years ago when on a float trip on the White River of Missouri and Arkansas, with Julian Crandall, president of the Ashaway Line and Twine Company, he presented me with a spool of this squidding line. This proved so perfect on several of my tournament type casting reels that I have been using it off and on ever since, indeed the line Crandall originally gave me has taken hundreds of fish, some of them over twenty pounds in weight. Yet in all the time it has been used no fish has broken it, nor has any pike or pickerel gashed it off as we are told so feelingly about by some writers. I should mention that this squidding line recommended, and which is soft to the tip of the thumb in thumbing the reel, is 14-pounds test yet it is in caliber about that of a nine pound test line.

In light lure fishing, using an outfit as I have outlined, one feels a resentment against using any manner of leader simply because it interfers with the free action of the lure. The so-called gimp wire leaders, eight to ten inches in length, never stay straight for one thing but loop back on themselves, and coil up, making them utterly without a semblance of worth, especially so far as ensuring an indistinct connection between the lure and the line. The gimp leader on the end of the line stands out like a sore thumb. Rather than use a leader of this sort use a small four-bead Bead Chain terminal line connection, the beads being of the small type, and the snap on the end a fly-rod snap. This is hardly more than two and one-half inches in length overall, has little weight such as might destroy the action of the lure, and has a ring in the line end to which the doubled over line is attached. Thus, you bring the end of the line back on itself about eight inches and tie to the main line across with a common knot. Now take the doubled end of the line, insert it through the eye on the bead chain device, bring the chain and snap through the loop and draw tight. With this bead chain snap you can change lures at will. Too, while the bead chain may be only a few inches in length it aids somewhat should the fish overstrike beyond the lure itself.

Lures for pickerel fishing are many and various. No specific lures are made for the pickerel save that he will take most any lure that the bass will take, and what the great northern pike is eager for, that will also stimulate the "go and get it!" fever of the pickerel. One thing is certain, namely and to wit, the pickerel is enchanted by the flash of a spinner or a small spoon which would indicate at once that such spoon or spinner lures are among the important ones for pickerel fishing, just as the same type lure proves of top merit in fishing for the great northern pike. There is little doubt in my mind but that the fluted or crimped type of spoon is by far the best of the spoon lot for fishing purposes, in that the reflection thrown from these flutings are more comprehensive than those

delivered by the plain blade. The Horrocks-Ibbotson Company handle some excellent fluted spoons finished both in
chrome and high grade nickel that are probably among the
best in this smaller type to be had. The Nos. 3, 4, 5 and
124½ are suggestions. They should have the treble masked in
feathers as usual with this type spoonhook. The Skinner spoon,
distributed by the Whittemore Company of Boston, Mass.,
in the 4 and 5 sizes are also excellent. These are also fluted.
While these light spoons can be trolled it is as a casting
spoon that they turn in their best results and afford the most
satisfaction in pickerel fishing. It should never be forgotten,
however, that in waters occupied also by the great northern
pike the latter will seize upon this smaller spoon as freely—
if not more so—than the pickerel, and that of course is saying
a great deal. That a ten or twelve pound pike might in this
manner be hooked is saying the least. It has happened time
and again in our experience.

Years ago when the Skinner spoon was selling by the barrel
we were in the habit of casting these smaller spoons a great
deal. But with the coming of plug lures in formidable array
and undeniable attraction, the spoon lost out to the extent
that in the present day spoon casting for pickerel may be
considered in the light of something of a lost art. I am sure
that fishermen have missed a lot in keen enjoyment as a
direct result. For casting spoons of this sort I like to use a
four foot (limp) monofilament leader with a fly-rod snap at
its tip on which the lure is attached and a swivel of small
size on the other end to which the main line is tied. This
new type leader is about as invisible as a leader can be. As
to whether a pickerel is deterred from striking a lure that
has a heavy line tied right to the lure is not so certain, for
I do not think the fish is that discriminating or observant.
It is certain that the limp leader does much to increase the
action and smooth-working nature of the lure, all of which is
the main thing striven for.

While the wobbling spoon is a killer of the first water on
pike, I never have considered it too useful in pickerel fishing,
therefore I rarely recommend it for such. The small regulation spoon with crimped or fluted blade is so much better
that I see no special advantage in pickerel fishing with the
wobbling spoon. Too, much of the water the pickerel lives

in is farily shallow, and unless hurried along the wobbling spoon will sink to the bottom. Where water fished over is only eighteen inches in depth a wobbling spoon has to be hurried fast or it will be on the bottom in no time at all.

It is an interesting observation that pickerel are inordinately attracted to the wriggling, crawling pork rind as attached to a spoon, either the standard regulation spoons mentioned above or to regular pork rind spoons of which there are a number on the market. In using a pork rind on the feathered treble hook of the spoon-lure, a small snap can be soldered into the crotch where the three hooks branch out. One can then snap on a pork rind with little trouble. So located the pork rind will ride straight, since it is centrally affixed. The usual practice of attaching the pork rind to one of the hooks of the treble does not cause it to ride centrally and the action is lost. The rind strip should stand out not less than two inches beyond the end of the feathers decorating the treble. In the event that one does not care to solder in a snap one can simply twist in a copper wire of small diameter at the crotch of the treble and on this affix the rind. It will do as well but the snap is far better. This should be a fly-rod snap if possible.

Of the pork rind spoons that are useful in this type of fishing there are a number to be had on the market. So that you will know what is meant by this type spoon, three are named, and seeing the type you will not be in doubt as to identity. Typical of these pork rind spoons is the Johnson Silver Minnow, the Rex Spoon and the Hellion. The name applied to the spoon made by the Louis Johnson Company, that of the Johnson Silver Minnow is rather misleading. Persons not having seen the lure imagine it to be a minnow-shaped creation whereas it is a spoon type. It would have been far better to have named it the Johnson Silver Spoon. The three spoons mentioned (there are others like it on the market) ride concave side up and convex side down, the single hook (not a treble) being attached to the concave side and is protected with weed-guard wires. I much prefer the single hook in that, riding with point up, it will not easily engage with the weeds. There are spoons in this class that have a treble hook at the tail rather than a single hook but these are vulnerable among the weeds and have little possible use. Spoons in this class generally have a tuft of feathers or hair masking the hook but this does not prevent attaching a pork rind strip to the hook which adds immeasurably to the overall action and attractiveness of the combination.

These spoons should not be over two inches in length or possibly not over a half inch longer. The little Rex Spoon, with a length of 2¼ inches is, I believe, one of the finest little lures in this spoon type to be had. Used with a light outfit such as previously outlined it casts perfectly. Its advantage in pickerel fishing is that you can cast into the thickest of the weeds, pads, grasses, brush and down-trees and it will come sliding in through the obstructions with the greatest of ease.

Two other lures of excellent merit in pickerel fishing is the Shimmy Wiggler and the Oriental Wiggler, both, however, to be obtained in their smallest sizes. Both of these are used in combination with pork rind strips and, being protected with weed guard wires, they can be used more or less freely in the midst of the obstructions. In fact any lure that is around two inches in length to which a fluttery pork rind strip can be attached is of the greatest moment as a lure for pickerel fishing. It might be mentioned that both of these lures (which were invented by the late Al Foss) can be considered as among the most important of the pork rind lures. It might also be mentioned that you better watch your step when in vulnerable pike water because the way the great northern pike slams into these lures plus those other spoon lures named, is a caution, same dressed up with a capital C.

The method of skittering for pickerel has been largely in use in the eastern part of the country for sixty or seventy years, in fact it is almost certain that this was one of the old standbys in the fishing field before the spoonhook took over.

Rupert West, in "Angling Success" (the Macmillan Company), edited by Mortimer Norton, has this to say about skittering as a method of taking pickerel:

"Do not think there isn't sport in skittering for pickerel. I well remember my first lesson in skittering. I had fished religiously all morning along the marsh shore of a lake that I knew teemed with pickerel. After three hours of fishing I had two pike on my stringer and was ready to give up in despair when I saw a flat-bottomed skiff with two persons in it loom up among the stumps that lined the opposite shore. I made my way over to them. One was paddling leisurely along, picking his way through the partly submerged stumps; the other was glued fast to the butt end of a 16-foot cane-pole. To the narrow, whiplike end of this pole dangled about six feet of stout linen cord. To the end of the cord a single hook was made fast, and from the hook a strip of fat meat dangled. I watched the antics of the old fisherman as he led that bit of fat meat in and out among those stumps. Presently I saw that canepole whip into an arc. There was a swirl of water and the fight was on. Every minute I expected to see the slender tip of that pole go. But the old-timer knew his bamboo and after a series of skillful maneuvers he had that black pike, as he called it, in the bottom of the skiff. That isn't all; he had a dozen others in there, any one of them larger than my largest one. On my next fishing trip to this lake I went armed with a skittering outfit and while I am still an advocate of the rod and reel, when I want a thrill in pickerel fishing that is out of the ordinary, I try skittering.

"While feather spinners are perhaps the most popular skit-tering lures," continues West, "I believe the most deadly that I have used is the one I first saw—the homemade fat meat affair. Of course, fat meat isn't used so much now because it has been found that the skin of the porker is better than the pork itself; better because it is tougher and lasts longer. Instead of the single No. 3/0 hook, I would suggest that to this hook a No. 1 hook be added by making it fast with a piece of fine wire to the main hook and allowing it to trail about one inch behind the larger hook. To the larger hook, make fast one end of the strip of pork rind, then slit the pork rind to where the trailer hook will thread through it, allowing at least one inch of the pork rind to trail the smaller hook. This puts an end to pickerel striking short. Too, it gives the bait more action."

Instead of wiring the trailer hook to the front hook as this writer suggests it is possible to flatten the barb of the main hook somewhat with pliers after which the eye of the trailer hook will pass over the barb with ease. The barb can then be straightened into place and the trailer hook will not come off past the barb.

The "fat meat" bait that Rupert West speaks of does not seem to awaken any memories in my mind, as, while I virtually grew up in the midst of skittering entry I never saw any pork used without rind attached. It would seem from reading West's remarks on the subject that this pickerel skittering attractor (fat meat) was a rather crude object. My own recollection was that pork chunk lures were mostly used, but this had the white pork attached to the rind which gave it shape and held it together. I will admit that these pork chunk baits were made in many and various ways, some with rather deep bodies and rather lengthy legs and others with flat bodies with only about a quarter inch or so of fat adhering. It was the fluttering thin rind legs attached to the pork chunk that finally led to the founding of the rind lure strictly without any pork at all, the rind in fact shaved thin to give it every possible degree of undulation in the water.

Agreeable with the statement of West acclaiming the skittering method with a long canepole as unusually successful, I must admit (and so will many an oldtimer) that, used with some degree of knowledge how to operate the pole and the lure, exceptional good luck can be had. This would apply not only to taking pickerel but bass as well. Too, full many a great northern pike of both length and girth has fallen foul of the skitterer and has paid with his life for his cupidity. As West has stated, the line at the tip of the pole would be about six feet in length, although no strict rule was laid down on this score. In fact I can remember an eight foot line being used.

One value of the canepole is that you can reach out over the water and very lightly drop the lure just exactly where you want it. Unlike in the use of rod and reel you can move the lure to right and left or pull it up on a lily pad and then dunk it for another move, and so on. All this can be accomplished very noiselessly so that the fish are not made suspicious, which is to be remembered when fishing in waters that are much operated. When the fish strikes, one has absolute control over the fish, since the pole is long and the upward impetus serves to keep the fish close to the surface and unable to plunge into the pads or weeds to snarl the line. If an unusually large fish is hooked while you are fishing for pickerel (and this can happen!) the fish can be brought out into deep water, the pole can be thrown into the water and the fish can be permitted to struggle as he may—he will never pull the pole under, for the air chambers between the nodes in the cane will cause the entire pole to act as a bobber.

It should be noted that all kinds of rind lures can be used with the canepole in skittering, including the spoons of the Johnson and Rex type previously called to attention. Indeed, it is possible to use a typical fly and spinner lure in this manner such as is used in fly fishing, that is, a bass size fly tied to a No. 1/0 hook which in turn is attached to a shaft with a No. 2 spinner on it. There are times when this will take pickerel when other lures may prove of little consequence. It is obvious that the possibilities in a long cane pole in pickerel fishing can hardly be exaggerated. For instance it can be used in live frog fishing for pickerel also since it is a well known fact that the pickerels are inveterate feeders on these marshland serenaders. But the limitations of the long canepole of course can be understood. It is useful, true, out in the open where there is lots of elbow room, and that of course would almost restrict its presence to lakes and ponds. For streams and spots where even a bait casting rod may at times be a doubtful thing a canepole is out of the question.

There are many and various cut baits and strip baits that seem to be taken with avidity by pickerel of all three varieties. Ray Bergman, famous fishing writer lists one that we have used successfully and it may be told about here. To accomplish this lure, you cut a strip out of the belly of a yellow perch taking in both of the forward or pectoral fins and a little ahead of the fins where the hook is seated. This is attached to a bare hook and the hook in turn is attached to a spinner shaft with a No. 3 spinner on it. This lure should ride in the water in such fashion that the fins are down. The best manner in using this lure in a stream is to let it wash on downstream through the racy water and into stiller water. As the lure works down, give it twitches of the rod-tip, drawing it a few inches upstream and then letting it back down, repeatedly carrying on this action of the lure. This characterizes the struggle of a minnow trying to make its way upstream but invariably dropping back through lack of stamina in making the grade. It is a killer of the first water on pickerel, and, in the streams, used as stated, is a big killer on rainbow trout. It can of course be cast with an effect every bit equal to that of using it in the downstream method depicted.

If the use of a lightweight bait casting outfit has qualifications of greatness in all fishing, then it can certainly be said that taking pickerel by means of the fly-rod has something about it that cannot but stimulate serious consideration and recommendation as a means to taking the pickerels, and naturally when I say that I am thinking greatly in terms of the chain pickerel. For fly-fishing for the pickerel I like a seven or seven-and-one-half foot rod of bamboo, glass fiber or seamless tubular steel construction. It should have sufficient backbone to put out a bass size fly and spinner as previously recommended, the fly being tied to a 1/0 bass hook, the flies without wings, only the inch-long hackles at the head. The fly should come on a shaft having a No. 2 spinner. I might mention that fly makers will make these flies for you, on order, tied without wings, something that few fishermen are in knowledge of. A fly-tyer in Opelousas, Louisiana has been tying flies following my specifications for years, these being without wings. They are attached to a spinner shaft with a No. 2 spinner on it. I believe that this maker now puts these out in six or eight patterns. No doubt these can be obtained by writing this fly-tyer (one of the oldest in the field), E. H. Le Blanc, Box 121, Opelousas, Louisiana. I early found these a remarkable success on pickerel. They are fly-rod lures of course.

Using a fly-rod in taking pickerel possibly gives one the greatest opportunity to test the fighting qualities of the fish. I have known eastern trout fishermen to tell me on the side that they have a sneaking admiration for the pickerels and when taken on the fly-rod often put many a trout to shame. In a case of this sort the fish is not cluttered up holding a plug across its mouth, nor is it "horsed in" as so many fishermen do when using heavy tackle. The fly-rod does not allow one the opportunity of doing any "horsing" and most of the time, if the pickerel is a good one, he'll really give you a run for your money.

To use with the fly-rod in fishing for pickerel are virtually a host of small lures. The largest producer of many and varied fly-rod items is the Weber Lifelike Fly Company, Stevens Point, Wisconsin. Examination of their catalogue should introduce to you many attractors that the pickerel will take. But chiefly you will find those bass flies I mentioned as being very nearly perfect for fly-rod fishing for the pickerels. My choice as a finish for a bass spinner to combine with the bass fly would be nickel, and the oval type spinner is my favorite.

If you select a lightweight bait casting outfit, remember this. You can work your way up small streams where it would be impossible to use the fly-rod. That, of course, is the advantage of the short rod, for the fly-rod, even if only seven or eight feet in length still is likely to provide a problem. As with the canepole, so the fly-rod. It can be used only in open areas, lakes and ponds where there is plenty of elbow room to prevent contact with the trees. And, what is true with both of the above, *i.e.*, the canepole and the fly-rod, can also be held as true of the spinning outfits. They also are in demand of latitude in casting, therefore, as a rule, they too are restricted to open water. Also it is restricted more or less to weed-free and obstruction-free water, clean going in fact and that is accomplished by doing ones fishing entirely along the edge of the weed beds. Only the canepole and the bait casting rod with its various pork chunk and pork rind lures is able to probe and explore the length and breadth of these cluttered places. And when I say that, I know whereof I am writing—from actual experience.

One thing that was accomplished by the introduction of the fad of spinning was that most all lure makers were finally gotten to put out miniature counterparts of their larger, famous lures, to the extent that if you examine the lists of the plug makers today you will find upwards of a hundred small lures, well under 5/8-ounce that will prove perfection plus in pickerel fishing. Because the Creek Chub Bait Company has put out notable bass and pike lures, and their product in plugs is outstanding for pickerel, the fisherman's attention is called to their light counterparts of their famous list of lures. If your plug selection in a lightweight order goes no further than these you would have little to worry about. Indeed, looking at these and numbers turned out by many and various companies I would say that they open up an entire new field, that field being pickerel fishing which shows every sign of becoming a resurrected branch of angling!

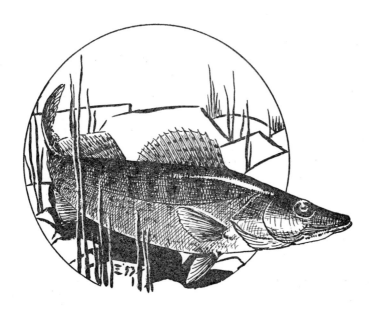

IX

THE WALL-EYED PIKE

As a game fish it is doubtful of the wall-eyed pike has
been given a fair show. In fact the fish has not been carefully dealt with nor has it been accorded the position due
it among our fishes. There was a time when the lake trout
occupied the same position and was universally considered
only as a commercial fish. It was sold in the fish markets, a
circumstance that alone served to lower it to the common
lot of suckers, carp and others in the rough fish class. So
with the wall-eyed pike. Its presence in the markets gave
it the commercial fish status and it has always been in that
category. But just as the lake trout was finally "discovered"
and was lifted to a game fish rating so was the wall-eyed
pike found out. Today this member of the perch family is
more sought after than any of our freshwater game species
and gives more fishermen fishing pleasure than many of the

other game species put together. Surely if a poll were taken among the average fishermen of the country, especially in the regions where the wall-eye exists, their choice as the fish they like best to catch and best to eat would surely be this greater member of the perch family.

In some of our leading wall-eyed pike states, Minnesota foremost, the wall-eye tops all in demand by the fishermen. On the large lakes of that state such as Lake Mille Lacs, Leech Lake, Cass Lake, Lake Winnibigoshish and others, sport fishing for the species almost equals that of an industry. Boats tour the fishing grounds carrying ten or more fishermen, all with lines out and all taking fish. Too, it is the surest way of taking them for if the grounds are known it is only a matter of operating back and forth over such locations and success is had. Because of this prodigeous demand for the wall-eye such states as Minnesota carry on a hatching program annually that turns out untold millions of these wall-eyes and still the cry goes up for more and more. With such fishing pressure exerted on it, Minnesota has largely concentrated on producing wall-eyed pike, letting other programs of stocking involving other game fish wait their turn or fare as best they may. Minnesota's feeling in the matter is: "If they (the fishermen) want wall-eyed pike, let's give them wall-eyed pike." And that's just what is being done in that state today. Possibly no state in the union is turning out more wall-eyes than Minnesota nor, possibly, is any state better equipped for this job.

Just how it happened that this fish was given the name, "wall-eyed pike" is something that has never been explained away and probably it never will. The presence of the word "pike" itself in the name no doubt was justified by the fish having something of a pikelike form. Instead of belonging to the pike family the wall-eye belongs to the perch family, *Percidæ*, of which there are almost a hundred species throughout the world, the most important of these being the wall-eyed pike *(Stizostedion vitreum)* and its close relative the sauger *(Stizostedion canadense)* which is found all through the north over a wide range and extends as far south as northern Alabama and Tennessee. The common yellow perch *(Perca flavescens)* is closely related to the wall-eye but where as the wall-eyed pike is found only in North

America, the yellow perch is found in Europe, especially in the Scandinavian countries and in the British Isles. Here, again, is an oddity, for while the yellow perch is found over seas, its relative the wall-eyed pike and the sauger are unknown there. One wonders whether the scientists have ever wrestled with that conundrum.

In the early days in Pennsylvania the wall-eyes of the Susquehanna River were known as "Susquehanna Salmon," at best a terrible misnomer. But if this was taking a liberty what then must we say about the name of the same fish in the South where it is called "jack salmon," to this day. At one time in Ohio the fish was called the "white salmon" and in the Great Lakes region it early went by such names as Blue Pike, Yellow Pike, Green Pike and Grass Pike. Even in our times you will run across these names. Still more odd appellations occur in Lake Erie and much of eastern Ontario and Quebec where the wall-eye is called *pickerel*. The Cree Indians name it *okow* while the French Canadians call it *dore* and *picarel*. In the far north where it is found the fur-traders of the Hudson Bay Company called it *hornfish*. Richardson recorded the wall-eye as far north as 58° and it is said to extend eastward from Great Slave Lake as far as Labrador. It ranges southward mostly east of the Mississippi River, but the states of Minnesota, Iowa, Missouri, Arkansas and Louisiana are the western borders of the wall-eye range. It is also found as far south as Mississippi and Alabama and is said to inhabit the streams flowing into the Atlantic in Georgia although this is not too certain. It is not, to our knowledge, found in Florida but in the rest of the states embraced in the perimeter noted it is fairly common to very common. The wall-eyed pike has never been introduced into western waters which is odd in this day when fish species are sown numerously over vast areas without any regard for whether they will do well in this or that state or region and if, in fact, the waters and food are suitable for its upkeep. Personally I would say that introduction of the pike in the West would be a tragedy inasmuch as the food demanded by these hordes is such as to be doubted even when the facts are laid down before one and authenticated. Western waters could never support such a fish species. Still, that would not stop individuals from introducing it on the sly.

Because the wall-eyed pike is so generally mistaken for a pike *(Esox lucius)* it is interesting to note the difference between the pike family (the pike, the muskellunge and the three pickerels) and this greater member of the perch family. The pike family all have their bodies covered with a slime which makes them slippery as eels, which slime is useful as a means of protecting the body from the inroads of fungus diseases. Very often members of the pike family fairly drip and run with this slime. On the other hand the wall-eyed pike, the sauger and the yellow perch (all in the same family) have no slime whatever on their bodies. The bodies of the perch family are protected by very tightly set scales and the surface of the scales being rough, very rough to the touch. Thus, by merely running your fingers over the body of the wall-eye you should be able to tell it instantly from a member of the pike family. Too, the wall-eyed pike has two dorsal (back) fins, the anterior or forward dorsal fin being set with strong spines while those in the rear back fin are softer as in the bass. The wall-eyed pike, therefore, has two dorsal (back) fins while the pike family only have one and that is set far back toward the tail. On another score, too, can the wall-eyed pike be told from the true pike family and that is by its eyes which, after capture, turn white, for all the world as though they were stone-frozen. It is this appearance of its eyes when out of water from which is derived the name "wall-eye."

To the best of my knowledge there is no technical information extant regarding the eyes of the wall-eyed pike. Surely no fish we have in our inland waters are in the least comparable to them. Those scientific gentlemen who study eyes might find much to interest them in dissecting the optics of this fish and probably they could answer the question that often comes our way: "Do the wall-eyed pike have eyes with which they can see in the dark, very much as does the owl on land?" There is no doubt about this, although to what degree is something that one must leave entirely to conjecture. But that wall-eyed pike can be taken at night is a well known fact, although even knowing this there are any number of fishermen who will not fish at night. In the chapter on fishing for the wall-eye there will be some notes regarding night fishing for this greater member of the perch family.

Coloration and physical characteristics of the wall-eye are as follows: Color olivaceous, mingled with brassy; sides of the head vermiculated; the dorsals, caudal and pectoral fins having bands; those of the dorsals and caudal not continuous; sides with about seven oblique dark bands, differing in direction; a jet black blotch on the membrane behind the last spine of the dorsal.

"In most cases an adult wall-eyed pike," writes Ben Robinson, famous fishing writer, "is heavy of girth if in good shape, is solidly constructed, with spinous dorsal fin, the second one in back being soft, a well shaped tail marked with small yellow oblong spots and with the color of yellowish olive. The belly is silver. This is what unquestionably caused Ohio anglers years ago to call it 'white salmon.' In fact the gleam of the hooked fish gives one the impression that it is entirely silver in hue. The head is shaped in close harmony with the pike, being rather flat and long, the under jaw coming well over the upper and the large wall-eye set at a good distance from the side of the head. The inside of the mouth is armed with bands of sharp, long teeth, the front teeth of the lower jaw hooking back at a sharp angle. The top of the head is of a dark olive green and bronze color, without scales. The gill covers are not scaled excepting the lower strip which is noticably scaled. The cheeks are entirely unscaled. There are five rays (bones) in the branchiostegals, which are of a salmon and silver hue, the underside of the head being a delicate pink color. The mouth of the fish comes directly under the line of the back part of the eye. The eye is usually large in this species. The eye of a four and one-half pound fish measures approximately three-fourths of an inch in diameter, and is of a full grey and brown color with a line of golden light separating the pupil. The pupil is jet black and large."

To describe one wall-eyed pike in one section of the country, however, and hold this as applicable to all wall-eyed pike in other sections of the country does not work out. I have taken the wall-eyed pike in the greater part of its range, north and south and must state that there is likely to be drastic color changes and variations depending upon the region the fish is found in, the variety of food that it consumes and water and bottom nature. We have taken walleyed pike in waters saturated with tannin and other chemicals of natural origin, which water has been the color of port wine. From such waters are taken wall-eyes that are darkish brown in color. In other waters where the bottom is gravelled and sandy and the sunlight has full play on the bottom, wall-eyed pike have proved to be very light in coloration, even silvery. Normally, however, the coloration is very much the same wherever the wall-eye is found with the exception of cases where water and bottom conditions make for a different colored fish. John B. Thompson who wrote so well on fishing under the *nom de plume* of "Ozark Ripley" once stated:

"The coloration of the wall-eyed pike holds the same almost everywhere; its dark, mixed black and bronze, and under golden shadings of almost, at times, a white tinge, are too well known to make further comment. But the exceeding beauty of this fish where the variety takes the name of *blue pickerel*, in certain waters of eastern Canada, is notable, especially around the falls of Little Messanabi. To attempt to depict the gorgeous coloration of this variant is impossible—the rich purple, dark and light blue shadings are made tremendously attractive by the lightening effect of subtle iridescence and can never be appreciated except by those who have viewed them just as they are taken from their cold water habitat!"

I believe the above instance can be duplicated in other localities by wall-eyes found in various and scattered waters. I once viewed a fourteen pound wall-eyed pike taken in Lake Hamilton, a reservoir lake on the Ouachita River, near Hot Springs, Arkansas, which, if laid side by side with wall-eyes taken in Kiarskons Lake in western Ontario would be so much alike as to color and shape as to make it impossible to tell which was which. The large wall-eye I saw caught in Dale Hollow Lake of northern Tennessee last summer had approximately the same coloration and shape of these Ontario wall-eyes. It is interesting to note that many northerners are of the belief that these southern walleyes were the result of the introduction of northern wall-eyes into southern waters. There is definitely no truth to this, inasmuch as the original range of the wall-eye covered both Tennessee and Arkansas, equally as it did in the north. Fact is, Mitchill (1818) first located the wall-eyed pike in the South.

The sauger *(Stizostedion canadense)* is, of course, closely related to the wall-eye being a sort of smaller understudy of the larger species. Distinguishing characteristics are: Color olivaceous above; sides brassy or pale orange, mottled with black in the form of irregular blotches, which are best defined under the soft dorsal. The spinous dorsal has several rows of round black spots on the membrane between the spines; no black blotch on the hind part of the spinous dorsal. Pectorals with a large dark blotch at base; soft dorsal with several rows of dark spots irregularly placed; caudal yellowish with dark spots forming interrupted bars. The wall-eye has also been distinguished from the saugers by the structure of its *pyloric cæca,* these being three in number, about of the same size and normally of about the length of the stomach. By way of explanation the *pyloric cæca* are wormlike tubes found toward the rear of the stomach. These can easily be checked when the fish is gutted. Another point might be stressed in telling the wall-eye from the sauger. The former has 21 soft rays in the second dorsal, the sauger has 18. Personally I do not believe that this holds good in all cases.

In size the sauger is much below that of the wall-eye, a very good fish in this variety being 18 inches in length with a top weight of two pounds. It is a very slim fish, the posterior portion of its body being almost cylindrical in shape. Very closely duplicating the sauger is the so-called gray pike or sand pike of the Great Lakes and southwestward (*Lucioperca grisea*) De Kay (1842) and (*Stizostedion canadense griseum,*) Jordan & Evermann (1896). I do not think that this variety is considered much different from the sauger. It is said to differ from the typical *canadense* by having smoother opercles and head bones, fewer opercular spines and less complete scaling of the head.

It is strange that the sauger should be so numerous in the TVA lakes of the state of Tennessee. These were originally found in the Tennessee River in great numbers and when the reservoir lakes were created they naturally were trapped in these lakes and there continued to produce their kind. To what extent propagation of the saugers and wall-eyed-pike has been carried on in the TVA lakes I do not know. Dr. R. W. Eschmeyer, formerly chief biologist of the TVA systems, comments that in Norris Lake the saugers are very well established but that fishermen have been poorly rewarded in fishing for them. Saugers, he states, have a very wide range of distribution in the spring, extending more or less evenly from the surface to a depth of over 40 feet. He remarks: "Saugers are somewhat concentrated in summer, but are in deep water. There is no evidence that sauger are concentrated even at spawning time, although we know nothing about their spawning habits in Norris Lake, though it is known that the spawning takes place in March or early April. In addition to being scattered, the species tends to remain on the bottom at whatever depth it happens to be. Deep-trolling near the bottom, involves constant snagging on stumps or rocks. It appears that sauger can be caught best by live minnow fishing at the proper depth, keeping the bait within a few inches of the bottom, preferably off of the sandy points.

"*From all indications the sauger crop cannot be harvested adequately by hook-and-line fishing.* Most of this excellent food will be wasted even if year-round fishing is permitted. There is one further consideration—the sauger completes with the bass for food, since the diet of both consists almost exclusively of small fish. Summer fishing is poor because small fish are very abundant. If the sauger eats only shad and bluegills it may be an asset to the fisherman even if it is not caught, because it helps to reduce the number of the small fish. If, however, small bass are taken in considerable numbers by the saugers, they may be very undesirable. Food studies should help provide information on the value of the sauger to fishing."

Eschmeyer also states that during the entire fishing season most sauger are to be found in deep water. During June and July very few are taken in water less than 20 feet deep. Most of the summer fishing has been too shallow for sauger. In mid-March it was found that saugers were equally abundant at all depths from the surface to 40 feet. By mid-May they tended to become more concentrated. During June almost all sauger were within the 20-foot layer, between 20 and 40 feet in depth. When spread more or less evenly over a wide range of depth, relatively few are present at any one level, hence fewer will be attracted to the bait. During most of the season, sauger concentrations tend to be greatest at 20 to 40 feet. The person fishing for sauger could, therefore, expect to do best at these depths. It was believed that reducing the size limit on saugers in Tennessee from 15 to 12 inches would result in more fish being taken, but this reduction in size availed little in cutting down on the sum total of the sauger crop in Norris Lake, and the same might possibly be true in all the other lakes of the TVA system. The contention of Eschmeyer was that "A greater removal of sauger in Norris Lake seems desirable." He adds: "Sauger tend to run to the tailwaters and to concentrate there. Where they are concentrated they provide good fishing. Anglers, therefore, should be encouraged to fish the tailwaters. Restrictions on the fishing should be few if we wish to harvest a considerable portion of the sauger crop in the reservoirs." By way of explanation, the "tailwaters" is the fast water below dams, the same being felt for a considerable stretch downstream. This water is almost always clear and fish come up to the area below dams to get away from the silt filling the TVA lakes.

As to whether it was Dr. Eschmeyer's belief that TVA waters should be seined every so often to remove some of the preponderating numbers of the saugers and other fish is something I know little about. There is a well defined movement looming all over the country demanding that excess numbers of fish be removed by seining from lakes and reservoirs. That this will aid in bringing the fish species back to normal is still unknown. Those opposed to any such seining contend that biologists and state departments are working hand in glove with the commerical fishermen whom they seek to get the job of removing these surplus fish. On the whole this suspicion can be dismissed as groundless and without other comment than to state that in only one state I know of, Florida, is such seining to remove surplus numbers being done by commercial fishermen, under state supervision. And this seining in Florida has been conducted in only six lakes the object being to test whether a corrected condition

and normalcy can be obtained in these lakes in which case of
course correction measures will be taken in all lakes in the
state. The main object to the Florida experiment is that commercial fishermen are permitted to do the seining, where, so
contend the opponents of the method, the state should do
the seining and realize by the profits of the sale of the fish
harvested instead of private individuals. It is to be admitted
that only if a state does any such seining should it be permitted.

That the sauger and the wall-eyed pike devour an immense
amount of food goes without the saying and if a lake is
over-stocked with saugers, at least, it can be seen where its
decimation of the food supply can over-topple the balance
in any water. It has been estimated that a single wall-eyed
pike will eat at least 600 three to four inch fishes in the
course of one year. Forbes and Richardson stated:

"Allowing three years of life to the wall-eye, the smallest,
reasonable estimate of food for each wall-eye would fall somewhere between 1800 and 3000 fishes and on this basis
100 wall-eyes, such as should each year be taken along a
few miles of a river like the Illinois, would require 180,000
to 300,000 fishes for food. Probably no fish in our streams
is able to meet so tremendous a food demand except the
hickory (gizzard) shad—so abundant in the food of this
fish—unless the carp may be an equally acceptable victim."

The carp has never proved to be a desirable food for wall-
eyed pike or sauger as the case may be, but in the South,
as in the reservoir lakes in Tennessee and Arkansas, the
gizzard shad has proved virtually a godsend to the fish. Not
only do these shad reproduce their kind by the millions annually but their numbers afford food not only to the wall-eyes
and saugers but are also food for all four of the bass species,
plus the crappie and the white bass. Were it not for the
presence of the shad in such fantastic numbers the fishing
in the southern lakes and streams would become quite hopeless, as there would not be sufficient food for the various
species to keep in the swim.

Gowanloch (Louisiana) states that "the wall-eye may
reach from 10 to 20 pounds" and, elsewhere, "a wall-eye three
feet long may weigh 25 pounds." In another observation
he stated: "Thirty-five pound wall-eyed pike have been

taken." A fish and game record around the turn of the century claims that wall-eyes 50 pounds in weight have been caught. Opposed to the above the world's record wall-eyed pike as established by the *Field and Stream* contest weighed 22 pounds, 4 ounces. It might be mentioned that 16, 17 and 18 pound wall-eyed pike are not uncommon, and most of these, year after year have come from the state of Tennessee. It should be mentioned, however, that the world's record wall-eye was taken in Ontario, just to keep the facts of the case in line. Arkansas streams and other bodies of water have produced wall-eyes up to 16 pounds to my knowledge. In the north the taking of an 8 or 10 pound wall-eye is considered rather unusual, although two I know of taken in Kiarskons Lake, in the pipestone Valley region of western Ontario, weighed 17 and 18 pounds respectively. One gains from this the knowledge that super-large wall-eyed pike do not come from Tennessee only or the south in General. It is reasonable to believe that only in the upper south do these large wall-eyes appear.

During the latter part of the summer of 1952, while fishing in Dale Hollow Lake in northern Tennessee a wall-eyed pike that weighed 14 pounds, 9 ounces was brought in at Jimmy Reneau's Holly Creek Dock. I might mention that the largest one I have ever taken weighed 13½ pounds. It is very rare indeed that one sees a wall-eye as large as this one I saw at Dale Hollow Lake. In an interview with John W. Parsons, Fish Biologist for the Cumberland District in Tennessee, he stated:

"Wall-eyes are taken by fishing methods in Tennessee that frequently weigh from ten to fourteen pounds and not infrequently up to seventeen and one-half pounds. I took one sixteen and one-half pounds by net last spring. As a matter of fact, our gill net catches in Dale Hollow Lake during March and April would make some of the wall-eye netting for spawn taking purposes in the north and elsewhere anything but outstanding. Probably most of the big wall-eyes are females. So far as the distribution of this fish in Tennessee is concerned, they are in all the large reservoirs and large rivers systems of the state. Occasionally they are found in the highland or plateau streams along with the musky but I believe most of the wall-eye spawning takes place in the large rivers, but they then migrate in the smaller and more upland streams. Although Watts Bar Lake of the Tennessee TVA lakes has received some publicity as being a wall-eye lake, it certainly must be said that Dale Hollow Lake and Norris Lake far surpass it in that respect.

"I do not pretend to know why Dale Hollow is so productive of large bass and wall-eyes. It is the only lake in Tennessee of this type that has abundant vegetation of various types. Whether the vegetation accounts for the excellent fish populations or whether the factor or factors that account for the vegetation is also responsible for the large fish populations; I don't know. Dale Hollow Lake is distinctive from other reservoirs of its type in Tennessee in that the water is relatively clear 12 months of the year. Lake Bedford, a lake owned by the Tennessee Game and Fish Department, produces many large bass from 10 to 14 pounds in weight. This lake is known to be productive due to the phosphate ground material surrounding the lake. Whether there is phosphate in Dale Hollow basin or not, I have no data."

This well known fish biologist continued:

"We do not propagate the well-eyed pike in Tennessee. Several states in the north have large wall-eyed pike propagation programs. Never in one case to date have they proven that their artificial propagation methods have been beneficial to fishing. Iowa State College is carrying on experiments in stocking a lake with fingerlings from hatcheries every other year. Annual surveys in the lake are being made to determine, by the 'scale' method, if the population in later years consists mostly of fish of the years when the stocking took place. So far I do not believe they have attempted to analyze the data collected. Usually two methods are used in stocking the wall-eye. First, the fish are stocked in the water as soon as they are able to feed by themselves. In other words, just past the egg fry stage. This takes place around a week after the fish are hatched. Another method is to stock these fry in a small, say 15, 20 or so acre lake that have few predators fish present. Then the following year, when the fish are 6 to 8 inches in length, they are seined from the lake (usually a shallow lake which can be easily seined with a 1,000 foot net). These yearlings are then stocked in the desired locations. I doubt very much if any hatchery raises wall-eyes over a couple inches long. Probably the reason that the propagation of wall-eyes is so common is that the fish are easily caught, easily stripped and the eggs are easily handled and hatched even though they may not be too justified in their efforts. I doubt very much if we will ever have a reason for propagating the wall-eye in Tennessee. So far as the location of planting small wall-eyes is concerned I expect most of it is inshore stocking.

"I do not doubt," he added, "but what Dale Hollow Lake is the best smallmouth bass lake in the United States and I believe it is the best large wall-eye lake in the country. The wall-eyes in Dale Hollow are much more abundant than the creel counts have indicated. Fishermen of the South have not yet developed the knack of wall-eye fishing to any great extent. For instance, June-bug spinners and minnows which are known killers of the species in the north and is in use everywhere up there as you know, is practically unknown in the South."

The practice of stocking wall-eyed pike fry in a minute size by pouring the contents of the cans into shallow inshore waters to shift for themselves has been in such common practice by many and various game and fish departments as to need no explanation. Out of these millions, so dumped, few survive inasmuch as minnows, panfish of all kinds and game fish young form a ring in the inshore waters through which none of these mites are able to penetrate. Those that, by miracle, are able to get through this ring may be the ones that survive. A number of years ago I suggested that instead of dumping the fry along the shores, in shallow water, that they should be planted out in the middle of small bays in which case preying fishes inshore would be circumvented. If this was ever followed up I do not know inasmuch as game and fish departments are of the opinion that no one save schooled culturists know what to do in the matter. Thus, presumably, as Parsons has stated, most of the stocking continues to be that of plantings in shallow water. If this is so then expecting to derive a normal number of wall-eyed pike in a lake may have its grave short-comings. The method carried on by some sportsmen and angler's associations of creating their own ponds for rearing wall-eyes to a size suitable for stocking, *i.e.*, from a few inches to 8 inches or so in length, is a method that should be expanded upon and publicized. In Minnesota this has been carried out most successfully. The sportsmen and angler groups obtain their fry from the state hatcheries and at their own expense raise the pike to the desired length and then stock them. As a result many lakes that were failing in pike numbers have now been brought up to oldtime normal quantities. This a method of stocking that may have to be followed up in many states. The cost of maintenance and the holding over of fry to the status of small fish is such that it could be done only on a very small scale if done by a state.

Dr. R. W. Eschmeyer's statement that anglers take comparatively few of the saugers in Lake Norris of the TVA system in Tenesseee gives one food for thought. Eschmeyer remarks:

"We must conclude from available evidence that most game fish in Norris Lake (and other TVA waters as well), are never caught. The belief that most fish are wasted is also supported by evidence collected everywhere. For example, in a large lake in Minnesota the population of walleyes was estimated by investigators Jerome Stroudt and Samuel Eddy to be about 900,000 adult fish. The catch in one year was estimated at 55,000, or about 6 per cent of the population!"

X

WALL-EYED PIKE FISHING

As a rule the wall-eyed pike is a sly, elusive fish, rarely
if ever seen by the fisherman save only when a specimen is
hooked and is brought to the surface. The reason for this
blotting out of their presence is traceable to the deep-roving
nature of the species which keeps itself more or less identified
with the depths and rarely in a shallow-water habitat.
Yet it should not be understood from this that the wall-eyed
pike lives its life mostly in the depths for this is not so.
The fact that it is a night feeder is known to many but is
certainly not known to the rank and file of the fishermen.
These nocturnal operations of the wall-eyed pike are interesting in that from nine of ten o'clock in the evening
around to two o'clock in the morning you are likely to find the
wall-eyes in shallow water, in the bays, around reefs and

sandbars and more or less generally inshore. They operate as a rule in schools of greater or lesser numbers, sweeping in and crowding the minnows up ahead of them and there feeding on them. By taking their food in this manner and at this time comparatively few fishermen are around or active and do not get in on the fishing. Having fed to repletion the wall-eyes then move back out into deep water, go down to the floor of the lake and lie there most of the day, bellies on the sands, digesting there intake of the night before. This is one reason why fishermen, trolling at a normal depth in the daytime rarely ever get any wall-eyes. Very simply, their lures never get anywhere near the fish they are after. It is merely a case of the feeding period coming at a time when the fisherman is not active. And when the fisherman is active the fish are not—they are fed up and are lying on the bottom of the lake. This is definitely one of the reasons why summer fishing for wall-eyed pike produces such inferior dividends.

There are two seasons in the year when the wall-eyed pike are in varying depths comparatively shallow water. One is in the spring when they are generally to be found in from ten to twenty feet of water following upon the close of their spawning which goes into effect as early as in April in Minnesota and through the northern states through which it ranges. Following the spawning period the fish are apparently famished for food and it is then that they are taken in the thousands by fishermen. This generally good fishing begins to taper off in June and with warm weather coming on they vanish from the grounds they have been taken over in the spring and go into the depths. From then on till autumn they are much of an unknown quantity. Those fishermen who take them know enough about the habits of the fish to go out at night for them or, if they troll by day, they bring their lures so deep down that they fairly scrape on the bottom.

The autumn movement of the wall-eyed pike into inshore locations can never be told by any sight of the fish in those inshore locations. This fall invasion of the inshore stretches no doubt goes into effect some time after the middle of September and continues into the month of October. We have taken them as late in the shallow water as the 25th of September, but during autumns having conspicuous Indian

Summer periods they may work around inshore till the early part of November. Interest attaches itself to the fact that while this is a general feeding run, and most any sort of food known to the wall-eyed pike diet is then taken, a chief food at the time is frogs that have come into the lakes to sink themselves in the mud and debris for a winter of dormancy. Like the bass and other fish, so the wall-eyes. They will hunt out these frogs and devour them, possibly by the hundreds. It is interesting in this respect to note that while the wall-eyed pike is classified as a minnow-consumer, taking huge numbers of minnows no doubt, still it also feeds on young panfish, crawfish, frogs, etc., in fact stomach contents on examination are likely to show up with a heavy diet of mayflies in season. That it does feed on frogs during the spring and fall periods is a fact that I early established.

Being sly and elusive, and extremely wary about exposing himself to the gaze of Man, the wall-eyed pike may never be suspected of being inshore until one is caught. But even this may not make one believe these fish are inshore until four or five are taken and then the secret will be out. Yet you may use all manner of lures and still not take fish. Why? The answer is wrapped up in the strange circumstance that live frogs are what the pike is seeking and he will take these in preference to any lure that is offered. Since not one one fisherman in a hundred thousand is using frogs for any kind of fish at this time of the year its value as a wall-eyed pike lure can hardly be bettered upon.

Yet in fishing this lure in the autumn remember that it should be reeled close to the bottom, if not right along the bottom. Of course this is possible only when the bottom is sandy or gravelled and there are few obstructions. Such bottom conditions do not always exist. If not reeled right on the bottom, reel it along in such fashion that the frog now and then touches on the bottom. Mention should be made that that where wall-eyed pike lakes in which the species is identified in numbers has streams flowing into them they often work around the mouths of the same, and even make short runs up these streams. Naturally such locations may be considered as among the best locations for fall fishing with frogs. Frogs used should, if possible, be medium in size. They need not be hooked on alive. They can be killed by being stunned. The fresh frog, though dead, practically works as well on the hook as a live one. Minnows up to three or four inches can be used, alive in like fishing around the stream mouths. If a bobber is used ajust it on the line so that the minnow almost touches on the bottom. If reeling a frog (which is very limp) it will be found that a continuous series of little jerks with the rod tip as you reel it will communicate action to the frog causing it to move along as though it is alive. This trick, once learned, will take many fish. Of course the possibility occurs that bass, also contacted by this method of working the frog may be candidates for the frying pan in that they, too, are operating inshore seeking frogs which they grub for with industry.

Because fishing for the wall-eyed pike has been but little commented on, even the rudimentary methods of such fishing have almost wholly been left in the dark. Not only are the habits of the species known only to a minor extent, but the methods of fishing have been woefully neglected by writers who know what they are talking about. It is generally known however that the so-called June-bug spinner with its single hook, to which is applied a live minnow, is by far the choice of all lures that are used in trolling for the wall-eye. But, as our friend John W. Parsons fish biologist for the Cumberland District in northern Tennessee, has commented, the lure and the methods of using it are practically unknown to the South. In fact it can probably be stated that most southern wall-eyes are taken with minnows still-fishing or cast in the natural way by hooking the minnow through both lips, which of course, is one way of casting for the wall-eye. But trolling, using a June-bug spinner, is known and religiously practiced apparently only in the north, with special emphasis on fishing in Minnesota, Wisconsin and Michigan where this lure can certainly be said to be omnipresent in all fishing sections where the fish is trolled for.

The June-bug type of spinner is not a patented device or if there ever was a patent on it the patent ran out many years ago. In any event most all companies putting out spoon lures also have their versions of the June-bug spinner. Some are very simple affairs, others more elaborate. A very popular lure in this class has an arm extending from the shaft to the middle of the blade, as a consequence of which the spoon

revolves in a limited area close to the shaft, whereas a
spinner without this arm from blade to shaft swings free
and flares out. Spoons with the free spinner are to be had,
also made by most companies dealing in spoons. While the
latter is very commonly used there is no gainsaying the fact
that the former mentioned type is the best. Usually there is
just a long stemmed single hook attached to the spinner shaft
in the June-bug spinner combination and on this the hook
is applied. And the minnow is attached to the hook but in
a manner, as a rule, that is clumsy and unnatural. Yet in
spite of this the lure and the hooking arrangement in general
will take wall-eyes and many of them. In fact this method
is in use on all the wall-eye lakes in the state of Minnesota
where, as I have stated elsewhere in another chapter, most
fishing for wall-eyes is done with the June-bug spinner, indeed I would say that fully 95% of such fishing is done
with this lure with live minnow attached.

When one states, however, that a "live" minnow is used
do not gain from this the impression that the minnow is alive
very long after the hook is seated in its side. Fact is it does
not live more than a minute on the hook before it has given
up its finny ghost. It would be better to say "fresh" minnow
than "live" minnow. The one is correct; the other is not. The
wall-eye is not attracted to the lure because of any lifelike
quality of the combination in conjunction with the fresh
minnow. It is the fresh scent that attracts it and this is what
spurs it on to strike. It will follow this fresh scent in a
manner that stamps it as unusual among other fishes, for it
is almost certain that the scenting powers are great indeed,
as a consequence of which the fresh minnow is sure to bring
on its undoing.

We tested this matter very thoroughly, in this manner. One
hook on one line was used on one side of the boat while
another with the same June-bug spinner was used on the line
on the other side. On the line on one side a pickled minnow
from a bottle commercially put up on the Pacific coast was
used. On the other line arrangement on the other side of
the boat a fresh minnow was applied. The trolling was done
at exactly the same distance from the boat. The results were
two fish caught on the rubbery pickled minnow to eight
taken on the fresh minnow. In still further fishing the results

were even greater in favor of the fresh minnow as against the commercially bottled product, proof that it was the scent that attracted the fish for the fresh minnow was just as dead as the pickled one. It should be mentioned that a landslide of pickled minnows were at one time dumped in the wall-eyed pike fishing regions of the north. Usually the fisherman would try them a couple times and then drop their use, invariably returning to the live minnow and the June big spinner. Then in some states a law was passed forbidding the sale of pickled minnows; just why I would not know.

The June bug spinner and the live (or fresh) minnow on it is successful for one reason and one reason only: the fresh minnow leaves a scent trail in the water and the wall-eyes are attracted to it. It becomes apparent on study of this fish that of all our game fish, it is least of all attracted by any manner of artificial lure, plug, spoon, or any like device that is without a live fish attachment. If you were to troll any one of these lures of an artificial nature without a live minnow attached, the lure assuring no live fish scent, on one side of the boat and a June bug spinner and live minnow on the other, the June bug and live minnow will take the fish and the artificial lure but a small fraction of the catch. This is not supposition, but fact. But if you were to cut out a part of the belly of a perch to hook on the June bug hook you would find things reversed. This piece of light belly skin should retain the breast or pectoral fins and then taper back to the anal section. This strip will make all the difference in the world, especially if it is fresh. In this respect it should be noted that perch fresh to us is apparently the sweetest of all fish flesh as among our common lake fish varieties. The same would be true so far as the wall-eyed pike are concerned— perch flesh does act as providing a scent and affords a trail in the water that brings the fish on.

In the light of the above it can be said that artificial lures in themselves without some sort of fish attraction added have their absolute shortcomings in the field of wall-eye trolling. This is especially the case where the numbers of wall-eyes paying court to your lure are scattered and few in number. If they are numerous and the competition is great they are likely to rush a strictly artificial lure and take it just to keep some other fish from seizing it.

Wall-eyes are definitely attracted by the movements of a lure. It is well known in this respect that the wall-eyed pike is susceptible to the rippling undulations of a strip of pork-rind attached to the hook. It will be found, however, that where a rind strip is used on the hook that the fish will follow the lure and nip at that wiggling tail. Because of this habit such fish are called short-strikers. At one time I was of the opinion that they nipped this "tail" (the pork rind strip) as they would nip the tail of some fish that they prey upon, so injuring it and making it easier for them to seize. I do not know if this is the reason but we do know that the habit wall-eyes have of following a pork rind lure and nipping or short-striking it is too well known to need comment. Many years ago the Pflueger Company put out what they called a "tail hook" pork rind that was, I believe, one of the brightest ideas, at least in wall-eye fishing, that could have been thought up. Whoever did invent it was certainly a wall-eye fisherman and he was well aware of the trick wall-eyes have of nipping the tail of a pork rind. When using this tail-hook rind the wall-eye nips the tail-end and gets hooked in that hook crimped in at the tail. Invariably the fish is hooked. Nor does this short-striking habit apply to fish in waters within civilization solely but in the wilderness as well where the fish probably never have seen a lure. It is this that has stimulated the idea with me that, as previously stated, the fish nips the tail to disable the minnow or fish (if he thinks it so to be) so that he can the easier seize it. As witness: On a canoe trip in northern Quetico Provincial park or reserve in western Ontario I caught over 40 wall-eyes standing and casting in one spot, and all save a very few of them were taken on the tail-hook of that Pflueger tail-rind item. This rind is hard to obtain save through the company. It is bottled in chemical like all other pork rind and has the hooks crimped into the rind ready to go. Apparently the chemical has no rusting influence on them although they are heavily coated with paint. The points should be cleaned and filed sharp before they are used.

Because the wall-eyed pike is a short-striker there is also need in using a two-hook arrangement on the June bug spinner. This second or back hook is called the trailer hook. You can bend down the barb of the forward hook with a pair of pliers, which will permit putting the trailer hook eye over the same, then the barb can be turned back into place with the pliers. You can then hook the two lips of the minnow on the forward hook, while the trailer hook is lightly attached under the skin on the side of the minnow. In this manner the minnow actually is alive as its body is not harmed. Opposed to this the common system used is that the long shanked hook on the June bug spinner (which is a single hook) is inserted into the mouth of the minnow and comes out at the gill covers, then is carried back and hooked somewhere around the rear portion of the dorsal (back) fin. Nothing holding the lips of the minnow in front the front portion sags back on the hook so that when trolled it assumes a sort of C shape on the stem of the hook, extremely clumsy and the surprise of course is that any fish could be taken on it at all. A Bead Chain arrangement can be made by selecting a bit of chain in this bead swivel type that is two-and-one-half inches in length, has a small ring in one end and a fly-rod swivel in the other. The ring on the bead chain slips over a crimped-down barb on the front hook, after which the barb is turned back into place which will hold it secure without coming off. To the fly-rod snap a No. 1 treble hook is applied, preferably Mustad imported hook if it is to be had. These are a bronzed type. Now attach one of the hooks of the treble under the skin near the rear part of the dorsal (back) fin and you will have a most excellent arrangement. If the fish is a short striker he will likely come forward enough ahead of the tail to become affixed to the treble hook. I believe this is one of the best hook set-ups I have ever used and, as a rule, it is never-failing in its sure-fire hooking capacity.

How cagey, observant and discriminating the wall-eyed pike is may be open to question. Let us take another experiment that we made in wall-eyed pike trolling. It involved the use of a black line right up to the lure on one side of the boat and the use of nylon leader line up to the lure in the other. This was of the new limp monofilament type that is very flexible and is just about as transparent as any leader material can be. It should be remembered that this new du-Pont monofilament differs from the older product in that it can be used on a reel, lays well and does not jump up in coils as did the older and less flexible type. For experiments we used 12 pound test line as this was heavy enough for all trolling purposes. By way of explanation this new duPont monofilament is called "line" up to 15 pounds test, but from (and including the 15 pound test) up to 60 pounds test it is called "leader" not "line". The duPont Company states that up to 15 pound test the material is too limp for leader purposes but that from 15 pounds test up it is suitable.

Here again the black line tied directly to the bait, used on one side of the boat, proved not nearly as successful as the bait that was tied to the limp monofilament line. This would seem to point to the fact that the invisibility factor of the line has much to do whether you will take as many wall-eyes as you should in your fishing. The conclusions reached are definitely that a monofilament line is superior to a regular bait casting line up to the lure. It is suggested that a 200 yard reel be used for this sort of trolling in that a long line out is another consideration of moment. One should never troll in a lake for wall-eyes with less than 150 feet of line out. When the wall-eyes are deep down, that is 30, 40 or more feet the system that is used in the famous bass and wall-eye lakes in Tennessee might be stressed. Here a type of saltwater rod with a handle 20 inches in length and a glass fiber tip of 33 inches in length, is used, the rod and handle totalling 4 feet, 5 to 6 inches overall. Some of these rods are a little longer than this but they belong to a familiar saltwater trolling type and are made by most all companies who make saltwater rods. The glass fiber tip naturally is light but incomparably strong for its length and caliber. It makes an ideal trolling rod not only for deep-trolling for the wall-eyed pike, but lake trout and other game freshwater fish of size as well. By referring my specifications above to any company making such rods one can get what he is looking for. I much prefer the glass fiber tip for this sort of rod.

Use a 200, or 250 yard saltwater trolling reel, preferably with a star drag to adjust for all degrees of trolling. One can use anywhere from 15 pound test up to 20 pound test limp monofilament nylon for the line. To the end of your line you can use 50 feet of steel wire line or monel line which will act as a "sinker" in taking the line down. Without wire line out in front one figures that the lure will go down ten feet for every 100 feet of line had out. Thus to go down 40 feet one would need to have out 400 or more feet of line. But there is less needed if you have on the 50 feet of wire in front as then between 300 and 350 feet of line and wire out will take your lure down to the required 40 feet. Better than either steel wire or monel, in my estimation, is leaded line. This is a wire of lead that has nylon woven over it so that one can hardly tell it from a regular line. The flexibility of this lead line is far superior to monel or steel wire, even though light in gauge and would be a distinct recommendation. Fifty feet of this would be equal as a "sinker" factor to fifty feet of either steel wire or monel. As to whether any company other than Ashaway makes this leaded line, I do not know.

The use of wire, monel wire or leaded line is ostensibly to get away from sinkers which are far from desirable in any manner of trolling. And that is especially true in deep trolling where one must on occasion go down almost to the very bottom to get results. If you can troll your lure so that it virtually bounces off of the bottom you are in line to take fish, especially when the wall-eyes are deep down, as in the summer but otherwise not.

It is obvious of course that not too many lakes can be trolled deep down toward the bottom. The reason of course is vegetation in greater or lesser quantity. However, it is interesting to note that most of the best wall-eye waters have gravelled, sandy or rocky bottoms and deep trolling, down to the bottom, is feasible. On the other hand some lakes may be partly obstructed with vegetation but other parts of such lakes may have a clear bottom. To know where to troll for wall-eyes in such waters becomes a paramount demand and it is because fishermen really never know where to go that such lakes never produce in proportion to their actual worth.

Wall-eyed pike invariably, and naturally demand a sandy, gravelled or rocky bottom as their habitat. Therefore, if you can find a bottom of the sort you have the right location for trolling. That is especially true where rocks are located on the bottom. To find the condition of the bottom it is possible to troll with a dipsey sinker (the pear-shaped type) without hook or bait attached, permitting it to bounce along on the bottom. You can easily tell if rocks are hit by the bounce of the sinker. Too, the condition of the bottom can be ascertained if no weeds are met with. If the bottom is clear, has rocks, gravel, sand, then that would be a place to troll, aiming to let the lure touch occasionally on the bottom. This certainty exists in deep trolling and it has been proved time and again by actual experience that your largest wall-eyes are deep down during the day hours, bellies flush on the bottom, digesting what they accumulated the night before. But though they are lying idle and not moving much above the bottom, except to change position, they will take a lure if it comes within their reach. Unless you troll deep and get close to the bottom you will have very little success in daytime trolling for wall-eyes, especially in the summer when even in the best wall-eyes lakes the fishermen show up with disappointing results for their efforts. Thus deep trolling is the thing, or if not deep trolling then deep fishing close to the bottom with live minnows.

There is no gainsaying the fact that fishing on the bottom with live minnows is important among the methods whereby this species can be taken. For one thing, one can actually get down to the rocky bottom in a lake. Once this is found the chances are strong that you will locate your wall-eyes there, as the affinity of wall-eyes with rocks is very nearly as bread is to butter. Having located a spot of the sort, every care should be taken to mark the place so that it can be returned to again. This is possible by tying a wire to a large rock and letting that down to the bottom and attaching an inflated inner tube to the wire at the top. If you do not wish this to show at the surface shorten the wire to the extent that the tube is held fixed ten inches or a foot below the surface. To make it the easier to be seen, paint it with white paint. Often you will find in a lake of this sort just certain isolated rocky spots and no others, in which case it is almost an absolute certainty that what wall-eyes are in a lake will be found in that immediate neighborhood. In searching for these locations carry along a cord with a rock on it and some manner of toy balloon that can be inflated. This can then be let down, permitting the balloon to ride on the surface. This, of course is only a temporary marker; the heavier marker is installed later if the spot turns out to be a producer. Often bottom springs, boiling up on the lake floor, are found in such spots, and this of course only adds to the value of the bottom location.

Use minnows in deep fishing for wall-eyes that are four to five inches in length, as such a length is not too large for the purpose. Place a sinker on the line (dipsey sinker preferred) about 18 inches or 2 feet above the lure. Let the lure and sinker down so that the sinker rests on the bottom, heavy enough (but not too heavy) to let the minnow swim around without pulling the sinker with him. The impulse of the minnow will be to swim upwards and he usually puts up quite a commotion doing so. If any wall-eyes are around they are sure to seize the bait. The minnow should be hooked just back of the dorsal (back) fin, into a little of the flesh and through the skin but never so deep that the spine is touched as this will paralyze it. Do not set the hook instantly upon its being seized but let the fish have it for a slow count of fifteen before setting the hook.

One value assured in the finding these deep-water retreats of the wall-eyed pike in the summer is that once you have found them you can go there any time and get your fish, either by still fishing or drifting around these spots, or by trolling over the location or locations.

Night fishing for wall-eyes really goes into effect around nine or ten o'clock and may last, as previously stated, till two in the morning. The wall-eye being a school fish, gathers with many of its kind and sweeps inshore to crowd the minnows up around the reefs and in the bays and shallow water generally. One might think that this is done with much noise and splashing of the water but this is not so. Indeed it is surprising with what degree of noiselessness these feeding operations are conducted. Here is one time when a lure that is painted over with phosphorescent paint so that it glows in the dark, will prove of value. At one time as the writer of an outdoor column in a northern newspaper, I mentioned the habit wall-eyes have of seizing upon glowing lures that operate underwater during night fishing. As a result hundreds of fishermen tried the method and had excellent success. Later on someone invented a bait with an electric light in it and something on the order of murder took place on the wall-eye grounds of the state. In fact so many wall-eyes were taken that a law was passed forbidding use of this manner of lighted lure!

If the wall-eyes are hesitant about taking artificial lures

during the day hours the same is not true at night. Surface lures, or those that you pop on the surface, are of no great use inasmuch as the wall-eye takes most all of its food underwater and rarely on top. It is not, however, necessary to use glowing lures as most any white lures will be useful. The glowing or luminous paint is far superior to the so-called modern fire lacquer on lures. The latter is hardly better than ordinary paint as used on plugs. The Pflueger tandem spinner lures, which have the inside of their propeller blades coated with luminous paint, are good both in lake fishing and in stream fishing. Indeed I would say that where wall-eyes are found in streams this tandem spinner is really one of the best lures that you can use and that is especially so in the pools where these fish often foregather and concentrate in goodly numbers.

To the fisherman who has not tried out night fishing for wall-eyed pike there is a treat in store. Let it never be forgotten that during the heat of summer, the night period is *the* feeding time for this species. Most fishermen do not know this, hence the fish steals a march on them to the extent that when the fisherman hits the water in the morning the walleyes have safely gone into deep water and are down there half asleep on the bottom waiting for another night to roll around. It is in knowing the feeding habits of the wall-eyed pike that one is assured success in taking it, in fact knowledge of those feeding habits are more a demand in wall-eyed pike fishing than in fishing for any other fish!

PART II

Muskellunge

INTRODUCTION

There were six or eight of us sitting on the porch of Calvert's Cedar Island Camp, in Lake of the Woods in western Ontario. For over forty years this camp has been known to fishermen the length and breadth of the continent. To it have come famous men, industrialists, doctors, lawyers and men from every walk of life. There have been hundreds of them who have come here throughout the years, all attracted as though by a magnet to this outstanding habitat of the muskellunge.

As I have stated above there were six or eight of us; and as was natural the subject being discussed, re-discussed and turned inside out was that of the muskellunge, its habits, its weight, its sub-species, its coloration, methods of fishing for it and experiences met with during years of following this great sport. There were some interesting theories propounded, and possibly some questions were answered. Maybe that evening we talked enough to fill a book should a stenographer have been at hand to put down the remarks pro and con.

When eventually there came a halt in the conversation a doctor who had been listening without saying a great deal said to me: "Mr. Lincoln, if you could put all that you have said on the muskellunge this evening, into a book I think that it would fill a long-felt want and I know that everyone sitting here tonight would buy a copy of it. To the best of my knowledge there has been no book printed regarding the species, and probably the reason for this is that no one has had an extensive enough experience to warrant taking on a work of the sort. But you have been fishing muskies all of your life. Have you ever thought of doing a work of this sort?"

I said that I never cared much about writing books, and that while I had done considerable wordage on the muskellunge it had been entirely in the magazines and newspapers. I had to agree that I knew of no complete book on the subject but I, too, felt that there were thousands who might be interested in a thorough appraisal of the life history of the fish and how to fish for it in many and various ways. Every person present at that little gathering on the porch of Calvert's Camp agreed that they would buy a copy as soon as it was off the press and one gentleman stated that he would buy twenty-five copies. Well, that was all very nice but I smiled it off, and after I left the little group I quite forgot all about it.

Now, after some few years have elapsed I am attempting that book. It may not be as exhaustive a review of the subject as I would like, but what is set down is gleaned from actual experience and from being on waters far and wide that contain this species. Maybe I always have hoped to write something on the subject that could be preserved between book covers, which would probably do half-way justice to the taking of one of our most noble game fishes and which apparently seems to be the least understood. This I will state in regard to the fish, that during all the time you are fishing for it your interest in the pursuit never lags. It never lags because you know full well that any time when you least expect it all hell will seem to have broken loose and a fish of the grey warrior breed will have glommed onto your plug or spoon lure. There is no slackening in interest when you are musky fishing. Virtually, you have to be on your toes all the time and be prepared for most anything.

As I write these lines I can hear in my memory the waters of a northern lake lapping on a rocky shore. I am casting a heavy duty musky spoon with a ganghook on it masked in red bucktail hair. It hits the water with a spat and is almost instantly started outward as it is reeled toward the boat. It has hardly gone more than a few feet beyond that patch of musky weeds when the big fellow strikes. In fact the impetus of his strike is such that he is carried upward free of the water, a huge fish, one of those remarkable finny creatures that are always a mystery and an endless source of interest.

Yes, there is something about musky fishing that brings you back to it time and again. In fact you never get enough of musky fishing. If you hook and lose one, you figure that you will come back next year and take another whack at him. And the funny thing about it is that you do come back just as sure as you are at least a foot high. In musky fishing there is intrigue, adventure, uncertainty, never-failing interest and a magnetic pull on the imagination that will not quell.

In this book there will be jotted down some of the things I have found out about musky fishing. These facts may not be in any way new to those time-hardened muskyteers who have followed the water trails the major portion of their lives. But if in general some new facts are given and if one gains something from reading this that will aid him in taking that big musky he has always been seeking, then the production of this book will not have been in vain.

R. P. L.

HOW THE MUSKELLUNGE GOT ITS NAME

It is doubtful if a fish has received more names in its day than the muskellunge. In the present day these names have been pared down most drastically to the extent that in this country we have now come to abide by the name, muskellunge, as the most likely and proper to use while in Canada there is a disposition to call the fish "muscallonge" and from this determination the Canadians cannot apparently be budged. With them its muscallonge or nothing. Some years ago the late Dr. Barton Warren Evermann, one of the foremost authorities on the fishes of North America, wrote me that the name applied to the fish should be muskallunge, although he offered no reason as to why this name was more correct than any other. Strictly speaking neither muscallonge or muskallunge is right. This is the reason why:

The fish owes its name partly to the French language, or, if you will, French-Canadian, and applies particularly to the formation of the head of the fish—*masque allonge,* which, in French-Canadian, means long face or snout; but this has been so translated and re-translated as to have lost much of its meaning. One of the earliest of the French historians of Canada distinguished the fish in question by its shorter snout, that is, shorter than that of the pike with which he was familiar. He called the fish the *"masquenonge,"* having recognized the last as the Indian name, the derivation of the Algonquin name, itself derived from *mas,* meaning great, and *kinonge,* pike or pickerel. If this were followed up the fish should more rightly be named *maskinonge.* As it is we, in this country, have chosen muskellunge and the Canadians demand that it be muscallonge neither of which, strictly speaking, is right.

The now-common abbreviation for muskellunge is musky, which is a lot better than shortening it to *muska* or *masca.* In other words it seems that we have settled on *muskellunge* because it is easier to get a smooth abbreviation out of it than any of the others.

Some of the names we have run across by which the fish was known in the past were: muskalonge, masquallonge, moskalonge, maskallunge, lunge, longue, moskallonge, maskalonge, muskellinge, muskellinga and muskellunge. Thank heavens that from this mess of handles we have been able to exact one and are abiding by it, MUSKELLUNGE.

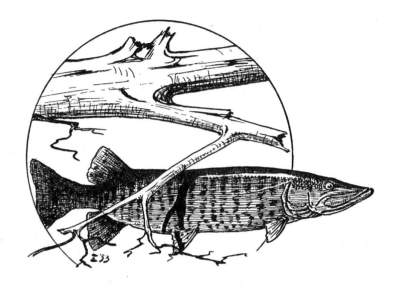

XI
GENERAL CHARACTERISTICS

It is doubtful if any fish outside of the tarpon and the Atlantic salmon have been more greatly, even voluminously popularized than the muskellunge, "the tiger musky" and the "grey warror" that we have heard so much about for the last thirty or forty years. That the fish deserves the meed of praise which has been accorded it as a fighter can be taken for granted as fact. Possibly at times it has its faults and is slow on the draw, as it were, but by and large it is certain that when you are hooked into a lively specimen of the species *Esox masquinongy* you know that you are on the receiving end of a very dramatic and pugnacious battle. You know that the battle is likely to be nip and tuck. Yes, there are chances in plenty that you will lose that fish, and there are many ways in which this can happen. It is for this reason that every avenue of approach to the taking this great fish should be weighed and it is in knowing these things that one may successfully land the fish of his dreams. But, just as there are men who have fished for tarpon for years without landing one, so are there fishermen who have failed signally in counting *coup* on the grey warrior. It just does not seem possible that this can be so, but experience and observation along these very lines have proved the truth of the assertion.

The muskellunge is one of those strange, odd fish that has always been, in the sense of things, mysterious and apart from other fish species. For instance one can acquire an excellent knowledge of the black bass, in fact many possess a close acquaintance with the species, but this is not true so far as the muskellunge is concerned. One never really gets to know the fish. They roam the waters in which they are found like a silent menace, rarely being seen, stalking their prey with all the cunning of a wolf, or lying in wait among the rocks or lily-pads, as the case may be, to fall upon the unwary. It takes a considerable amount of food to keep a thirty or forty pound muskellunge well fed and in good humor, one reason why it can be said the fish is always on the prowl and seemingly is always hungry. In this of course it partakes of the same characteristics as the great northern pike, its fairly close relative and likewise, in a lesser sense, the pickerel family which is also closely related to it. Dr. David Starr Jordan once stated that a lake could hold only so many muskellunge. If they were too numerous they would soon decimate the population of other fishes for food purposes and the balance of nature would be thrown out of kilter. There are those among our desk-working and library-operating white collar fish biologists who contend vociferously that there is nothing to this matter of balance in nature, but anyone who is able to put two and two together to make four and not six knows that it is a fact. We know that the muskellunge not only has a prodigeous appetite, but one that takes in a rather well-rounded fare, including both finny food as well as contributions from the land in many and varied forms. One time we caught a muskellunge that had a considerable knob that stuck out on its side in the region of the stomach. On opening the fish we found that it had swallowed none other than just about the largest muskrat we have ever seen and which would have graded "No. 1 northern large" in the fur market. While having this generous morsel in its innards, it had not been content, but with all the savagery in the world had sought to make mince-meat out of one of our surface plugs. This one, however, he failed to masticate!

Of land animals that have been collected out of muskellunge stomachs in the course of a lifetime fishing for the fish, we have removed besides the muskrat: mink, gophers, chipmunks, squirrels, rats and mice. How the fish has been able to garner these unto itself is one of those mysteries never accounted for. Among the feathered life has been found: ducklings, both wild and tame, goslings, coots, grebes and shorebirds. A fisherman told me one time that he had seen a muskellunge of about ten pounds leap out of the water in the attempt to catch a red-winged blackbird swaying on a branch over the water surface, but the fish failed to make connections. Snakes and turtles have also been found in this fish.

Now the interesting thing about the above is that all of the items of food listed were inshore in habitat, or of land origin. This brings up a very interesting point that has not been stressed, namely and to wit, that in spite of the fact that it is one of the truly large fishes in our waters, it spends the greater part of its life in shallow to fairly shallow water, and it is from these inshore haunts that it finds most of its food. And still for all that, its presence seems to be masked from sight, which makes the fish all the more strange and mysterious. Feeding and operating inshore much of the time it goes about its inshore cruising operations with such stealth, in spite of its size, as to practically blot it out from human sight. Bass and other fish you may see now and then, but as a rule you will rarely see the muskellunge in its native haunts. Indeed I have known fishermen in the north who have fished muskellunge waters year after year and yet they claim they have yet to see the fish alive swimming about!

Something not known to many fishermen is the fact that the muskellunge is an early riser and is out at daybreak trying to corner a square meal for the day. How heavily he feeds at this time is uncertain, but it is probably far more than just a fragment of nourishment. So far as the fisherman is concerned there is not one in a thousand up and abroad at daybreak, so few cash in on the early morning feeding program of *Esox masquinongy*. Some do get on the water around seven o'clock but most of them are ready to go to work at eight or nine o'clock at which time the species will be pretty well fed up and in a mood to rest. It is interesting in this respect that few, if any, guides can be influenced to do any fishing before seven o'clock and so far as daybreak fishing is concerned a guide would rather have an arm cut off than go out at that time. I just wanted to mention the status of early morning fishing to let the fisherman know just where and when he loses out.

There is another time of fishing for the musky that might be called to attention, which is generally left out of consideration, and that is evening fishing, just before dark. In this respect it should be noted that the great northern pike, a close relative of the muskellunge, tapers off in its feeding operations rather early in the evening and is very rarely taken around the time when dusk is gathering on the shoreline. Opposed to this, the muskellunge continues its feeding almost up to the time when it is so gloomy on the water surface that it is hard to see where to place the lure. This, again, is something the musky fisherman misses out on, for by the use of surface lures during the hours of dusk some of the largest of the members of the species can be induced to strike. No doubt it is during this time that many waterfowl and water birds, are seized by the fish. Too, in the dusk the fish can carry on its feeding without being disclosed to the sight of its chief enemy, Man. The bait caster who will make it a point to study inshore fishing for the musky during the evening hours and into the dark is likely to take fish that would not be possible of capture during the day hours. The fisherman of course has a distinct advantage over the fish in such an environment inasmuch as his presence is masked from the fish. Our favorite method of evening fishing for the musky in the north is to use a canoe as a craft. With it one can steal in on the many and various vulnerable shore locations without a semblance of sound, as the result of which the fish is taken completely unawares.

A characteristic or life habit innate in the muskellunge is that it is not by nature migratory. True, in the past it got into the various places it did by coming from one place to another but such movements of the fish were in the past. Today it is static; it is grounded in the places where it is known to have been since first the white-man came: Other fishes have been known to extend their range in a natural way, quite without the aid of man in his propagation and planting program. For instance, if it would be entirely possible for it to get out of the lake of its birth and move down a stream and so into other waters it will not do so. As stated, the species is not, in its greater sense, migratory.

Too, there is a peculiarity observed in the fact that unlike the great northern pike, which has no place that it can call home in a lake save the lake itself, the muskellunge almost invariably finds for itself some nook, cove, set-back in the shore, a location among the pads, a haunt among the rocks, under the top of a tree fallen over the water, etc., etc. Here it will be at home. This is his lair. He feels that he owns it completely, lock, stock and barrel. True, he will operate from the location and make wide swings up and down the shore in either direction when the need for sustenance becomes uppermost to his vitals. But invariably, after the feeding period is over, he will come back to his lair just as will a tiger or any other animal.

This lair-establishing habit of the muskellunge is not exactly to its enjoyment of a long and happy life ever thereafter. For instance should you "raise" a musky at a spot that might be considered its lair you can go there again and at an opportune moment place your lure right close to his front door. He is liable to hit that lure with a power and vim that will lift the hat on your honorable head and what happens directly thereafter may be a song and dance number, a clatter and bang of oars, and decks being cleared for action. That you may lose your fish is entirely within reason and to be expected. One thing is certain, let a muskellunge so much as get into the pads and obtain slack line and he will snap that hook out of his jaws as neatly as a dentist

removing a tooth. You can rest assured that if you ever
stumble onto the lair of a musky and put your lure right
in his face so to speak, he is going to be boiling mad. We
have seen them charge out from a lair fairly bristling with
anger and if eyes of a musky really flash, they were flashing.
It is one of those cases where the fish feels insulted if not
completely outraged to think that you have invaded his
precious domain. In Lake of the Woods in western Ontario,
one of the greatest musky lakes in North America, which
is a hundred miles long and almost as wide, guides invariably return time and again when a musky has revealed the
place where he hangs out, and they keep after the fish
until he finally, probably out of sheer exasperation, gloms
a lure cast to him, and is so relegated to the bourne of
yesterday's ten thousand years. It's just a tip to the fisherman, namely, find where a musky has his lair; then keep
after him until he weakens or becomes so mad that he will
attempt to grind the plug into dust.

I have mentioned in the above that the muskellunge seems
to keep away from the sight of man and is rarely seen. However, this statement could very easily be modified since there
are times when you will see the fish, or a number of them,
and not in the course of spawning either. I have had muskies
follow a lure right up to the boat and they have shown no
fear in the least. An incident, however, that stands out particularly in my memory has to do with an occasion in which
we had the most unusual experience of seeing no less than
ten muskies in one spot in a small bay in Mantrap Lake,
near Park Rapids, Minnesota. The occasion is particularly
vivid to me inasmuch as out of the ten muskies we saw,
three of these I took with a fly-rod, the largest twenty-six
pounds, one of twenty pounds and another of eighteen. I
can remember we had started out in the morning to fish for
smallmouth bass and I was using, as stated, a fly-rod. The
lures I was using were bass flies tied to No. 1-O bass hooks,
O'Shaughnessy pattern, hand-forged, the flies having chenille
bodies with a red-feather tail tag and inch-long hackles at
the head, and no wings. I never use flies that have wings
in the bass fly patterns when they are used in combination
with a spinner on a shaft, and that was what I was using
in this instance.

As we proceeded down the shore and into this bay we detected the fish swimming about, as in a group. If it had been in the course of the spawning season one might have claimed to know the answer, but this was during the month of July. Spawning had been carried out long before that. No reason could be ascribed for this camp meeting of the elite in fishdom, nor to this day has anyone I have put the matter to been able to fix the reason for this gathering of the ten muskies.

It occurred to me that I might be able to fool one of these fine fellows to take a fly and spinner. At the time we were in the shadows of the pines on shore so that it was reasonable to believe that we had not been seen. Taking note of the largest musky, I cast the fly and spinner ahead of the fish aiming to have it pass by his honorable snout at the moment he reached a certain point. This worked out to perfection and the lure appeared just about two inches ahead of point of contact. The fish made no dash at the lure nor did he seem excited in the least. He merely nipped the lure, and I instantly set the keen-pointed hook in the rim of the upper jaw in the center. The fish made no wild spurts of speed to get somewhere as a result of which we were able to lead him away from the scene of the other fish without disturbing them. We beached the big fellow some distance down the shore, and then immediately returned to try for another. The same procedure followed with the other two, although the last one, an eighteen pounder, put up a struggle and the rest of the fish, frightened by the commotion, melted away into the lake depths.

This incident, as above related, convinced me definitely that the muskellunge can be taken on small lures, and especially fly and spinner lures. In later days, when in northern waters fairly well populated with the muskellunge, I tried out further experiments with the fly and spinner and invariably took muskies, but I followed exactly the same method of bringing the lure directly by the jaws. You will find that the fish will not go out of his way a foot to take this lure, which of course makes blind casting here and there rather useless. If, however, you can stalk your fish and actually see him and cast to him, the chances are very strong that he will strike, and that of course would go for large muskies as well as smaller ones.

In a study of largemouth and smallmouth black bass it will be found that the species are, by nature, cannibalistic, which is to say that they will feed upon and make food of their own kind. Indeed, like the bass, it might be said of the musky that they stalk their own young and feed upon them apparently in preference to other food. This is one of those strange oddities met with in a natural state for which there seems to be neither rhyme nor reason. If one would give his imagination free rein one might suspect that this is nature's method of preventing an over-population of any one species, even unto letting the parent fish do their own curbing of its numbers. If one would accept this theory it would of course promote and give credence to the theory that there is conscious planning and design in nature, and that of course is something which must be taken with a grain of salt. Meehan tells about putting five thousand muskies in a pond out of which eventually only one remained. This was a survival of the fittest with a vengeance. One might gain from this some idea as to why the muskellunge never was in great numbers and never will be regardless of how conducive conditions may be to the continuance of the species in either lake or stream.

Every angling writer meets up with the question time and again: Why isn't it possible to plant muskies in Smith Lake, Pine Lake or Skunk Lake? Just like that. No one, I believe, has ever plausibly answered that question and I doubt if any logical answer can be cooked up that will meet with approval or will hold water. It may be possible to plant bass in such lakes, great northern pike, walleye pike and any one of eight or ten other species; they will become established, and the endeavor will be recognized as successful. On the other hand, there is not one vagrant chance in a million that you could establish the muskellunge in such waters. Why? Try to find the answer and you will have solved what is the greatest puzzle extant in fish cultural circles. The muskellunge is one of the most difficult of all fishes to raise from the hatched egg to a size of eight to ten inches. The state of Wisconsin, after years of painstaking study of the musky, finally was able to successfully put out fish suitable for planting. But what plans and methods were followed in producing these fish has never been committed to public print, which is how closely the secret of muskellunge propagation is guarded. It is a case of: We have found out how it is done; if you want to be as successful as we are then go and find out for yourselves. That sort of selfishness is met with in all branches of fish culture in this country, proof how narrow-minded and uncooperative we can be. True, there are instances of absolute cooperation, but such instances are rather the exception than the rule.

One thing is certain, namely, that if a muskellunge was never in a water of its own volition before the coming of the white man, then it is not likely that it will establish itself in that water with any degree of success, if at all. If muskies were placed in waters that would seem to be every bit the counterpart of lakes containing the musky, there is hardly a chance that they would successfully establish themselves therein. However, it is known to be a fact that lakes that did have the muskellunge in them originally, but which fish had been caught out, have been found to "take" when stocked. This would seem to indicate some natural condition in lakes that are demanded by the species, but just what, no one seems to know. Therein, in a nut-shell abides the eternal question: why will muskies establish themselves in one lake and not in another? If you can answer that question correctly you will have done more than any one has to date who has been trying to solve the conundrum.

For instance there is a small lake in central Minnesota, in the Akeley region, that is named Shingobee Lake. There is nothing outstanding about it, nothing that would set it aside as different from any of the other 11,500 lakes in the state. Yet it has produced numbers of muskies throughout the years. Yet Howard Lake, a body of water with all the physical characteristics and attributes of a true muskellunge water, and which has a direct connection with Shingobee Lake, never has been known to have a muskellunge in it save one that I inserted in it (from Shingobee Lake) years ago. But in a natural state it was utterly free of the fish species in question. All of this of course is exasperating, for in a musky region or in a state possessing muskies the publicity value of the species cannot be computed in mere figures. The immense value of the species as a drawing card has led opportunistic, and not too honest, resort or fishing camp owners to take muskies in accepted musky lakes and bring them to their own waters and pan them off as taken therein. However, in almost all instances these transfers and double-dealings are found out and the lakes that the fish is found in are not increased apparently by one iota. Merely to give you an example. Minnesota, as above stated, has, by count, 11,500 lakes, and yet you can virtually name the musky waters of that state, believe it or not, on your two hands!

XII

THE RANGE
OF THE MUSKELLUNGE

The muskellunge, first, last and all of the time is strictly a fish known only to North American waters. This is a fact beyond dispute and contradiction. Opposed to this the great northern pike has a range that takes in the greater part of northern Europe, England, the Scandinavian countries, Russia and Siberia. It extends in range south to Italy. It is not a different pike from that found in our waters although it is to be admitted that it looks rather grotesque in shape and head appearance to the more trim and streamlined specimens found in our waters. But it is the same pike nevertheless, though of course it is not called great northern pike as are our North American representatives of the species.

In spite of the fact that the muskellunge is closely related to the pike, there has been no proof in the slightest that the former has ever turned up in European or Asian waters, in fact some years ago I was given a resumè on the subject by a European student of fishes and his conclusions bear out the fact that whereas the great northern pike is present in waters across the Atlantic, no specimens of the muskellunge have ever turned up nor it is possible that it occurs in the wide range of the fish in the areas stated. Nor has any attempt to my knowledge ever been made to introduce the muskellunge into either Europe or Asia. The species remains with us for better or worse, to dwindle in numbers and disappear or to be propagated and kept circulating in our waters as long as there are ways and means of creating the fish and increasing or preserving its range.

Those who are interested in the whys and wherefors of any fish or animal species inevitably propound that elusive and puzzling question: Where did the muskellunge come from? That might easily take the form of a sixty-four dollar question, for so far as has been ascertained, few students of our fishes have arrived at any conclusions on the subject at all. No one seems to know where the species were derived on this continent although the general conception is that its birthplace must have been in the westernmost part of the St. Lawrence River and the lower Great Lakes. The spread apparently south and west was from this part of the country, since from the Ohio River drainage of the Great Lakes the species got into the Ohio River, thence worked down into the Mississippi River, and so up the Mississippi River to get into the state of Minnesota, Wisconsin and the area in close proximity. By going down the Ohio the muskellunge made its way up the Tennessee River and went as far east as the upper portions of that stream where it is found today in sections of western North Carolina. It is not found there in great numbers, true, but appreciably so and certainly to the extent that specimens are annually accounted for through Tennessee and North Carolina. As stated, these came up the Tennessee River from the Ohio River, in fact that is the only way that they could have come into that southern section of the country.

In this respect the fact should be emphasized that whereas the muskellunge is known to be found sparingly in the state

of Pennsylvania, the species are found only in the waters
that are part of the Ohio and, therefore, the Mississippi
watershed. This would include the upper Alleghany right up
through the Indian Reservation in New York State, Oil Creek
and French Creek in western Pennsylvania. The conclusions
might be arrived at that the muskellunge, as found in Pennsylvania, was the result of migrants coming up from the
Ohio River. While we have no record as to the state of
numbers of the muskellunge in the early days in the Ohio
River it is possible that during pioneer times it was fairly
numerous therein. Today the Ohio River is so violently pol-
luted as to preclude the possibility of any fish being found
in it, let alone the muskellunge. It can be taken for granted
that what migratory jaunts the muskellunge made in an
early day, belongs to that early day only. No such migrations are now to be looked for. Not only have the species
so lessened in numbers as to make migrations impossible
but pollution and the presence of dams on our streams halt
any movement of the fish from place to place. As an example there are 27 lock dams between Alton, Illinois and
Minneapolis on the Mississippi that would definitely halt
any upward trend of fish life. The same would be true of
the movement of fish up the Tennessee River. There is a
twenty mile stretch of the Tennessee River before it joins
with the Ohio River that is one of the best fishing stretches
of the Tennessee for all manner of fishes known to the
region. And in that twenty mile stretch are found muskellunge, probably as many as any recognized to exist in the
Ohio Valley. They can go upstream as far as Kentucky Dam
that creates Kentucky Lake, a TVA impoundment, but no
further. Were there no dams spanning the river and holding
the fish back there is every reason to believe that the movement of the muskellunge up the Tennessee might still be
in force. They would move out of the Ohio if for no other
reason than that it is such a stinking, running sore as to
kill most fish life in it.

Connecting with the Ohio River, there are a number of
West Virginia streams that are known to have muskellunge
in them, never numerous of course, but sufficient to let
the world know they are at least there. The same would be
true of some streams in the state of Kentucky, but to recom-

mend the same as a possible place to go to in the interests of landing one of these fighting grey warriors is something one would be extremely cautious in even suggesting. Mostly the muskellunge taken in both West Virginia and Kentucky streams are caught while one is fishing for bass or other fish, and most of the time on live bait. The same would be true of streams in the state of Ohio, the Scioto and others that are tributaries to the Ohio, indeed if there ever were any muskellunge in the Ohio River in recent times they certainly have gone into the tributaries. Of these the Scioto has produced some exceptionally large muskies of the Ohio drainage variety. The last one I heard from taken in that stream weighed close to forty pounds, and a forty pound muskellunge is a considerable fish in any section of the range of the species.

There are two lakes in Pennsylvania that have been rather notable in muskellunge history that belong in the Ohio drainage system. These are Lake Le Bouef and Conneaut, two relatively small bodies of water which produce a few good fish annually, the same ranging from 25 to a possible 50 pounds in weight, though the latter figure has been attained only once or twice to our knowledge in these waters. A 50-pounder was taken in Conneaut Lake, Pennsylvania, in the mid-thirties. Most of these muskies I am told are taken in the fall of the year on live suckers about a foot in length that are rigged out with a chain or wire harness which has several hooks attached. The sucker is permitted to swim about in a vulnerable location and when a musky hits, it is given line for twenty minutes or more before the hooks are set. When the fish jumps the fisherman knows that the lure has been swallowed and the fight is on. The fish taken in Pennsylvania, in Conneaut and Le Beouf Lakes, run larger than the river and creek fish. I understand that few large ones are taken on artificial lures in Pennsylvania. Every so often a plug fisherman, however, meets up with a powerful one in the Allegheny River and most of the time the fish comes up the victor.

One might believe that the state of New York would be well populated with the muskellunge species since the St. Lawrence River has been represented as a chief muskellunge center since the eighties when fishing for it first went into effect. But in the state proper, outside of the St. Lawrence, few waters contain or have contained the species. Lake Chautauqua has probably been the most notable in that state for muskellunge, in fact one of the largest hatcheries in the country or in North America, devoted exclusively to the propagation and distribution of the species, is managed on that lake. Many muskies have been taken in Lake Chautauqua but as one fisherman has stated "one can fish till one is blue in the face and never take a musky." A circumstance such as this, however, does not necessarily apply to just that lake. Something of the same sort applies even to waters where the fish is numerous to fairly numerous. As to whether unusual fishing methods carried out will aid in the capture of the fish, as opposed to less intriguing or common methods of fishing now in force, is entirely a matter of conjecture.

Several streams flowing north out of New York state into the St. Lawrence are known to have muskellunge, but the taking of them is almost as uncertain as that known to the streams of West Virginia and Kentucky. While the Niagara River also is claimed as a muskellunge water its productiveness, too, is virtually relegated to the class of questionables. No one seriously recommends it any more than the streams previously listed as minor possibilities in Ohio, West Virginia and Kentucky, and of course North Carolina and Tennessee might as well be bracketed in the same category.

According to Howard Pyle, who fished the St. Lawrence in the region of the Thousand Islands during the eighties, he never knew of a musky taken in those waters over 35 pounds in weight. At the time musky fishing hit the St. Lawrence, this type of fishing became the rage and fishermen from all over the east flocked to the region. It is possible that fishing for the species in this country dated from that time, although it was extremely slow in making an impression in the fishing world. Indeed it is only within the last twenty-five or thirty years that the fish has come to the front as a game species of most unusual and outstanding merit. Indeed, through the early 1900's one heard practically nothing regarding the fish. Between 1912 and 1920 the muskellunge made its debut in the fishing world, strange as this may seem but true nevertheless. Examination of out-

door publications at dates earlier than 1912 will show practically nothing regarding the fish. At that time the chief
fishing area where it was most numerous were Minnesota,
Wisconsin, Michigan and western Ontario. But at that time
they were practically dormant so far as musky fishing was
concerned. The fish at that time apparently still remained
to be discovered.

While the lower Great Lakes region has been named as
the birthplace waters of the muskellunge they never have
taken any manner of rank, as these waters produce less
than a moderate number of the species. This would apply
to both Lakes Erie and Ontario, although Lake Huron, in
an earlier day, was fairly well populated with the fish. Lake
Huron today turns up occasional fish but that is all. There
is little doubt but that the activities of the commercial
fishermen have had much to do with the elimination of the
species from the Great Lakes. Commercial fishermen are
no abiders by ethics and the principle of sportsmanship and
can be considered as not only a foe of the game fish but
of the sport-fishermen as well. A guide of mine up in Lake
of the Woods in western Ontario once dropped into a
fishery on that lake on a casual visit. No one being at home
he took the occasion to look into some of the boxes that
had been iced and were ready to go out to the market and
so be shipped into the states. What was his surprise on finding a great number of muskies in the boxes ranging from a
few pounds up to fifteen or more pounds in weight. It is a
well known fact that eating places of the elite, clubs, etc.,
in this country are a ready market for muskellunge that
are sold on the sly by the racketeers to these places. Where
there is a demand such as this the commercial fisherman is
quick to fill the bill. The sport fisherman could never begin
to kill out the muskellunge but permitted to do as he likes
about it, the commercial fisherman can contrive the disaster to any fish species. And that is just what they are doing.

While eastern and southern Ontario produce some muskies,
the numbers are fairly limited, and as is the common occurrence in the lakes, they are found in, they are hard to
take. Lake Superior is never known to have produced a
musky, the water apparently being too cold. For that matter,
all of the region in Ontario above Lake Superior, in Ontario,

is quite barren of the fish or at least that is the extent of present knowledge and investigations. Draw a line north and south through the eastern limits of Rainy Lake on the Minnesota-Ontario border, the same reaching north as far as you like, and then draw a line north and south from Lake Huron up through Algonquin Park in eastern Ontario, as far as you care to go north; and in that immensity of fishing region in between, no muskellunge, to the best of our knowledge, have been taken or are to be found. This blanking out of the species can of course be applied likewise to Quebec Province which has not produced the species so far as we know, any more than the whole region of New England, Maine, New Brunswick and the maritime provinces generally.

So we finally come as we must in a study of the range of this massive species to the peak production region in North America, namely, Michigan, Wisconsin, Minnesota and western Ontario. But even here the numbers and locations of the fish is spotty and questionable, so much so that if one wished to draw in shaded areas where the fish is found, those areas would be rather remote and far apart.

Old Wrinkled Meat, a Chippewa Indian chief in Minnesota, who was said at the close of his life to be 135 years old, contended that the muskellunge in Minnesota never was found in any waters save those connected with the Mississippi River. We made a study of this over a period of several years in Minnesota and the result was that the old Indian was very nearly correct in his assertion. It would seem from this that the muskellunge came down the Ohio River via the Ohio drainage, and so into the Mississippi. It went up the Fathers of Waters and so populated lakes and streams in what is now Wisconsin and Minnesota. Yet, strangely enough, in spite of the fact that Minnesota has 11,500 lakes and Wisconsin a matter of 8,000 or more, only a handful are inhabited by this fish. Wisconsin of course is a more spectacular producer of the species and claims the world's record, besides having taken prizes, for a great number of years, for specimens very close to top records. There is little doubt about it, Wisconsin is the prime and leading muskellunge fishing region in North America. Too, with its musky propagation and distribution program it is possible that the

state has built up a muskellunge population of sizable proportions. However, the statement that Wisconsin will some
day have as many muskies as great northern pike can be
taken not only with a grain of salt but a level teaspoonful
of it.

There does not seem to be the slightest doubt but that
the muskellunge came up the Mississippi and so populated
what waters are known to contain this fish. Even today the
Mississippi River in its Minnesota locale is probably the best
location for the species in that state. But quite aside from
that, one might even go further, and claim (as I did originally a number of years ago), that the muskellunge never
was native to western Ontario and the Lake of the Woods
region, in fact that the species came up the Mississippi
River and so, by devious migration, got into streams that
connected with Lake of the Woods and populated that
famous water with this great species. The manner in which
this apparently was accomplished is interesting. I pointed
out to Dr. Barton Warren Evermann and Dr. David Starr
Jordan, two of the leading authorities on fishes of North
America, that there is a lake that lies virtually on a height
of land in northern Minnesota, not far from the town of
Deer River. The lake is Bowstring Lake. From it the waters
flow in two directions, namely, south into the Mississippi
and north, via the Big Fork River, a long winding border
stream that flows into Lake of the Woods. In this manner
the muskellunge of the Mississippi, coming north, got into
the stream leading into Bowstring Lake and the stage was
set for its taking over of Lake of the Woods. Both Jordan
and Evermann agreed with me in regard to this and contended that the argument was practically unassailable. Even
today the Big Fork River is a good producer of muskies and
annually records many specimens in the thirty pounds. The
stories of large muskies seen and lost to fishermen on this
stream are quite numerous. At the time I was on the *Minneapolis Tribune*. Some years ago I had occasion to write
regarding large muskellunge as known to the state. A gentleman who had read this article came to see me and here is
the story:

He had gone north to the Big Fork River not far from
Bowstring Lake (previously mentioned) and had taken a

spear one evening, just after the ice had gone out, with the object in view of spearing pike. By shining his light into the water at the mouth of the stream where it left the lake to flow into the Big Fork River he was able to see into the water with great ease. He did not see any pike but what he did see as the beam of his flash-lantern swept over the water was something that held him transfixed to the spot without taking his light from the place where the object had been sighted. And the "object" was none other than the largest muskellunge he had even seen. I asked him how long the fish was and he said to the best of his ability to estimate, it must have been eight feet in length. He said when first he detected the fish lying there in the water he had the flood of the beam on the approximate center of the fish. At that point he estimated that the fish was no less than a foot deep. Moving the light toward the head he saw that stand out perfectly also. Pulling the beam of the light toward the back of the fish he was able to see that portion of the fish also. He estimated four feet either way from the center where the beam of his light had originally marked the fish.

Of course I did not attach much credence to the size of the fish as related but when asked how he knew it was a musky he said that he had taken a number of the species in his life and this one had the spots of a musky without the slightest doubt. It was just when he was deciding if he should spear the fish or not that it moved out of the area of light and disappeared. I am convinced that the man had looked upon an outstanding muskellunge, but that it was eight feet in length is something else again. It may have been six feet in length and at that length it probably would take the world's record prize. Years ago one met up with statements by writers on the muskellunge, especially the "doctor authorities," who, without hesitation, would state that the muskellenge has been known to reach a length of eight feet and a weight of eighty to one hundred pounds. I found this statement in the Seventh Annual Report of the Game and Fish Department of New York State, a massive volume, put out at the turn of the century. It told of many one hundred pounders being taken. A hundred pound musky was said to have been taken in nets in Wisconsin by commercial fishermen many years ago, and the fish is said to be mounted and still preserved, though where it is I do not know. Certain waters in the northern part of lower Michigan have always produced large muskies. Some time ago in *Fur-Fish-Game Magazine* I showed a photo taken over forty years ago, of a fish that was supposed to be in the hundred pound class. A man standing alongside of the fish seems rather dwarfed. The fish, I might mention, was hung up on a stable wall on a nail and the man was reaching up and had his hand on the jaws of the fish.

But regardless of one hundred pounders, and forgetful of the fact that "there were giants in those day," there are larger muskies being taken in modern times than were actually recorded many years ago when the species certainly was in its prime and had not been cut down drastically by either the commercial fishermen or the sport fishermen. The 69-pounder taken by Louis Spray in Lake Chippewa, Wisconsin is a fish that will not soon be beaten in the contests, although I am convinced that Wisconsin has some to its credit that will top this mark by ten or fifteen pounds. Too, I believe that Minnesota likewise has such tremendous fish in its waters. Possibly most of them eventually die of old age. As they grow old they become blind and then become bottom feeders. Maybe they starve to death. Pushing along on the bottom it is possible they will eventually become snarled up in the weeds and so die, the weeds falling over them and enclosing them. Once in a while a huge musky will wash up on shore in any musky waters. One such fish in Minnesota weighed almost sixty pounds.

In Minnesota the species is found, as stated, up and down the Mississippi River. Originally a type muskellunge that was plain in coloration and was technically designed as *Esox masquinongy immaculatus* was found in Lake Pepin a natural broadening of the Mississippi below Red Wing. This fish was very foolishly called a "northern pike," by Garrard, which for years, led to endless confusion. In the present day the chief distribution of the musky is from the Rum River where it flows into the Mississippi at Anoka, above Minneapolis, on up the stream to Lake Bemidji on the Mississippi. An excellent float trip for bass and muskies is from St. Cloud, Minnesota, on the Mississippi down to the Rum River. From St. Cloud on up the stream are found excellent grounds, as in the Brainerd district. Leech Lake, which connects with the Mississippi, is one of the largest lakes in the state of Minnesota and it has produced muskies up to 55 pounds in weight, so it is one of those so-called "best bets." Little and Big Winnibigoshish on the Mississippi produce ten or more muskies a year up to forty pounds although in 1951 a 50 pound fish was taken in Little Winnie.

Cass Lake has many muskies, and so has Lake Andrusia, through connection with the Mississippi River. But above Andrusia the species are blanked out and never seem to have been found. Of course, as previously stated, the Big Fork River is a best best too, as are also some lakes in the Deer River section such as Deer and Moose Lakes. Step by step as one checks on the muskellunge in its Minnesota locale he finds that the statement made by old Wrinkled Meat, *i.e.*, that the muskellunge is found in waters connecting with the Mississippi only, is profoundly correct. However, there has been one flaw in this conception, namely, that the Mantrap chain of lakes at Park Rapids, Minnesota, was early possessed of the species but it has no top connection with the Crow Wing River save an underground passage. Old Wrinkled Meat was not able to solve that one. When asked if the Chippewas planted the musky in the Mantrap Lakes he grunted: "Chippewas no plant. Maybe white man plant, not Chippewa." While the Mantrap chain of sixteen lakes—some of them now dried up—originally had many muskies, in the present day they are only taken on rare occasions, and most are relatively small in size.

Save the areas mentioned, the musky is almost entirely missing from the greater part of the state. The entire northern part of the state, especially taking in the area of Superior National Forest with its five thousand lakes, can muster not one instance of a fish of this species being taken. That would be in those waters of course not having a connection with the Mississippi.

It is possible that Wisconsin became the possessor of the muskellunge by two tributaries of the Mississippi, the St. Croix and the Chippewa. Of these two the Chippewa River might originally have been called the "mother stream" that introduced the musky into the most famous section of all

Wisconsin, that is, the Hayward region. The Chippewa River flows into the Mississippi near Read's Landing, above Wabasha, Minnesota, and but a short distance below the foot of Lake Pepin. The Flambeau region around Flambeau, Wisconsin, also places on the map such spots as Mercer and Rhinelander, well known to seasoned muskyteers. But topping all of the course would be the Hayward region which has produced some of the largest muskies taken in North America.

The Lake of the Woods country in Ontario ranks probably as high in prominence in the taking of this species as any on the continent, although admittedly none of the top fish of the species so far taken in Lake of the Woods can compare with Wisconsin prize winners. There have been muskies caught in Lake of the Woods over fifty pounds in weight, and of course such fish are magnificent, but they occur just as often. We can remember 'way back when fishing in Lake of the Woods, taking two or three muskies in a day of considerable size. But with the thousands taken out of the lake it has dwindled in productiveness almost to an alarming degree. We have known times when for ten days or two weeks of steady fishing no muskies have been taken. This, of course, is not to say that they are not circulating around in this famous water but only that they are what might be called "educated" muskies. Usually these have been hooked once or several times before, hence their caution and awareness of deadly lures in the water. There are instances where fishermen in a day of fishing on Lake of the Woods have had as many as thirty muskies follow their lures. An experience of the sort practically leaves the fishermen nerveless as he watches them idly following a lure and inspecting it at close range. I might mention that it is things like this that carry one back to the scene time after time and year after year.

The existence of muskies in the Lake of the Woods country is as everywhere else, spasmodic. East of the Manitou stretch of waters directly above the western end of Rainy Lake in western Ontario, you will find no waters that you can definitely put a finger on and say: "There are muskies here." West of the Manitou there are a number of waters such as great Eagle Lake, Pipestone Lake and Crow Lake for the large ones and many small ones that occasionally produce fish. Chiefly, however, it is Lake of the Woods that is the focal point in muskellunge fishing in this region. Points of entry to this region are Rainy River and Fort Frances, both across the Minnesota border in Ontario. The largest musky camps on Lake of the Woods are Calverts Camps, Rainy River, Ontario, Canada.

North of Lake of the Woods there is a considerable stretch of musky water in the Vermilion Lake area. The muskies in this lake region have mostly been planted. As a rule they do not go much over fifteen pounds in weight, and the average will be very far below that. Still further north, muskellunge have been planted in upper lakes or have moved up of their own accord from plantings below to the extent that new musky locations in this western Ontario region are being talked about every year. No doubt the introduction of the species to these upper waters will act to populate the entire region with them. Surely if this is being acomplished then this is an unusual example of the species taking over and extending their range in a manner that must have been followed in its approximate by the fishes originally coming down the Ohio and up stream throughout the northern Mississippi valley.

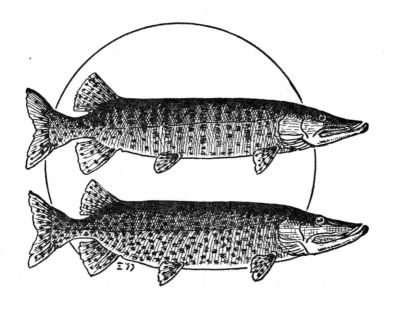

XIII

COLORATION
AND PHYSICAL FACTS

Scientifically there are supposed to be three varieties of the muskellunge in North America, namely, the Spotted Muskellunge, the Northern or Unspotted Muskellunge and the Barred or Lake Chautauqua Muskellunge. However, Dr. David Starr Jordan tells us that there are two varieties of this species, the common muskellunge (*Esox masquinongy*) and the Ohio Muskellunge (*Esox ohiensis*). In Jordan's words "unspotted, but vaguely cross-barred muskies occur sparingly in the Ohio River and the upper Mississippi Valley. It is especially abundant in Lake Chautauqua in New York state." A co-worker with Jordan, Dr. Barton Warren Evermann listed three, namely the common muskellunge, the Ohio muskellunge and the unspotted muskellunge but also held out for a fourth variety, which he chose to call the "tiger musky." Later, even Jordan apparently recognized this fourth variety which had tiger stripes running perpendicularly on its sides, that is, up and down. These so-called "tiger muskies" were said to come from Eagle Lake, Wisconsin and some waters in close proximity in that state, and also from the Mantrap Lakes, a chain of sixteen lakes located near Park Rapids, Minnesota. It is to be admitted that this certain section of Wisconsin has produced these oddly marked or striped fish, some of them with such vivid stripes of black that it would seem they were laid down with a brush. The color pattern certainly is unusual in this variety. I must admit for the first time in print that while the Mantrap Lakes of north central Minnesota, were said by Jordan and Evermann to contain this variety with tiger stripes, it has never been my experience to take one in any of the waters of the Mantrap chain although it is possible they were at one time found in those waters.

It is highly possible that the "tiger musky" of the Eagle Lake region, Wisconsin might have become a species apart were it not for the fact that I took a number of these tiger-striped muskies in the Lake of the Woods region of western Ontario, as did Ernie Calvert of the famous Calvert's Camps in Lake of the Woods proper. This I called to the attention of Dr. Evermann. Later, a number of muskies were taken in the Vermilion district north of Lake of the Woods that were as definitely tiger-striped as those that came out of the Wisconsin section. When photos were sent Evermann showing these tiger-striped specimens from Lake of the Woods and the Vermilion section he wrote back that it was obvious that the markings were misleading and that it was no more, no less than a freak color phase in the fish, hence it could not be given sub-species rating. As a humorous commentary on this an advertising man named Joe Godfrey gave this fish a scientific title and called it *Esox masquinongy Mike Amentus* in honor of a resort owner in the Vermilion area. Also finding a black-spotted muskellunge in the section he promptly called it *Esox masquinongy godfreeus*. Of course neither designation is recognized, although I understand attempts were made to railroad these "handles" through the accredited scientific channels. The thing, I might mention, was passed off as an uproarious joke.

One of the most unusual incidents in my fishing life was the taking of three muskies in one day in Kakagi (Crow) Lake in western Ontario, one a vividly-striped "tiger musky" as is supposed only to come from the Eagle Lake section of Wisconsin; one spotted musky on which the spots were so plain and roundish that it seemed they had been painted on with black paint; and I finished out with a plain muskellunge without any stripes, spots or bars or what have you on it and which could surely, for all purposes, be passed as a true specimen of *Esox masquinongy immaculatus*. It is interesting to note that the so-called plain or unspotted muskellunge was named out of Minnesota by an army officer by the name of Garrard sometime in the eighties or nineties and was taken in Lake Pepin a natural broadening of the Mississippi River below Red Wing, Minnesota. This specimen, which was given the designation *Lucius immaculatus*, was said to have: "Body unspotted, or with vague, dark cross shades; tail a little more slended and fin a little higher than in the Spotted or Lake Mascalonge. This is probably not distinct from the Mascalonge of Chautauqua Lake." Garrard named this fish as a "great northern pike" but this was possible since at that time the muskellunge tangle had not been solved. In fact most writers called it "the Great Pike." Others confused it with the common pike, *Esox lucius*. Even Prof. Cope mentions it as the "Blue Pike." Dr. Tarleton Bean called the unspotted muskellunge *Lucius lucius immaculatus* and thus bracketed the variety with the pike.

If one would want to draw some very fine distinctions one could easily say that what is known scientifically as the spotted muskellunge is not spotted at all but blotched, as though the "spots" were dabs laid on with the three finger tips. The spots in other words are mere irregular dark dabs or blotches rather than round black spots as found on specimens we have taken in the western Ontario region and which I have mentioned are as though they were painted on with black paint. These same spottings are found on some muskies up in the Lake Vermilion region of western Ontario. These are really spotted muskellunge as opposed to the dabbed-over ones usually known as spotted muskellunge.

Mention of Garrard's naming the Minnesota type of musky *immaculatus* and the calling of it a "great northern pike" straggles into the present day with its unfounded representations. Just to show you how the above misconception persists in the "best circles" among the fish classification experts, I was down at the National Museum in Washington, D. C. one spring. On this particular occasion one of the young fellows in the department told me that they had received a fish the day before that would rather surprise me. The fish, which had been sent down from the state of Wisconsin, he said, weighed 48 pounds and was a great northern pike. I might mention that all of my life I have been searching for a great northern pike (*Esox lucius*) that would go anywhere from 30 pounds and up but have never taken one, so when I was told by this fellow that they had received a 48 pound great northern pike I can assure you I was surprised. The case containing the fish was taken down from a shelf, the lid removed and there before my eyes was, not a great northern pike but a muskellunge, and, if one would want to get down as fine as frog's hair, this was what you would call *immaculatus* the unspotted muskellunge. Sure enough, Garrard was referred to when I asked where in the world they had gotten that information. I do not know if this muskellunge was ever placed in the freshwater fish collection in Washington or if it was labeled as a great northern pike. I can assure you that if they ever entered that fish in the collection under that name, they would be due for a lot of lambasting. I do not think that it would be in the collection under that name one week before it would be removed and rightly named. I might also mention that the last time I saw this collection, which was at the time they showed me this alleged "pike," there was a so-called "great northern pike" in it that must have been caught by George Washington as it was mounted as they did in the early days, and was falling apart. I suppose the *immaculatus* "pike" (Garrard) was intended to replace it —just an example of technical idiocy.

There is a belief that Garrard invented the "great northern pike" term but I believe that Henry William Herbert ("Frank Forester") so named the true pike in the fifties. I doubt very much if he ever named a muskellunge variety a great northern pike, an error that Garrard certainly was guilty of. Herbert named the true pike the "great northern pike" and it was not named by Jim Hill for his Great Northern Railroad. This is a question I have been peppered with and have answered ever since I took my pen in hand to do some writing *re* fishes starting when I was fourteen years old.

There is a muskellunge found variously in Wisconsin and Minnesota, particularly in Chippewa Lake, Wisconsin and Shoepac Lake, on the Kabetogama Peninsula, in northern Minnesota, that is oddly without coloration and is brownish instead of grey. By way of explanation, Chippewa Lake, as it now is called, was originally known as the Chippewa Flowage, a reservoir lake on the Chippewa River created by a dam installed years ago by the Northern States Power Company. When this reservoir was made, a tamarack and spruce forest was inundated, since the trees were not cut out. This left a ghastly wilderness of dead trees, possibly as wretched a sight as one would care to see anywhere. Where much of this has now been cut out, the underwater hazards are such as to make one very nearly despair of ever landing a fish. The horrible part of it all is that there are muskies there of both width, girth, length and superpoundage. If you don't believe so let me state that this is the lake where Louis Spray caught his world's record muskellunge which weighed exactly 69 pounds, 11 ounces. Quite apart from this, however, muskies up to 45 pounds have been taken in this water. In the years that I fished this "flowage" I lost every truly large musky I hooked in it, the same deftly snarling the line on every occasion in the underwater forest. Those specimens I have taken were up to ten or twelve pounds weight. It is these that I have reference to in stating that they are brown in color, some specimens being almost chocolate-brown. Because of this unusual coloration for a musky it was common practice to call these members of the species "mud muskies." There are those who did not like this name any too well, but it should be stated that it was given chiefly because of the mud or clay color, not that the fish lived in mud. Of course the tannin in the water, derived from the submerged trees, was the reason for this coloration of these particular fish. In volume this water (in Chippewa Lake) is much the color of port wine, but taken up in a glass it seems perfectly clear. I am quite sure that had our fish students and doctors been given an opportunity to add further sub-species to our muskellunge, the time would have come when these mud-muskies of Chippewa Lake would have been granted a very splendid and meaningless name, a "handle" in fact on which you could chin yourself.

The disposition in the present time most everywhere is to forget all about any such thing as colors and markings in the muskellunge and call it a muskellunge whether it has tiger stripes, is barred, is blotched, spotted or is plain in coloration. I will say for one that it has helped us immeasurably in putting persons right on the subject who were at one time very confused indeed. It was of course the application of the title "tiger musky" to this fish that probably accounted for the fierceness of the fish when in action. While this "tiger" appellation originally applied only to these muskies having the perpendicular stripes, it was not long until all muskies, regardless of color or markings became "tiger muskies." It only served to give the muskellunge an added and more substantial build-up and increase its prestige among the greatest of all fighting fish to which even the tarpon must take second place.

In reflecting on the vicissitudes of misconception as regards the great northern pike and muskellunge one cannot help but recall the strange case of Thaddeus Surber and his contention that save for several minor characteristics and physical differences the muskellunge and the great northern pike were identical. Surber at the time was head of fish propagation and distribution for the state of Minnesota. One of his most amazing statements was that everything depended upon the water the fish was in whether it became a great northern pike or a muskellunge. Possibly the case of the muskellunge in the Mantrap Lakes of Minnesota did something toward leading Surber wrong in his deduction, because, so far as I have been able to ascertain through years of questioning, the Mantrap Lakes never did harbor great northern pike (*Esox lucius*). Now if anyone not a high-brow fish student or "doctor" had made a statement of the above caliber he would promptly have been laughed down and no one would have given the assertion a second thought. But when an accredited fish culturist made the statement, people naturally sat up and took notice.

One of the oddities accruing from the above was that the Minnesota Game and Fish Department felt called upon to do something about the matter as they probably believed that it undermined their prestige. So they sent Surber to the muskellunge hatcheries at Chautauqua Lake in New York to be put right on the question. I don't know whatever took place at Chautauqua, but no elaborate papers, interlarded with terminological jaw-breakers came from the gifted pen of Surber. The surprising thing was that Surber returned from the wars in the hatcheries at Chautauqua stating: "I am more than ever convinced that the great northern pike and the muskellunge are identical!" In the face of such enormous self-confidence in the belief that black is white and that the sun rises in the West, the Minnesota State Game and Fish Commission could do nothing save sit back and contemplate the waywardness of science.

An odd thing happened as the result of Surber's statement: Why were there no great northern pike in the Mantrap Lakes? There were none because these were muskellunge waters and presumably the great northern pike, if placed in it, would turn into muskies! There were those who believed with Surber that black is white and that the sun rises in the West, hence the feeling spread that, *Why not increase the musky population in these lakes by stocking them with great northern pike?* Of course, that was the answer, and since the muskellunge in the Mantrap Lakes drew more fishermen than you could shake a stick at, the more muskies the greater would the business of catering to the incoming hordes. So on the sly, or by methods we never did fathom, the Mantrap Lakes suddenly became afflicted with great northern pike. They seemed to come out of nowhere and it is to be noticed that they did not change into muskellunge, but remained strictly, and in classic conformation, pike in every sense of the word.

Now the above was quite some years ago and in the meantime the great northern pike has produced his kind through the years and it is to be noticed that while the pike are increasing the muskellunge is passing out as a factor in the Mantrap Lakes. One might even ask, is it possible that the muskellunge in the Mantrap Lakes are becoming great northern pike? The first prize in the great northern pike division recorded for 1951 in the annual prize contest run by Earl Fuller, at Park Rapids, Minnesota, in the Mantrap section, was a pike from Lake Belle Taine, lowest lake of the Mantrap chain, that weighed 19 pounds, 13 ounces. Another of 19 pounds, 7 ounces was taken in Lower Bottle Lake, one of 19 pounds was also taken out of Lake Belle Taine and so on and on. It is possible that some of these large pike were among the original baby pike that were planted in the waters so that they would change into Surber muskies. Alack and alas, such are the vagaries nursed into life by the desk-bound scientists!

It would, I suppose, be sheer heresy in a book on the muskellunge not to include specific information regarding the method whereby the muskellunge, the pike and the pickerel may be identified. If you cannot go by the coloration or markings of the fish, what sure system of identification is there that is practically infallible and can be depended upon? There is one, and this positive means of identification is by the squamation, i.e., the arrangement of the scales on the cheeks and gill covers of the three members of the pike family, the muskellunge, the great northern pike and the pickerel.

In the pickerel the cheek and gill cover are completely scaled over; in the muskellunge only the extreme upper part of the gill cover and the upper part of the cheek, back of the eye, are with scales. Thus almost the entire cheek and gill cover of the muskellunge are barren of scales. In the great northern pike the cheek is entirely scaled over and so, too, the upper part of the gill cover but the lower half of the gill cover is unscaled. In fact the division line between the scaled upper part of the pike's gill cover and the smooth or scaleless lower half is easily detected. In the pike and the muskellunge you can easily note the scaling as the scales are large enough. In the pickerel the scales on the gills and cheek may be very fine, depending of course upon the age and size of the fish. A reading glass or lens will easily show these scales.

Another method of identifying the three members of the

pike family is to count the number of rays or bones that support the gill covers; in fact they control the action of the same much as do the ribs in an umbrella. Without seeing which member of the pike family you are asked to identify, and with eyes closed, open or spread the gill cover and feel along the gill cover with your thumb and forefinger. By exerting fair pressure let a ray or bone slip by one at a time and count.

The eastern of chain pickerel (*Esox reticulatus*) has 14 to 16 rays in its gill cover. The banded pickerel (*Esox americanus*) usually has 11 to 13 rays which number is very nearly the same also in the little pickerel, brook pickerel or grass "pike" (*Esox vermiculatus*). In the muskellunge the number of rays in the gill cover are 17 to 19. The great northern pike has 15 to 16.

With regard to the method of identifying the various members of the pike family by means of scalation on the cheeks and gill covers, and by the count of the rays or bones in the gill covers of the pike family, it should be mentioned that Surber disregarded this method entirely and said that it had nothing of merit to recommend it as infallible. I made arrangement with Earl Fuller, previously mentioned as conducting an annual fish contest at Park Rapids, Minnesota, one of the most notable in the country by the way, to check on both scalation and ray count in the great northern pike and muskies brought in during the course of the spring, summer and fall seasons. This was done and invariably the ray count stood 17 to 19 per gill cover in the muskellunge and 15 to 16 in the great northern pike. I doubt whether any such extensive check has ever before or since been made, as this investigation covered over five hundred specimens. Of course no pickerel were included in this survey inasmuch as no member of the three varieties of pickerel are found in the state of Minnesota. Quite the reverse of the Surber dictum, the means of scalation and ray-count are quite infallible in identifying any of these members of the pike family. And you can identify the fish with eyes closed. The fingers will reveal both the number of rays and the degree of scalation.

Singularly enough, in spite of the fact that the muskellunge is comparatively limited in numbers as compared to other fish species, the fact remains that it is very prolific in its egg production. Meehan found that a fish weighing 35 pounds will yield 265,000 eggs, each about an eleventh of an inch in diameter, 74,000 of them filling a quart-measure. Muskellunge eggs, according to Meehan, are separate, non-adhesive, and semi-buoyant and, under favorable circumstances, 97 per cent have been hatched. At 55° F. they will hatch in fifteen days, and the yolk sac is absorbed in about fifteen days more. When first hatched the fry is so heavy that it is unable to swim from the jars into the battery trough in the hatchery. The eggs, therefore, have to be transferred, when the fry are ready to emerge from the shell, to trays set in boxes placed in the troughs. The degree of cannibalism evinced by the muskellunge must be terrific and this may be nature's way of controlling the species, for as Jordan has stated, a lake can only stand so many of these voracious fish or the whole balance of nature would be over-turned. With a perfect hatching of 97 per cent of all eggs shed by the species it is understandable that the waters could be crowded with the kind. Obviously not only the muskellunge themselves but all other fish pursue the young and destroy them almost down to a minimum. In a way it is not odd that the species is so limited in numbers.

In a wild state the muskellunge go about their spawning activities as soon as the ice goes out in the spring. Some time between the middle and the last of April the act of procreation is completed. The eggs are shed in water from six to ten feet in depth, in and out among the water vegetation. For some reason or other muddy bays are preferred.

The movements of the muskellunge after spawning has something of mystery connected with it. They possibly spend a fair amount of their time in water fifteen to twenty feet deep although almost ninety-five per cent of all muskies are taken either by trolling inshore or by casting plugs and spoons as the case may be in the same comparatively shallow water. In warm to hot weather they do most of their feeding inshore during the very early morning, and again in the late afternoon and evening.

During three weeks or so in the month of August, mostly during the so-called "dog-day" season, the muskellunge, in common with many other freshwater fishes, are afflicted with a sore mouth or sore gums, even loosened teeth. Ernest G. Poole recounts that some specimens of muskellunge having loosened teeth and a typical sore gum condition, were sent to the department of dental research at Harvard University for examination. The result of the studies made of these specimens is set down as follows:

"The reason the material was forwarded for examination was that the looseness of the teeth in the jaw and the apparent inflammation associated with the tissues of the gums, were noticed by the donors aforementioned.

"It was found that the looseness of the teeth," continued the report, "was a normal anatomical condition, and the associated hyperemia was not a pathological lesion, but the normal blood supply to the teeth. Further it was found that the teeth of this fish are of successive growth and attachment. They develop in the floor of the mouth, become hinged teeth and are finally attached to the jaw-bone by a bony union. The tooth shows two types of dentine and an enamel cap. The blood supply to the tooth is profuse, the reason for which is undetermined, especially when considering that the teeth of this fish are used for offensive purposes and not for mastication. When a tooth is shed, a bony base remains, and this is later removed by absorption, and a hollow results in the jawbone. In this hollow, or depression, a tooth, attached to a fibrous membrane, soon appears. This is known as the hinged tooth, the base of which is later attached to the jawbone by osseous union and so becomes an ankylosed or fixed tooth."

It is interesting to state that the above, to my recollection, is the only attempt ever made to explain away the so-called shedding of teeth in the muskellunge. Coming from a school of leading specialists in dental matters I do not have the slightest doubt but that the approach is correct, though why this shedding should be accomplished during the dog-day season in August does not seem to dove-tail with the physical facts of the case. If a condition such as this would occur at any other time of the year than in the dog-day season one would not be given to questioning the facts related. It should be remembered that all fishes more or less during this dog-day season have sore mouths or sore gum conditions. The great northern pike often has purplish, bleeding and swelled gums that over-lap the teeth points and must be sore and sensitive in the extreme. One might ask, is the fish forced to go through this sore mouth affliction annually just to get new teeth? And that would apply to the other fish as well. The jaw-rim under the rough, toothbrushlike rudimentary teeth of the bass will show up with a purplish tinge, indicating sore jaw-rims. Later, after the sore mouth condition is gone, the jaws of the bass under the "teeth" will show up flesh-colored. Wall-eyed pike have the same failing. The panfishes are afflicted to the extent that some apparently cannot open their mouths.

Our own understanding with regard to the muskellunge and its shedding of its teeth is that the outer enamel on the tooth is in the form of a cone or cap. This cone advances, as in the case with the rattlesnake, the cone eventually falling off and the new tooth is underneath. How this fits in with the above appraisal of the subject by accredited dental authorities I would not know.

Voracious as the muskellunge is during the rest of the year, during the dog-day or sore-gum siege through which it must pass, it does comparatively little feeding and probably keeps itself in deep water or its close proximity. However, occasionally they do strike, possibly from sheer need of food. Specimens have been taken in our experience that were well nigh emaciated and showing positive signs of lengthy fasting. An interesting commentary might be made to the effect that during Augusts that are cool, even chilly (and such do occur at times), this sore-mouth condition in the fishes may occur but only to a trifling extent as compared to what happens during typical hot dog-day weather.

Following the period of sore-gums and, presumably, a more or less noticeable shedding of teeth, the muskellunge will again be in shape for action, teeth firm, gums hard and ready for anything that comes its way around the tenth of September. Then watch out!

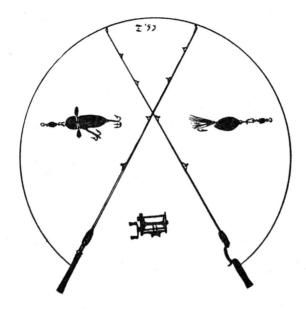

XIV

TACKLE REQUIREMENTS

It all happened when, some time ago an enthusiastic fisherman took a forty pound muskellunge in Lake of the Woods in western Ontario, Canada, on a small lure and a spinning outfit. If this event did nothing else it certainly served to create interest in lightweight fishing for muskellunge and gave the possible writer on muskellunge fishing something to think and write about. I shall cover lightweight fishing, therefore, at the opening of this chapter so that the international brotherhood of lightweight tackle and its use will not feel that they have been left out in the dark.

Whatever may be said for lightweight fishing for the muskellunge, one must face the fact that such tackle, however noteworthy, nevertheless has but little significant place in all-around fishing for this dominant species. That the fish can be taken both on fly-rod tackle and spinning tackle as well the writer has ascertained to his entire satisfaction, in fact in a previous chapter an incident is given where three muskies of good size were taken by the writer on a No. 1/O bass fly attached to a spinner-shaft, the same, cast with a typical fly-rod. All of this we admit to, and also that we have taken many other muskies in the same way. But to believe, because of this, that it is worthy of going into on an established scale is not only foolish but holds little tangible justification as to its success.

There will always be light tackle enthusiasts. Just as there are fishermen who find a world of excitement in taking or attempting to take tarpon, in saltwater, on the fly-rod, so there are inland fishermen who go on musky fishing expeditions aiming to take the species on tiny lures or fly and spinner combinations of which there are, of course, a wide variety to be had on the market. Lest the reader believes that the number who are bitten by the lightweight tackle bug in musky fishing, are rare, let me state that many letters come in to us annually and demand to be set right on the matter. As one correspondent stated: "The height of my ambition is to take a muskellunge on the fly-rod. Tell me how to go about it." Just like that. As though one could lay down fixed rules for such fishing that would be foolproof and would be a comprehensive guide to go by!

Previously I have stated that one will have little success fly rod fishing for muskies unless the fish are actually seen in the water and can be directly fished to, placing the lure so far as possible directly in front of the tip of the nose of the fish. That calls for cruising around looking for subjects to practice on and any such scouting expeditions all too often end up in failure. Usually, too, when you do see a specimen of this species swimming around you will have no fly rod along so you end out by using regulation bait rod, musky plugs and spoons. I do contend that if a fly rod is used then your best bet for a lure would be a fly and spinner combination, the fly being a bass type fly tied to a No. 1/O O'Shaughnessy hook, hand-forged (flat) variety, the fly with a husky chenille body, red tail tag, no wing feathers or "wings" of bucktail hair, only inch-long hackles at the head of the fly. The spinner on the shaft should be either No. 2 or 3 and can be used in either a gold or nickle finish. However, the No. 3 spinner, being larger, is best for stream fishing while the No. 2 is most likely to succeed in lake waters. The most successful fly pattern I have used in fly rod fishing for muskies is the Yellow Sally or, as it is sometimes called, the Yellow May. This, however, is not to say that many other standard regulation flies will not be successful, only that in the Yellow Sally one has a fly and spinner combination, and color, of known repute as based on actual experience. Under no circumstances should a bass fly be used on a shaft and spinner that has stiff, upstanding wings, as these wings cause the fly to wobble and turn from side to side in the water. The fly, as stated, should have inch-long hackles at the head only. Most fly users do not know that makers of flies will tie bass flies without wings, on one's order. This will save having to cut the wing feathers, something which, all too often, causes the fly to come undone.

So we again come around to the incident of a muskellunge fisherman taking a forty pound musky on a bass fly on a shaft and spinner, an interesting performance to say the least and one that might be closely examined to see what it might turn up by way of knowledge as to the lure and tackle used. To the writer it is more than ever interesting because it was as a result of reading one of my articles on taking muskies on the fly rod that this forty pound fish was taken.

In the article mentioned I brought out this fact, that in lakes, such as Lake of the Woods in western Ontario, many muskies have become bait-wise, whether through constantly seeing lures in the water or from having been hooked and lost might be a matter open to doubt. If large musky spoons and plugs are cast to them they are curious and come out of hiding and follow the lure, keeping close to it, studying it, but almost invariably failing to take it. When fishermen in Lake of the Woods have as many as thirty such follow-ups in a day of fishing this certainly establishes something, if nothing else, that these muskies are wise to large lures and are suspicious or afraid of them. It was in telling about taking such hook-wise or lure-wise muskies with the fly and spinner combination that the idea emanated whereby a lucky fisherman fooled a "follow-up," hooked and landed it. However, instead of using a fly rod this fisherman used a spinning outfit, but did use a fly and spinner as I had suggested originally. When a follow-up occurred he quickly picked up his spinning rod and was able to place the lure just back of the fish and reeled it forward thus catching the fish unawares. Seeing the small lure the fish nipped it and was hooked. They always "nip" a fly and spinner lure; never take it in a wide-mouthed gulp. This, of course, is excellent effect so far as the angler is concerned, for being hooked in the rim of the jaw and not deep in the mouth the lead is taken away from the fish. If deep in the mouth the leader would come in contact with the fangs and the chances are very strong that it would be gashed and in anything approaching strong action that leader would snap.

It would seem to me that where bait-wise muskies do occur, as in Lake of the Woods, the fisherman could easily carry a fly rod all set up ready for action so that if a fish did appear he could try the fly and spinner combination to its greatest possible advantage. The conclusions arrived at in this phase of fishing is that whereas the musky may be set in its mind, by instinct, on turning down the blandishments of a six-inch-long plug or a spoon-lure, he is, by no manner of means, immune to the seductive qualities of a fly and spinner, which size lure he may never have seen before. If it is new in his eyesight he may take it without question. But, as previously stated, that fish must be seen and directly cast to, to acquire desirable and noteworthy results. Personally I would much prefer the typical fly rod as used to cast the fly and spinner lure rather than a spinning outfit. My reason in stating so is that most fishermen will get more accuracy, by far, in casting with a fly rod than they would with a spinning rod. Indeed, it is possible to cast within so many inches of a spot desired to be reached with a fly rod, but this is almost impossible with the spinning rod. As a rule, if the average fisherman would get within four feet of the target with a spinning rod he would do well. This is not to state that there are not experts who are able to do rather spectacular things with the spinning rod, which is to be expected. But this does not apply to the rank and file who usually make a botch with the spinning rod especially so far as absolute accuracy is concerned.

A few words might be said with regard to fly tackle to

be used in musky fishing in the manner outlined in the above. Obviously no light rod with a limber action is a demand. If a bamboo rod is used, then it should have a generous backbone and would fall in the category of the "bass rod." I do not think that the glass fly rod would compare here with the bamboo rod, as most glass rods in the fly rod class that I have seen, while excellent for bass fishing, would not do too well in the musky fishing division. The same might be said to apply also to seamless tubular steel fly rods, but they would be far better, I would say, than the glass fly rod. It should be remembered that when a musky strikes you need a stiff action to properly set the hook in the jaw-rim. The tough, roundish rim along the jaws might turn the hook one attempts to set with a rod of too-flexible action, but would be properly penetrated by the hook set by a rod with plenty of backbone.

Normally you would use a C line in bringing out the action of a stiff-backed rod. This line can be level in caliber. One does not need a leader of more than four or five feet, preferably ten pounds test. Although I have a lot of faith in the automatic reel, the average of this type would not carry enough line should a good fish make a run for it which would call for not less than 150 feet of line should the demand arise. To accomplish this, there is need of a large size single action reel to which the fly-line can be attached first to a filler line of, say, 25 or 30 pounds test; the filler goes on the reel barrel and the enameled fly line on top. Usually muskies taken on the fly rod and fly do not become too excited. A mouthful of hooks on a plug lure might (and does) frighten them, but that little fly and single hook does not seem to whip them into a frenzy. But you never can tell; some may take off at a wild clip, in which case it is always well to have sufficient line on the reel.

There are a great many kinds of bait casting rods that are used in the business of trolling for muskies and for casting large plugs and spoons. The question as to the type bait casting rod you should employ depends upon several considerations, which might be specified and examined.

Musky plugs range in weight from ¾ ounce up to 2¼ ounces and in length from 3½ inches to 6¼ inches. These are sizeable lures to cast. Of course most musky plugs in use would go under ¾ ounce but those who want a wide selection to practice with will find that the larger models also need be considered.

One of the first obvious things about casting a musky plug of any size is that the rod propelling it to its destination must have backbone to it that will generate sufficient power to shoot it forward. That calls for a rod that is stiff. In the Lake of the Woods country, where you see more musky fishermen than anywhere in the accredited range of the species, a scattering of different sorts of rods are found involving the three most important types, namely, the bamboo rod, the solid steel rod and the seamless tubular steel rod. When the seamless tubular steel bait casting rod first came into view and (in its day) took over in the bass field, it was also introduced into the musky field as a rod with which to cast musky plugs and spoons. Time and again we had fishermen come in ranting, showing broken off rods, and claiming that they were not worth the proverbial slug copper. My verdict in the matter was always the same: that the fisherman expected the rod to cast heavy spoons and plugs as easily as a rod with stout backbone, that the rod never was meant to cast such heavy lures, and that the company making the same never did recommend those rods for such work. They were excellent, of course, for the casting of typical bass lures, but were absolutely "out" so far as casting musky lures of a heavy caliber were concerned. Another thing that militated against the success of the seamless tubular steel bait rod was (and is) the fact that it has only a moderate backbone, sufficient for setting the hook in the jaws of a bass, but lacking to a marked degree in driving the barbs into the jaws of a hulking old musky. It seems that one learns only through grim experience that a musky has a bony jaw and that a most forceful jerk, or six or eight of them, is needed to drive those hooks in. No half-hearted jerk of the rod will turn the trick. It demands powerful jerks. This, no rod with a limber action will accomplish, but the rod with good backbone will do the deed. We'll cover that phase more thoroughly later on.

First, let's consider the bamboo bait casting rod of a type suitable for the casting and trolling of musky plugs and spoons. I must confess that I have only tried out the Heddon product here, and the two rods by this company I have tested and reported on have been their No. 22A-DB, known as the "Riptide," and their No. 900, their "Musky Special." The Riptide model comes with a solid tip, no joints, and a butt section, detachable, that is 15 inches in length, with rear and forward cork grips. The rear cork grip is 9 inches in length, an additional three inches over the normal six inches. This gives the fisherman a chance to sink the butt of the rod against the mid-riff and give the arms full play in fighting the fish. There is little doubt but that this is a distinct advantage. This Riptide model can be had in either 5 or 5½ foot lengths and in either medium or heavy actions. The one I tried out was in heavy action and I used it both in musky trolling and in trolling for lake trout. I doubt whether I have used a better lake trout trolling rod than this heavy action Riptide model. It should be remembered in buying a rod of this sort that you can aim to use it on all manner of large inland freshwater fishes. I mean by this that the rod is not just meant for muskies, in fact it makes a wonderful saltwater rod also.

The No. 900 Heddon "Musky Special" differs from the Riptide with its one-piece tip and detachable handle. In the No. 900 is observed a two-piece rod, part of the rod being continuous with the handle. To this the tip of the rod attaches. This rod is also to be had in 5 and 5½ foot lengths, but in heavy action only. It will handle any manner of musky plug and spoon perfectly. This is a very popular all-around rod. Understand, these are the only two musky rods in bamboo I have tried out. This does not mean to say that there are not other rods made by other companies equally as good, only I have not, as yet, tried them out.

The only criticism I would have with both of the above models is that they are rather heavy to cast with, that is unless one has a powerful arm and casting hand. I have seen men cast all day with one of them and were still going strong. I have been able to cast for two hours all right with either of these rods but after that I had to admit the wrist tired. One failure, of course, is the fact that in both of these rods, by reason of the rod wood having to run continuous through the handle, there is forced to be a straight reel-seat. If you have been in the habit of using a rod having a sunken reel-seat, known as the offset handle, you'll have trouble getting yourself accustomed to this straight reel-seat, in that since the reel sits high, you virtually have to reach for the spooled line to control it. While the Heddon Company does make three of their one-piece tip bamboo bait casting rods with the offset handle (the No. 851, the 551 and the 451) these are only to be had in extra light, light and medium actions, thus being of no possible use in casting heavy plugs and spoons. It would have been a distinct advantage had these musky models, by Heddon, been made with offset handles.

A type of rod possessing real merit in the casting of musky plugs and spoons is the solid steel rod, with especial emphasis on two such rod makes, that by the True Temper Corp., formerly the American Fork and Hoe Company, and the Gephart Company who make the Gep Rod. The former company pioneered in the making of solid steel rods, producing a rod out of highest quality rapier steel, and were known under the trade name of Toledo. I had one of these rods given me by Fred Arbogast one summer in the north at which time he was bait casting champion. He carried six of these rods with him, that is, the solid steel Toledo type which he claimed had been ground to his specifications. In later years I sent this rod to the company to have another ground to the same specifications but they claimed that it was no different from regular rods they carried.

I caught something like two hundred muskies on this solid steel rod and it never did snap off in spite of the fact that in general heavy lures and spoons were cast with it. In a way it was just a little bit on the fairly flexible side but I had no trouble setting the hooks in the muskies that glommed my lures. I still consider this True Temper solid steel rod one of the best heavy lure casting rods I have ever used.

The Gephart Company produces a solid steel rod that I have found excellent in the casting of heavy musky lures the same being made in a triangular type, a cut said to protect the rod from snapping off. By the way, this snapping off business should be explained away so that the fisherman will know beforehand that it is not necessarily a flaw or crystallization in the steel that always causes this breakage. Or should we say that there might be a flaw in the steel that would cause breakage if undue power and whip were thrown into the rod. Here is what happens. When you throw your rod back on the back cast, if you should then cast sharply forward before the full weight of the lure eases up and slows down in back, you contrive a species of wrenching or twisting of the rod as the rod has to carry the lure forward before it was completed its backward impetus. This is terribly hard for a rod to take, even a best quality solid steel rod. The thing to do to off-set this wrenching and twisting is to let the lure slow up in back or until you feel that it has reached its back termination. When you then cast forward there will be no twisting. It is generally on the forward cast when the lure is cast forward before it has reached its backward impetus, that the snap will occur. No solid steel rod to my knowledge has ever been broken playing a fish because there is just no such strain that will ever break it.

The Gephart rod is a little bit on the heavy side and is more tiring in casting then with the True Temper rod but it has strength and if not forced by the twisting I have stated, it will stand up perfectly. I might mention that the Gephart rod also makes an excellent trolling rod for muskies and lake trout as well.

One Lou Feirabend in telling about solid steel rods comments as follows: "Solid steel rods probably had their origin when some enterprising mechanic installed a handle and a set of guides to an ordinary fencing foil. The latter, being extremely flexible, is almost totally lacking in casting ability. Weightwise, a solid steel rod is the least efficient material distribution possible."

I am quite sure that if this engineer had taken as many fish as I have in my day on solid steel rods he would have more faith in the product. I will admit to the fact that in my own case I have used such solid steel rods entirely in casting large lures, as I do not think they possess a flexible enough quality for casting lighter lures than those in the musky class. The only time we have used such solid steel rods for all around casting has been on canoe trips where one has to make one rod do for all purposes, thus, of course, cutting down on both space and weight factors. Another thing about the solid steel rods; they have the off-set handles, permitting grip-control on the handle, that certainly is not achieved on the bamboo rod with the straight reel seat.

Lines to be used for the casting of heavy musky lures invite no little need for attention. I have always recommended a 24 pound test bait casting line to be used in the casting of musky lures as I firmly believe that it has the proper weight for carrying through with a weighty plug or spoon.

In line with the above the late Mitchell (Mitch) Jamar of the Heddon Company criticised me for recommending a line as heavy as 24 pound test. He thought that a 12 pound test line would do better and was heavy enough. At the time it was apparent that he had cast very few heavy lures, so I explained my point of view to him. If you cast a heavy lure with a light line the bait will shoot forward much like a pebble thrown off the end of a lath stick. In other words, the line will belly and will not carry through on a plane with the lure. A heavier line, which has body to it, follows through with the lure and has a feeling of being a part of the lure, so well do the two merge together. After a fishing trip up to Lake of the Woods, I had a card from Jamar. He said: "I see what you mean about that 24 pound test line. We all had 12 pound test lines up here but changed to 24 pound test. You are every bit correct about the need for a heavier line for musky plugs and spoons."

Understand, it was not (and is not) a question so far as pounds test is concerned, as I would go up against any muskellunge swimming wet water with a 12 pound test line and would, I believe, come out the winner. What is true is that one needs a heavier line to carry through with the lure as outlined. In fact only by the use of this heavier line is one able to achieve anything like accuracy is heavy lure casting. You certainly cannot do so with a heavy plug on a light line.

Pure silkworm lines such as we used years ago were known to have a considerable stretch to them, a degree of elasticity that certainly was not to the best effect when one wanted to set the hook in the jaw of a rampaging musky. Depending upon how much line you have out, this elasticity of the line works against you. On a short line, as in casting, you have more control over the line and you can overcome the elastic nature of the line, though even under these conditions one needs to give a most powerful jerk to the line, in fact should follow it up with a succession of jerks. But if you have a long line out as in trolling you lose in getting the power of the jerk forward to the jaw of the fish, as you will be fighting water pressure on the line plus the elastic nature of it.

Nylon lines, while having less elasticity than the silk lines are nevertheless, also elastic by nature. There was introduced several years ago what has been variously known as a "hot stretch" treatment which is achieved by the use of infrared rays. Normally a nylon line has upwards of a 30 per cent stretch to it but under the hot stretch treatment the amount of give is cut down to about 12 per cent maximum. Too, there is less elasticity by far in a 24 pound test line than in, say, a 12 pound test line. I would say that fully 50 per cent of all losses accruing through musky throwing the hook has been because of inability on the part of the fisherman to understand the fact that the jaws or mouth of a musky is quite bony and that unless sufficient and powerful enough jerks are given the lure, those hooks will not affix to the jaw. We have used the "hot stretch" lines put out by the Western Line Company very successfully; in fact I believe they were the first to exploit this method of taking the "give" out of a line. As these words are written we have noticed an ad of the Western Line Company which states that a new world's record sailfish has just been taken on a Western "hot stretch" line testing only 12 pounds. This sailfish weighed 124 pounds and has been approved by the International Game Fish Association as a new record!

While it is true that a longer line is needed in trolling for muskies than in casting for them, even so a matter of fifty yards of line on a 100 yard, typical, bait casting reel is all that is needed. In spite of his so-called fighting spurt, the muskellunge can be handled on a fairly moderate length of line. Inasmuch as nylon line does not absorb water as does the real silk line, one can get more on the reel barrel of nylon than actual silk. The manner in which the line is spooled on the reel is as follows: Tie the new line to the reel barrel and reel it completely on. Then tie to the end of the new line the filler or base line and reel this on until the line is within a quarter inch or so of the cross-pillars of the reel. Now attach the end of the filler line to a tree and walk away thus removing all the line from the reel. Tie the end of the new line to a tree, walk back, string the end of the filler line through the guides and reel the entire line on. This will leave the new line a quarter inch from the reel pillars which is as it should be. While the line should be high in the reel, it should not be so high that it brushes against the cross bars or pillars between the plates and clogs. One can control a reel well filled with line far better than if the line is deep down on the reel barrel.

The use of gimp-wire leaders, six to ten inches in length at the end of the line to which to attach the spoon or plug as the case may be, is not recommended. In the first place, adding this wire leader makes it impossible to reel the lure up as close to the tip-top guide of the rod as is needed. Ostensibly the leader is needed, so some writers claim, to off-set the possibility of a fish over-striking and hitting onto the line. I must admit that in a lifetime of fishing for great northern pike and muskies no such thing has ever happened in my experience, and I have taken great numbers of these fish without the benefit, if benefit it be, of any manner of metal leader, steel wire or braided gimp. If any manner of leader should be used it need only be a brass wire about two inches long, with a snap and swivel at one end to which the lure attaches and a swivel with eye on the other to which the line is attached. I think that every fisherman should look into the so-called bead chains and terminal line attachments. The company making the bead chain items turns out a number of these and they are more or less invaluable especially to those trolling to the extent that these bead chains ("every bead a swivel"), absolutely prevents twisting or kinking of the line.

I generally protect the bait-end of the line by throwing a loop on the line and drawing the knot tight. Through the swivel eye insert the loop, pull it out, then bring it over the lure and back down to the eye and draw tight. It proves infallible.

XV

MUSKY PLUGS

I do not know where the expression originated but I have heard it all of my life. It is "large fish like large lures." Therefore, obviously if you would take large fish a short-cut to doing so would be to use large lures. So if you would take those tremndous muskies of great renown then if you would offer to these grey warriors musky plugs of both weight and size you might be in line to hang up a world's record—you think.

The above, however, is not borne out by the facts of the case. Large muskies have been taken on fly and spinner combinations and little spinning lures. I know of a large musky that was taken on a bass bug. As to just what a musky will take is by no means certain, and for that matter the musky itself would not be able to state his preference if he were able to make a statement as to his likes and dislikes in the field of eating pleasures. It is all a matter of circumstance, pure and simple. The muskellunge I took that had a muskrat in him that would have graded No. 1 Northern Large might just as well have seized upon a minnow or a small fish. Probably we figure that a large muskellunge has a considerable gut to keep filled and this is best done, not by picking up tiny bugs and minnows, but by seizing upon the largest food items he comes across, sensing probably instinctively that the larger the item the more space internally will be filled. I confess myself to a leaning toward the large lure for this very reason.

While there are not too many musky plugs to be had on the market there nevertheless are more than enough to go around. These range in weight from ¾ ounce up to 2¼ ounces and a length of from 4 inches to 6¾ inches. Of course we are speaking here in terms of large lures and are not considering those in the bass fishing class of which there is a barrel of good ones that could be exploited. However, I have this to say with regard to the taking of muskies on the typical bass lures in the ⅝ ounce class and smaller: most of them that do attract muskies to strike them are taken when you least expect it. I mean by this that there are musky waters that also harbor bass. It is while casting for bass that you might win a strike from one of the big fellows. I am convinced that this does not too often happen. Certainly your large plug would be more tempting to a musky that is stalking food and has to manage as best he can the annexing of a meal that has four corners to it.

Musky lures in the plug class come in two types, that is, the top-water lures and those under-water plugs that travel close to the surface or a foot or two below the surface. I never have cared anything about deep-running plugs for musky fishing, simply because there is hardly a musky in a hundred that is taken at any unusual depth. The musky spends some time in fairly deep water, but it does not feed there and it is rarely caught while one is deep trolling. Ninety-five per cent of all muskies are taken in four or five feet of water down to a possible twelve or fifteen feet, and mostly in the inshore waters of a lake, which is the natural feeding ground.

One failure of most musky plugs is the fact that they are not, in any sense of the word, weedless, inasmuch as their gang hooks are well exposed and will dig into any manner of vegetation, pads, weeds, reeds, etc., and get hung up. For this reason there is a limitation placed on the scope or area of vulnerable water in which they can be used. I am aware of the fact that there are gang or treble hooks that can be purchased that are supposed to be weedless, there being three small, short wires going up to each point of each of the three hooks composing the gang. To look at they would seem the answer to the problem, but in actual use they are of little comprehensive value. Furthermore, if you would desire to install these on a plug you would first have to remove the gangs already on the plug to accomplish the deed. This is not easily done and in some plugs cannot be done at all without injury to them. It has been my experience that when you tamper with a plug in this way you seal its doom, and that is surely true if the lure is made of wood, since wood will invite water intrusion. Of course many lures are now made of plastic, but an equal number are made of wood. Personally I would use the plugs with their bare gangs where they can be used and do what fishing one would want to do in the heart of the weeds with a pork-rind spoon and a musky-sized pork-rind strip. That's your best bet in fishing the vegetation anyhow, in fact it is almost the only way of circumventing or conquering the same.

First let us look at the top-water musky plugs of which there is a fine little group that have weathered the storms of time through the years and have held their own against competition of a most aggressive order. If it is interesting, fascinating, and a great experience to take bass on surface lures (and who can say there is a better way of bass fishing); taking a big musky on a top-water lure is something that is little short of nerve tingling and breath-taking. Now I must confess that I have never witnessed a musky seizing something alive on the surface and going his full length out of the water in doing so. At least I have seen no musky do this in a lifetime of fishing musky waters both in the United States and Canada. But I have had muskies time and again throw themselves full length out of water in seizing a surface plug. When a musky of thirty-five or forty pounds contrives a thing of the sort you really have dynamic action and something that will live in your memory the rest of your days. It is fascinating to use a top-water plug simply because the musky in its inshore operations is a surface watcher, and we must be conscious of the fact that a generous part of its food is taken from the surface, such as muskrats, mink, waterfowl of all kinds, to name just some of the living provender its annexes. Because it is no stranger to taking large food items of a heterogeneous type the surface lure can hardly be too large to attract its fancy.

Our intent in this appraisal of musky plugs is not to give all of those to be had on the market, which would be a manifest impossibility, but to single out types and point out their qualities. It is a well known fact that in lure manufacture in this country, the moment a manufacturer puts out a successful lure, there are likely to be ten imitations of it put on the market in very short order. Imitations fairly glut the trade, each maker feeling that he is justified and entitled to the same wide renown as the originator in spite of the fact that he has been an out and out copy-cat. As one they holler "me too, me too" lest they be forgotten with their flagrant simulations of the originals. This, however, is not to forget that some of the imitations of this, that or the other lure may even be better than the original, such indeed is the irony of the thing.

Of surface lures in the musky division there are two kinds (1) the puddling lure that wobbles along on the surface or otherwise stirs up the water in an animated fashion. And (2) the popping plug that is jerked to cause it to give a *plop* or boiling disturbance on the surface, a deadly lure on muskies anywhere and certainly recommended for evening fishing up into the dark period. Below are given six leading top-water musky plugs, namely, the Jitterbug, the Crazy Crawler, the Globe Bait, the Flaptail, the Injured Minnow and the Hula Popper. These are six; but to say that they compose the only lures in this class that will take muskies is absurd. They are, however, notable because of their action and those qualities that surely inveigle a musky to strike, if strike he must. Checking down on the list of six and examining them more closely; here are some facts about them:

The Jitterbug: This notable top-water lure belongs in what is known as the puddling class of lure and was invented by Fred Arbogast during the latter days of his boyhood, according to Hank Werner, but apparently was not put on the market till the early 1930's. Werner tells me that Fred made the mouthpieces of these first Jitterbugs out of the narrow lids from his father's Prince Albert tobacco cans. The lure was successful. Fred called it a "Floater" but it was not until about 1934 that it was put on the market. It proved an instant success and is certainly one of the foremost top-water lures to be had. In the fall of 1951 while fishing in the Currituck Sound country of North Carolina I found that the demand for Jitterbugs for bass in that part of North Carolina, and the whole state for that matter, was very great. For bass of course a standard size is made, that is, one weighing ⅝-ounce. Musky fishermen set up a clamor for a large or king-size Jitterbug, which eventually the Arbogast Company acceded to, and this large lure is now being used more or less consistently throughout the whole range of the fish. This musky-size Jitterbug is 5 inches in length, has a wood body and three No. 2/0 treble hooks. It can be had in red head, frog, black, yellow, black scale and perch coloration. I have much preferred the all-black musky Jitterbug, and the frog spotted one. However, this is a personal preference, and does not mean that the other colors listed are not every bit as good. Hank Werner has a method of attaching one of their large-size rubber strand skirts to the rear end of the musky Jitterbug that I have yet to try out but which has every semblance of being a ripping good idea. At the rounded tail-end of the Jitterbug a very fine hole is drilled. This points straight in, horizontal with the lure. A one-inch long narrow screw with a rounded head just large enough in size so that the sleeve of the skirt-holder can be worked over it without coming off, is then screwed into the fine drilled hole, letting it stand out sufficiently beyond the end of the wood (about 4/8 of an inch) to accommodate the rubber sleeve of the skirt without much forcing. One fisherman is said to have taken eight muskies on one trip with a musky Jitterbug thus fitted out. It is a very ingenious idea and one that bears careful examination and trial. It would be a recommendation that waterproof varnish be worked into the drilled hole and the same applied to the screw part as it is inserted. Then the edges around the screw should be touched up with paint to prevent water intrusion and cracking or scaling around the screw edges.

Unlike the great northern pike, which ceases feeding around twilight, the musky is on the move well into the dark, feeding heavily in the inshore waters. It is at this time that the Jitterbug is at the height of its intriguing seductiveness. As stated, when in action the Jitterbug belongs in the puddling class, wobbling from side to side as it moves along with a gurgling sound. More will be told about its use in a later chapter. The Jitterbug is one of the most deadly of the top-water lures, and that is certainly the case so far as the musky is concerned.

The Crazy Crawler: This is another puddler, made by the Heddon Company and has long been a musky standby. According to the company many prize winners have been taken on this lure, including a world's record. The largest size in this lure is not as large as the larger musky plugs, being 2¾ inches long and has a weight of ¾-ounce. It has a most surprising action, moving over the water, when reeled, in a sort of swimming-crawling manner brought about by its two metal arms or flippers that simulate something of an exaggerated Australian Crawl, no doubt the basis for the name of the lure. Because of its animated action and its stirring up of the water it must be quite difficult for the fish really to make out what it is save that it is something going somewhere and unless stopped will presently (probably) take off and be no more within easy reach. Many a musky has tried to stop such foolish notions on the part of the Crazy Crawler to his everlasting sorrow. The Crazy Crawler comes in several colors and color combinations: Frog, gray mouse, black with white head; yellow with red head; silver shore minnow and red and white shore minnow. My pick of these would be the frog color and the silver shore minnow. Here is another lure that is probably best fished around twilight, up around the shores, the pads, reeds, set-in coves and all those places where muskies like to hang out. One thing is certain, when a musky hits the Crazy Crawler he is likely to go his full length out of water.

The Globe Bait: This is a revolving head bait, the head having propeller blades that causes it to revolve as it is reeled. It is made by the Pflueger Company, although many years ago a revolving head bait was made, advertised and sold by Ans Decker. At one time I believe the South Bend Company made a large edition of the revolving head bait, but dropped its manufacture.

The Globe Bait is another of the surface commoters, *i.e.*, those that boil up the water, and by reason of so doing mask their identity, making it impossible for the fish to rightly interpret what it is. In this it acts in much the same way as the Jitterbug and the Crazy Crawler. If the fish is confused as to identity he is likely to be intrigued into striking. Like the previous baits this is another evening and bridging-on-dusk bait. By its sound-provoking animation it can possibly be heard for quite a distance by the fish. The Globe Bait while being deadly is also one of the easiest of all lures to work on the water. Its a good idea to pause now and then while reeling it, jerking it very little now and then in between and sometimes permitting it to lie still. To reel the lure straight in may take fish but I am quite sure that if this lure is worked as detailed above, far superior results will be had. I think that this slowing up of the lure and jerking it slightly now and then carries out the illusion of something maimed or injured. Too, while it is not a popping lure the Globe Bait can fairly well be popped, just as can the Crazy Crawler and the Jitterbug.

There are three sizes of the Globe Bait, the musky size being 5¼ inches in length, weighing 1 and 1/3 ounces.

The Flaptail: This is a Heddon product and a truly notable musky lure. The standard-sized Flaptail has a length of 4 inches, and a weight of ¾ ounce. While it was designed primarily for the taking of bass there arose a clamor for a larger size to be used in musky fishing. As a result the company put out what they call the "Giant Flaptail." This is really one of the huskiest of the musky numbers, being 6 and ¾ inches in length and having a weight of 2¼ ounces. When in action the Flaptail rides the surface, a pear-shaped spinner or "spoon" at its tail-end producing a species of flapping side to side motions as the lure is reeled. It is the animation of this flapper at the tail that draws the attention of the fish and no doubt inspires it to strike. The Heddon Company in telling about how best to use this lure states: "Try the stop and go method with the Flaptail. At the completion of the cast, jerk or chug the bait gently, then reel slowly. This will cause the spoon at the tail to revolve and will give the bait a swimming motion. Then reel fast. This causes the spoon to create a great commotion, then slow, then fast, etc., etc." The above, we have found, is sound advice.

The Injured Minnow: This famous top-water lure is made by the Creek Chub Bait Company and remains throughout the years one of those inevitable standbys that one just does not seem to be able to leave out of the tackle box. This is a plug lure that is minnow-shaped, with a chubby body. and lies on its side like a minnow that is hurt. As a result I would imagine that the fish gets a good view of its side looking up at it. There are propellers at the head and tail of this Injured Minnow. It can be reeled solely if desired in which case the spinners revolve, fretting up the water and so lending "enchantment to the view." But this manner of operating the Injured Minnow is not recommended, in fact it is possibly the least attractive. Here again there is need of practicing all sorts of ways of giving the lure that action needed to inject into it the something different that will cause a fish to forget everything and haul off and bat it one that will properly imbed it in the jaws of the mighty. To accomplish this, at the very start forget about reeling it straight in, back and forth, as most fishermen do who use it. Rather cast the lure to water and let it lie there for a minute or so. Then give it little quivering jerks or moves with the rod-tip as though it were, in reality, a maimed minnow kicking a little to try to get into action. Occasionally in between give a shaper jerk. While the Injured Minnow is not a popping plug, and does not give off a popping noise like the Hula Popper, it nevertheless can be given action to some extent in this manner. In between, let the lure lie still. These methods, as above, should always be used if you are casting into real vulnerable grounds, in fact the better the grounds the more persistent should be this slow fishing of the lure. This, again, is one of those lures that are killers in dusk fishing for muskies when they are certain to be inshore feeding bent.

The Injured Minnow is not made in a musky size, but should be. There is a baby size and a standard size, the latter being 3 and ¾ inches in length and weighing ¾ ounce. It is a strictly surface lure and is to be had in nineteen colors and blends. I have always preferred the silver scale, also the perch and pikie coloration. I have always avoided use of red, white and blue and like garish colorations. The Injured Minnow is provided with three treble hooks.

The Injured Minnow should not be confused with the Wounded Minnow that is made by the Heddon Company. The latter, which also lies on its side, is somewhat different but is smaller in size, being 2 and ⅞ inches long and weighing one-half ounce.

In using the Injured Minnow do not forget to cast it up in those deep indentations in the pads for it is in these deep bays in the pads that one is likely to spot a hulking musky.

The Hula Popper: This famous top-water lure made by the Arbogast people is another of those lures you would not think of leaving behind if you are going to go out for muskies and are going to use plug lures. While the Arbogasts made a concession in behalf of the musky fishermen and put out the Jitterbug in a king's size they have not done so with the Hula Popper although there is a real demand for it in a husky status. The Hula Popper is made at its largest only in the standard size, same having a weight of ⅝ ounce and a length of 2 and ¼ inches. Its body colors are red head, white body; frog color, with white belly; frog color, with yellow belly; black; yellow; pearl and luminous. It is provided with two treble hooks, one on the belly and one near the tail.

The Hula Popper is one of the foremost of the popping plugs, its hollow head providing a means to assuring real sound and gurgle that will stir any musky on the prowl into action. Here again is a lure that will do well for both very early morning fishing, and for fishing around dusk and until such time when it is getting so dark it is difficult to see the bait land on the water. We have always considered that the cue to stop fishing so far as daylight operations for muskies are concerned. One singular value of a popping plug in this evening fishing is that the sound carries far, hence might attract a fish to it. The muskellunge is always a curious critter anyhow and he certainly thinks it the height of something or other for a creature of any kind to invade its prowling and hunting grounds. One can always gauge the ire or irritation of a musky by the viciousness with which it takes a lure. I have noticed that every time a musky hits a Hula Popper it is with a savage snap and a suddenness that is likely to take you completely unawares.

Just as that rubber skirt is a go-getter and an attraction in fishing for bass so is the same undulating strands of rubber something that the muskellunge is powerfully attracted by. Indeed there are many instances I have known where the rubber strands may have been the cause for a musky hitting the lure. Suppose one casts the lure and lets it lie on the water. Even lying there silent on the water the sensitive rubber strands will still move in a provoking manner!

Like all the other lures mentioned previously in this top-water class, the Hula Popper should not be fished too hurriedly. It should be given plenty of time, given a pop, and then permitted to lie still. In between give the lure little jiggles of the rod tip to stir it into action and make it look like something injured. Just to pop it along in a steady succession of noise-making spurts is not to get the most out of it, and may cause the fish to become suspicious rather than anything else.

Three colorations in the Hula Popper I prefer over any of the other colors are the all-black plug with the black and yellow rubber skirt; the frog spotted color with a black skirt and the all-yellow plug with the yellow skirt. It might be mentioned that you can also get the Hula Popper in a luminous body color, which will glow in the dark. Generally a lure of the sort is placed in the sun and it will hold its glow equal to the time it has absorbed the sunrays. Since the musky feeds on up into the dark, you'll find this luminous Hula Popper worthy of consideration.

The Mud Puppy: This lure is made by C. C. Roberts, Mosinee, Wisconsin and has been on the market since 1928, I believe. I don't know but that I would class it as one of the most outstanding and original of all muskellunge lures.

It has turned in such numbers of muskies as no other lure in this class could begin to compare with. I might mention that in the Lake of the Woods country the Mud Puppy has been active since it first came on the market. Operating on the surface of the water the Mud Puppy has a revolving tail piece, a half-propeller spinner attached to this tail section aiding in the turning of it. But there is something else that is distinctive about the Mud Puppy. Roberts, in his early muskellunge fishing with plugs, took note of the fact that when a musky was hooked and shook his jaws to dislodge the lure, the heft of the lure aided in jerking back and forth and so dislodging the hook. This is how Roberts defines the situation:

"When the musky is hooked it opens its mouth to the fullest extent and violently shakes its head, which causes the bait to snap back and forth. The strain on the hooks becomes so great that often hooks and bait go sailing skyward and a prize fish may be lost. Nothing like that happens if you are using my Mud Puppy. When the fish shakes the Mud Puppy free of the hooks the hooks stay in the jaws of the fish while the bait floats on the surface. After the fish is landed the Mud Puppy is picked up."

A split ring on the leader is inserted on a pin at the nose of the fish. This wire leader is three inches long. The treble hook is attached to a hook clasp and the ring of the leader in turn to the hook clasp. This clasp is pressed up into a slot on the belly of the bait which holds it securely in place while the lure is cast or trolled with. When the fish strikes, the hook is firmly set. The hook clasp jerks out of the slot, the ring comes off of the nose pin in the bait and you have direct contact with the fish *sans* the body of the lure, which floats on the water and can be picked up after the fish is landed. In many ways I would say that this is definitely a "must" if you want to build up a complement of sure-fire muskellunge killers. Length, 7 inches, weight, 2 ounces. Best color, natural.

The Surf-Oreno: This lure made by the South Bend Bait Company is a surface operator that has long figured in the musky field as a threat of no mean order. Too, it is one of the oldest of the musky plugs. It has spinners fore and aft which, when reeled, churns the water. A waterproof metal tube runs through the plug through which the shaft of the lure passes and houses the wire for hook attachment. The lure is armored with three treble hooks. This lure can be reeled in slowly over the water, but our favorite way of operating it is to reel it a foot or so, let it rest, jiggle it somewhat or even pop it, then reel it again, occasionally letting it rest on the water without a move. It is killing on prowling muskies around twilight and into the dark. Length is 3½ inches, weight 1 ounce.

The Halik Frog: In the chapter on fishing the pads for muskies this lure is carefully considered. It has possibilities that make it a lure to add to your collection of musky killers, which collection, at best, is none too extensive.

Underwater Plugs For Muskies

If there is a limitation in the number of surface plugs suitable for musky fishing the same is hardly applicable to the underwater plugs in the musky field, a number of which are to be had. Two of the largest and most prominent makers of underwater musky plugs is the Heddon and the Creek Chub Companies. Indeed the number of prize winners and records that have been accounted for by Creek Chub Pikie lures through the years is something that brings one to a realization that these lures are really killers with an outstanding and almost unbeatable record.

I believe it was the Creek Chub Company that introduced the jointed type of underwater plug although I stand to be corrected on this point. In any event there is not the slightest doubt but that this jointed type was a most remarkable innovation. When reeled through the water a lure of this type has a swimming motion that is very nearly flawless in lifelikeness, hence is one of the most seductive of this type of musky plug. Certainly several of these should be carried on any musky expedition.

The Giant Jointed Vamp: Made by the Heddon Company, has chalked up a record as a musky getter that is more than noteworthy. This is a large plug, being 6 and ¾ inches in length and has a weight of 1 and ⅞ ounces. Has three 2/0 treble hooks and is to be had in white body with red head; blue herring scale; shiner scale, with red head and red side stripe, and, lastly, in shad coloration. Preference would lean to the red head, shiner scale body finish and the red stripe down the sides. This is a jointed lure, and floats when it is not being reeled. There is an advantage to this in that if for any reason (as a backlash) you cease reeling the lure will float and will not sink to the bottom. Too, floating it combines top-water action along with underwater action. You can work this lure very easily by slow-reeling and it will stay on the surface, swimming along with a very seductive movement of its jointed parts. It can also be jerked to cause it to boil up the top water. The trick in fishing this lure therefore is to work it (1) on top of the water, and (2) as an underwater operator. By combining the two you will have by far your greatest success in the musky field.

The Giant Vamp: This is another Heddon lure having a length of 5 and ¾ inches and a weight of 1 and ⅝ ounces. It has three 4/0 treble hooks and is to be had in shad, white body with red head, blue herring scale, and shiner scale with red head and red stripes down its sides. I much prefer the latter coloration, same as in the Giant Jointed Vamp. This lure is not jointed but comes in one piece construction. It is lighter in weight than the jointed Vamp and has a more seductive action. It is also easier to cast. Mention should be made that this lure, and the jointed one, are excellent for slow-trolling with a long line. I say "slow-trolling" and I mean by this, trolling just sufficiently to keep the lure near to the surface or just breaking at the surface. Indeed I would go so far as to state that I believe both of these plugs make better trolling lures than spoons for a very, very definite reason. If weeds are to be found even two feet under the surface, there are hardly any spoon lures, if trolled, that will not go down and annex them. In fact in many such weedy waters it is quite impractical to troll with a spoon. But by trolling a plug lure of the Vamp type, as outlined, you can do so by staying close to the surface with the lure, with just enough movement of the boat or canoe, as the case may be, to keep the lure just under the surface and sometimes right on the surface or breaking the surface water. In this way, in spite of the fact that these Vamps possess bare ganghooks, few if any weeds are picked up. In fact one can troll fairly close to the outer edges of the pads with between 75 to 100 feet of line out and take fish that would not possibly be caught under the same circumstances with a spoon lure.

The Husky Pikie Minnow: Much fame attaches itself to this Creek Chub Company lure. It is a solid piece construction, not jointed, having a length of 6 inches and a weight of 1½ ounces. It has three treble hooks. While it is to be had in six colorations, I have always been satisfied with the pikie coloration, that is to say, a color like a small pike. I do not think that this pikie coloration can be bettered. My largest musky taken on this solid Pikie weighed 42 pounds. Because it is trim and more or less streamlined this lure casts far better than one would suspect and one can, in fact, make fairly accurate casts with it. It operates at mid-depth. Here is a lure that is almost a "must" when you are picking your underwater plugs for that musky expedition.

The Jointed Husky Pikie Minnow: Like its sister bait above, this lure also has a length of 6 inches and a weight of 1½ ounces. It has a most lifelike swimming motion through the water when reeled and its pikie coloration is very nearly flawless. Here is action of the kind that intrigues the most hard-bitten old moss-back of a musky. I do not know if it is true that the musky is a foe of the great northern pike, and kills and consumes it in numbers. Sometimes I doubt it. But it is a fact that the pikie coloration arouses the musky to strike, just as the standard Pikie makes an old largemouth bass see spots. In many ways I consider this an outstanding musky plug in the underwater class and proof of its killing quality is seen by the great number of prize winners that have been caught on it. I have noticed that almost nine out of ten of all muskyteers on Lake of the Woods have this jointed Pikie in the musky size in their tackle boxes.

Other lures in this underwater class that would bear investigation is the Musk-Oreno, the Muskie Jinx, the Muskie Sucker and other lures in this class. Mainly these are copies of lures already in the field and established. It might be mentioned, however, that the South Bend Bass Oreno with its weaving, wobbling action in the water is different and is still preferred by a great number of musky fishermen. It should also be remembered that it has hung up a lot of records in its day. I do not care much for the white body, red head Bass Oreno. Of course the Musk-Oreno, being larger, takes the place in the musky field of the typical standard Bass Oreno.

The Musky Flatfish: Charlie Helin's Flatfish is now being advertised as having been sold to the tune of 9,000,000 separate and individual baits. Most of these have probably been in the standard or bass size, which is the most popular number. It should not be forgotten, however, that the Flatfish is now being produced in a saltwater and musky size and as such is due to carve for itself a place of no mean merit and prestige in the muskellunge set up. Already it has taken muskies over forty pounds with hundreds of other near-records that add immeasurably to the surprising reputation of this most famous of all American plug lures. While this is not strictly a surface lure it does work so close to the surface that it might easily be considered in the surface class. Like all Flatfish lures the musky Flatfish has a most seductive wiggle to it, a sort of side to side animation that is intriguing. One thing that I have always liked about the Flatfish is that it works slowly in the water; you just simply cannot work it fast; in fact it is not meant to move faster than a leisurely gait. Old muskies that are not able to flash through the water or are not disposed to do so by reason of a lazy condition find this lure just about cut for their speed. Moving side to side in a most animated fashion, even when reeled slowly, the fish is unable to tell what in the world it is. They decide that here is creamed-sucker-on-toast, and promptly clamp their wolf-trap jaws on it. When they do they are met by no less than four gangs of hooks that have a way, I might mention, of every one seating themselves in the jaw. I do say this with regard to this musky Flatfish: you better have several of them along. The last musky that shut the trap on the one I was using fairly ground it to an unrecognizable Flatfish, in fact it was flatter than any Flatfish I have seen cozily incased in the sporting goods store. Yes, you'll not do badly if you add that musky-sized Flatfish to your set-up, and for my money I would certainly pick the frog-colored one.

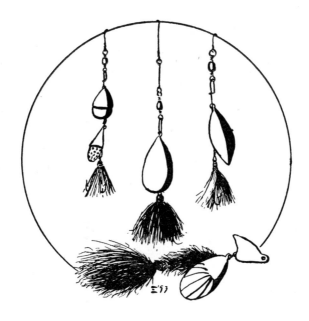

XVI

SPOONHOOKS
FOR MUSKIES

It is an interesting commentary that up until the time
fishermen started casting plugs in the Lake of the Woods
country of western Ontario little attention was paid to casting spoons in the same way probably because no one had
thought the idea feasible, or that it could be done. It was
after the method of casting plugs and spoons, too, for muskies
in this Ontario country had established itself, and the news
of its effectiveness had spread over the country, that casting
spoons and plugs in other musky waters besides Lake of
the Woods became rather a fixed and recommended method.
As one of the first to popularize this method I did my share
toward acquainting the fisherman of the country with the
effectiveness of casting instead of trolling.

Of course there was a reason for casting both plugs and spoons in Lake of the Woods. Owing to reefs and a jagged shoreline, trolling in these waters (if you are going to work close to shore) is a practical impossibility. You'll hook up endlessly, to the extent that trolling if followed up is little short of a hopeless venture. It was no doubt this fact that led fishermen to concentrate on casting plugs and spoons instead of trolling with the same in this notable lake. That it proved an invaluable method is attested to by the thousands of muskies that have come out of it. One might say in consideration of Lake of the Woods that it is suitable for casting plugs and spoons rather than trolling them, but that other waters, elsewhere in the range of the musky, are better trolled. This I sincerely doubt. For one thing, as pointed out previously, a great number of musky lakes are weedy and this is certainly the case so far as most inner or shoreline waters are concerned where ninety percent of all trolling is conducted, and has to be conducted if muskies are held at the horizon of one's endeavors, for the fish feed in these inner waters and are rarely taken in deeper waters. Trolling these weedy waters is far from practical simply because the bare hooks on the spoon lure or plug, as the case may be, will pick up those inevitable weed trailers. It would seem that if your hooks pick up so much as a weed six inches long, that lure becomes null and void as a fish taker until it is cleaned. The spectacle of fishermen trolling endlessly along the outer edges of the pads with a weed a foot long attached to the hook is rather a common occurence. Because of this weed assembling nature of the spoon lure, trolling at best is little short of a miserable failure and is never to be depended upon. Of course where waters are free of weeds, at least to a considerable extent, the feasibility of trolling is increased many fold. But not where the chances of hauling around weed trailers is the order of the day. Casting the plug lure or the spoonhook then will produce results where trolling is little short of a sheer impossibility.

Let us get a close-up view of trolling as it is generally carried on in typical musky waters. Mostly, but not always, there is a belt of pads that skirt the shore, reaching out in places a hundred feet or more from the lake edge. These pads never come in a perfect line so that you can troll up close to the outer edges of them. Rather they are in jagged outline, with deep indentations, or less prominent ones, along the whole pad area. This would mean, in trolling, that you have to keep outside of the pads, that peninsula out at the furthest point, else you'll hook into them. Also you have to keep far enough out so that you will not comb the tops of the weeds reaching for the surface. Your average spoon lure with 75 feet of line out will go down, of its natural weight about two feet under the surface. Trolling with a long line is most practical, but in weedy waters this is out of the question. Even with 75 feet of line out you will be picking up weeds. What then is to be said for 100 to 125 feet of line, which will sink the lure at least three feet below the water surface if not more. Obviously the deeper down you go the more of a chance there is of picking up weeds heading for the surface.

Now let us look at the method of casting the spoon and plug. Employing a line out of not more than 40 to 50 feet from the reel, you can cast deep up into the pockets and indentations in the pads that are never reached by trolling and you can work them thoroughly. Even if weeds are spiralling to the surface you need not hook into them because you can operate your spoon a few inches to six inches under the surface. Standing up in your boat you can easily see the water you are casting over and you need not hook into any weeds at all. The same of course is true with your plug lures. Where the waters in the deep indentations in the pads are fairly weedy, you can use your strictly surface plugs to advantage and get right up in the stronghold of some of the big fellows. Let me mention that up in those V-shaped indentations in the pads is where you will find your muskies, if at all, and the only way to reach them is by casting.

On all points save where the waters are quite weedless, the trolling method has little if anything to commend it. In the light of serious fishing practice trolling in weedy water is the most fruitless and unsuccessful method that can be managed. True, an odd fish now and then is taken but that happens only when, for a wonder, a spoonhook has come through without picking up a stringer of weeds.

Of two types of spoon lures that are used in fishing, one being the wobbling spoon type as originally made by Julio

T. Buel, the inventor of the spoonhook, and the other the so-called regulation spoon type wherein the spinner or spoon revolves on a shaft, it can be said, without arousing a controversy, that the latter is to be immensely preferred in taking muskellunge to the wobbling type. Personally I do not think that the wobbling spoon can begin to come up to the regulation spoon as a musky killer, this in spite of the fact that many muskies no doubt have been taken on the wobbling spoon. Opposed to this, the great northern pike would rather commit suicide taking a wobbling spoon than be tempted by a regulation spoon, indeed the way the great northern goes for the wobbling spoon is something to marvel at. True, they take the regulation spoon also but it does not inspire them to strike the way the wobbling spoon does. Why there should be this difference in the tastes of these two larger and most important members of the pike family is hard to say, but I believe in the experience of most musky fishermen the facts as stated will be universally agreed upon.

It is certain that Julio T. Buel invented the wobbling type of spoon but it is not so certain that he invented the regulation type spoon that revolves on a shaft. The present head of the J. T. Buel Company says Buel did make it and that patent papers show this fact. Be that as it may this type of regulation spoon did not make any impression on the fishing front till William T. Lowe of Buffalo, New York, went into production of the same around 1883. On Mr. Lowe's death in 1915, the Enterprise Manufacturing Company (the Pfluegers) of Akron, Ohio, took over the Lowe Company and have, for years, produced three types of these regulation spoons, namely, the Lowe Star Spoon, the Lowe Canadian Special, and the Lowe Buffalo spoons. It is interesting to note that the Pflueger Company has never, to my knowledge, advertised or played up these Lowe spoons which is rather odd considering the fact that they certainly are outstanding in the field today and certainly enjoy a prestige that belongs with the Skinner spoons that followed close on the heels of the Lowe product.

The G. M. Skinner Company was producing the Skinner Spoon in the nineties and production was great in the nineteen hundreds up to about 1914. The rage for Skinner spoons

was one of the surprises in the fishing lure field, especially
at that time when comparatively few baits of any kind were
being made. To go fishing without a Skinner spoon in one's
possession was tantamount to going forth without a chalkline by which hand-lining was achieved. In the present day
the Skinner spoon is being put out by the Whittemore Company, Boston, Massachusetts. Specimens now being made
are said to be far superior to those put out some years ago
when the company in question supplied the ten cent stores
with their ware. Not having seen the latter we reserve our
opinion. The Whittemore Company had threatened to hail
the writer into court for stating that the Skinner spoons they
made were of the gauge of tin can material. Later they
wailed that their attorney had stated it was impossible to
bring suit, which is to laugh. However, if it is true that the
present Skinner spoon is made in the same metal gauge
and quality of the old G. M. Skinner spoon, surely it would
demand recommendation.

A feature of the Skinner spoon was its crimped or fluted
tip, obviously on the convex or outside portion of the blade.
There is little doubt but that this had the effect of sending
rays of light shooting out from it. The Pflueger Lowe spoons
have a beaten brass effect, for example the convex tip on
the Canadian Special. The Pflueger Muskill spoon has a
"spotlite" finish, gold or bronze spots on an aluminum background. Now whether these spots twinkle and flash in the
water is a matter open to question. We have never viewed
this lure under water to make sure on the point. This I do
know however, the Pflueger Muskill spoon is just about as
killing a musky spoon as can be found, spots or no spots.
I don't know how many records it has hung up in its day
but I do know that if fishing in Lake of the Woods is any
criterion, you will find just about every fisherman in the
country well supplied with this Muskill spoon. And this
would certainly apply to those old-timers who still fish this
water for better or worse. But note this: in any spoon of
this type as intended for large muskies, be sure that it is
fairly large in size. I would say that the No. 9 and 12 sizes
are both excellent and should be carried, as they will do well
both in trolling and in casting. This would more or less
apply to all standard regulation spoons that revolve on a

shaft. One of the largest of the spoons in this class is the musky standard spoon made by the J. T. Buel Company, Canton, New York. The spoon here is 5 inches in length and two inches wide at widest point. It revolves only so far from the central shaft (1¼ inches) because of two wires soldered to the spoon attached to a central tube or sleeve of brass that goes over the shaft of the spoon. This spoon is ideal for use in trolling in water that is fairly clear of weeds. Our only fault with this Buel Musky spoon has been a too-small feathered ganghook at the business end. This, however, can easily be remedied as bucktail treble hooks can be obtained from the Brainerd Bait Company, St. Paul, Minnesota in natural color or in fancy and mixed colors of red, yellow, white and black. The addition of one of the Brainerd Company's heavy select bucktails, as used on their "bucktail trollers," is suggested.

A spoon that I have been partial to for years and on which I have taken a great number of muskies is what is known as a heavy duty musky spoon. The spoon (picking a typical one) is three inches in length by one and five-eighths inches in width at its widest point. The metal of the spoon, as indicative of its "heavy duty" qualification, is 1/16 inch thick. It revolves on a shaft, has a large bucktail masking the treble; it is deeply cupped but revolves nicely, and has a real silvery gleam in the water. Few companies now make this heavy duty spoon, but the South Bend Company some years ago put out a very choice one; they have now virtually abandoned all standard spoon making. So far as I know the Horrocks-Ibbotson Company still make a heavy duty musky spoon with large bucktail. The Brainerd Bait Company, St. Paul, Minnesota, made heavy duty spoons but they may not now be in production. Pfluegers make no heavy duty spoons. I regard this type spoon as one of the best in the whole battery of musky spoons, but in spite of its genuine effectiveness it seems to be passing out. That, however, happens to all too many excellent baits. One distinct value of the heavy duty spoon is that because of its heft it cuts through the air with bulletlike precision, and is one spoon that you can really get accuracy out of. This is not always true with other spoons which are lighter and which when caught by vagrant air currents are likely to be thrown off course. Not so the heavy duty spoon. It flashes through the air with the greatest of ease to destination in spite of the fact that it is carrying a sizeable bucktail adornment along with it.

One of the truly amazing spoons in the musky field is the Musky-Houn, made by the Marathon Bait Company, Wausau, Wisconsin, which has long been in operation. This bait has hung up more *Field and Stream* records than any other lure. It is provided with a fairly large bucktail at the tail, with a smaller one attached to the shaft above it. Above that is a fluted spinner of the Skinner type, 2 and ¾ inches in length. There is a leaded keel-piece in front, the object of which is to keep the lure riding without turning in the water. The Musky-Houn has the right heft for casting nicely without a maximum of effort; indeed it can be classed along with the heavy duty musky spoon in the accurate division. There is a split ring attached to the crotch of the ganghook of the Musky-Houn that has an excellent purpose, This is a take-off on my idea of soldering a snap (medium to large size) in the crotch of the treble hook. To this snap you can attach a commercially bottled pork-rind strip long enough to stand out two or three inches beyond the bucktail. I might mention that the Louis Johnson commercially bottled rind strips are among the best to be had on the market. For this Musky-Houn spoon lure I think that the Johnson "musky rind" is just about ideal. With this rind addition the Musky-Houn is given just that much more attraction and effectiveness.

For casting a spoon, one never uses more than a one-spoon lure. That is to say, you never use a tandem spoon in casting.

What is the value of the tandem spoon? Sometimes I think that it has much to recommend it and then again I think that the use of two spoons on one shaft is superfluous. So far as I know the Pflueger Company is now the only one making tandem spoons in the standard regulation class. Obviously about the sole purpose of the tandem spoon is for trolling. Possibly there is more flash and glitter to two spoons than one but the reader may be surprised to know how few muskies, to my knowledge, have been taken on such tandem lures. It is rather interesting to state that we have found it a better lake trout lure than a musky lure.

By going deep with the tandem spoon it will really be seized by some of the biggest of the lake trout.

The finish on the spoon that you use for musky fishing is of some little importance. Those who are specialists in musky fishing (and there are those who fish for no other fish), have their spoons silver or gold-plated in plating establishments. In many ways I do not consider silver plating a great advance over nickel plating of the highest grade. Apparently there are many grades of nickel, from a mere film to a coating that will stand actually a test equal to that of silver. Silver will tarnish and needs to be polished at all times to give it a shiny lustrous surface. Most plating establishments can do this job for you in first class shape. Gold plating can also be done, but this of course costs more. As to whether a gold finish is superior to silver or nickel I would not know. Certainly nickel or silver causes a flash that may be comparable to the flash from the glittering sides of a silver-scaled minnow or small fish. As to whether the musky believes it to be a minnow or fish is something no one will ever be able to prove. I think that if one were to pick his spoon in a nickel or silver finish he will get results equal to, if not superior, to any other finish or material. I might call attention to a singular fact. Your spoon lure is good, indifferent or useless according to the brightness of the blade. Chemical action in the water, and certainly more so in some waters than others, may have a deleterious effect on the spoon finish. For this reason it is always well to polish the spoon after use, coat it with pure white vaseline, and wrap a cleansing tissue around it. The habit, fishermen have of throwing a spoon in the tackle box without due attention and care is all too well known.

There are finishes and materials other than silver and nickel such as copper, bronze, aluminum and brass, plus spoons that are made of pearl, that is, shells. It may be expected that we have tried them all, but not one of them has been any better or even equal to nickel and silver finish. The theory that one finish will re-act to better effect on one day and state of weather than another is interesting but has little basis in fact. About all accomplished in the putting out of many finishes is that the makers of spoons are afforded the opportunity of selling more.

Just as in the use of plug lures for muskies, so in spoon
lures, one always meets up with the statement that you need
a gimp or steel wire leader of sorts so that the fish will not
over-strike and hit onto the line as the result of which the
line might be gashed and the fish lost. Yet the least distance between the hook and the eye to which the line ties
in in the musky spoons lying before me on the desk is fully
six inches. That is sufficient space between line and hook
so that it is quite impossible for the fish to over-strike to
hit into the line. Indeed, should a leader be placed on the
spoon it will be quite impossible to cast it because it will
hang down too low at the rod-tip, in fact it will be completely off balance for anything even suggestive of accurate
casting. Of course in trolling, it is possible to have an additional wire leader with a swivel on it to attach to the safety
pin device on the spoon shaft proper. Yet this need not be
a steel or brass wire of over two and one-half inches in
length. A suggestion of importance should be made that
musky fishermen, whether they troll or whether they cast
the spoon, they should examine the various terminal end
devices made by the Bead Chain Company, a Division of
the Ashaway Line & Twine Company, Ashaway, Rhode
Island. The steel bead chain idea is a most successful one,
in that each bead is a swivel in itself. There are so many
of these "end of line" connections put out by this company
that they have to be seen to be appreciated. Their value lies
in the fact that they definitely prevent twisting and kinking of the line, and this is something that anyone using
spoons, either in trolling or casting, is up against. These
steel bead chain devices, often a few inches of beads as a
chain attached to a swivel, in turn attaches to the lure. It
is impossible for the line to twist and kink. The value of
these terminal devices can hardly be exaggerated.

The feathers masking the ganghook on a spoon are often
thought by fishermen to be merely there as a decoration.
As a matter of fact it is highly possible that the original
intention was to use these feathers as a means to preventing
the twisting or kinking of the line, since these feathers form
a type of three-cornered vane and do prevent twisting of
the line. Of course at the same time the feathers act as a
decoration. Because of this, a spoon with a feather vane

will not twist, whereas a spoon with a bucktail, with no
trolling plane facility, will twist the line. In a case of the
sort there is ample need for a bead chain hook-up.

Recapitulation: To summarize on the various lures in the
spoon order that you may have access to is important chiefly
because spoon lures in the regulation type, that revolve on
a shaft, are now comparatively limited in number, which
makes increasingly important the existence of those that
are available.

Wobbling Spoons: I do not consider the wobbling type
of spoon too valuable as a musky spoon although, in due
justice to it, it must be stated that many muskies have been
taken on this type. Best numbers would be the Red Eyed
Wiggler, a wobbling spoon with red-bead eyes, made by
the Hofschneider Corp., Rochester, N. Y., especially that
one in a gold finish. The Lou Eppinger Dardevil spoon
is famous, and recommended, preference red and white
stripes. The Doctor Spoon, large size, is a good one, best
in either gold or nickel finish. It is made by the Brainerd
Bait Company, St. Paul, Minnesota. There are a large number of wobbling spoons on the market, in fact almost a
surfeit of them as compared to the regulation spoons. While
these wobbling spoons are a howling success in the taking
of great northern pike, and a sure killer on lake trout, they
are only fair in taking muskies.

Pflueger Spoons: I have recommended the Lowe Star
Spoons, the Lowe Canadian Special, the Lowe Buffalo
Spoons and the Muskill Spoons. You are not likely to find
these too commonly displayed in the sporting goods stores
for, as stated, these spoons get very little push from the
company. The recommendation would go to all three of
these spoons, both in the single spoon and the double-spoon
or tandem type. In the Muskill type in the Pflueger spoons
the "spotlite" type is a killer, but there are also spoons in
the Muskill order that are plain, without spotlite finish, in
nickel and gold that have real qualifications of greatness
that can well be an investment by the serious minded musky
enthusiast. A suggestion would be to obtain a Pflueger
catalogue to check on these spoons. This can be obtained
by writing the company, The Enterprise Manufacturing
Company (The Pfluegers), Akron, Ohio.

The Skinner Spoon: We have not seen the reconstituted and improved Skinner Spoon now made by H. A. Whittemore Co., Inc., Boston, Mass. If it is made of good quality material and is actually comparable to the old type Skinner Spoon made at Clayton, N. Y., it would be well to invest in the same, using the largest sizes possible.

The Buel Musky Spoon: This is made by the J. T. Buel Company, Canton, N. Y., it is recommended chiefly for trolling as it is difficult to cast. The feathered decoration is not large enough. Substitute a red or gray bucktail. Be sure to use bead chain hook-up on this spoon otherwise you will certainly kink the line.

Heavy Duty Musky Spoons: These have been described. They may be obtained either through the Horrocks-Ibbotson Company, Utica, N. Y., or the Brainerd Bait Company, St. Paul, Minnesota. You are lucky if you can now obtain this type.

The Brainerd Bait Company: It certainly would be best to obtain their catalogue, addressing them: Brainerd Bait Company, 2470 University Avenue, St. Paul, Minnesota. Recommended would be their Ten Thousand Lakes Fluted Trolling Spoons; Gold Bowl Trolling Spoons and their Ten Thousand Lakes Bucktail Trollers. Especial attention is called to their separate bucktail treble hooks, which can be had in both natural and fancy colors and can be had in hook sizes No. 1/0 to 8/0. By being separate these can be applied to any trolling spoon arrangement. They are among the best bucktail trebles made.

The Musky-Houn: This is one of the most famous of the musky spoons and, as stated in the body of the present chapter, has taken more prize-winners than any spoon extant. Made by the Marathon Bait Company, Wausau, Wisconsin, it is especially desirable, as detailed, if a strip of musky sized pork rind is used on it to stand out beyond the bucktail in back. The lure re-acts well when cast, and has a flat lead trolling plane at the head that prevents the bait from turning around and around and so twisting the line. This is a lure that you cannot leave out of your battery of spoons, as it has a reputation in the field second to none!

XVII

LIVE BAIT
FISHING FOR MUSKIES

Whatever may be said for the use of artificial lures in muskellunge fishing the fact should not be lost track of that one finds in the use of live lures, especially minnows and small fish, one of the deadliest of attractors for the great grey warrior of the lakes. Indeed it should not be forgotten that the world's record muskellunge taken by Louis Spray in Chippewa Lake, Wisconsin, which weighed 69 pounds, 11 ounces was caught on none less than a live sucker. Too, let us not forget that a very great number of muskies have been caught by fishermen who have not intentionally been fishing for muskies at all, but have been fishing for walleyed pike, great northern pike or bass as the case may happen to be. This may have been while the fisherman was still-fishing or while trolling. We have known of many large muskies taken on a June-bug spinner rig to which has been attached a four or five inch minnow. The fact remains that if you should ever come in contact with one of these large fish with a live minnow or live fish lure the chances are strong that the fish may sample it, and what happens thereafter is a story that you can indeed write home to your newspaper. We knew a farmer who one time was fishing with a long cane pole and a six or eight inch minnow on a sizeable hook. He was, in fact, after great northern pike in the deep water that dropped off from a point of land, where he had taken many large great northerns before. On this day a big fish of some sort clamped down on his lure and he promptly and powerfully set the hook in the jaws of the fish. However, the fish refused to be brought out of the depths. Realizing that the fish must be an unusually large one the farmer did as he had learned to do before: he threw the pole in the water and let the fish have its way. In a case of the sort the fish cannot pull the pole under, or, if he does, it will bob to the surface again like a cork since the air-filled pockets between the nodes on the bamboo act to float the pole. All this fisherman had to do was lead the fish out into deep water away from the weeds and obstructions and let him wear himself out. This the fish eventually did but it took several hours of see-sawing around before it could be led to a sand beach and there was beached. It weighed no less than 45 pounds. One might gain an idea from this just what to do if, inadvertently, you should happen to hang into a husky one while minnow fishing. And don't think that can't happen while you are minnow fishing for anything from crappies on up to walleyes and great northerns.

The taking of the large muskellunge by Louis Spray, on a large sucker lure is interesting, for a rather outstanding reason. It is obvious that the larger and older a musky becomes, the less able is he to dash hither and yon and seize food with a dash and verve possible only in a far younger and more active fish. We must realize that as a musky gets hulking large in size and weight, and in proportion his food must be taken in a very leisurely fashion, with the minimum of effort. Indeed as such a fish finally becomes blind and incapacitated it becomes a bottom feeder. This is one reason why, in Lake of the Woods, large muskies feed on the underwater reefs, on which they are able to pick up bullheads, also pushing along in their unenlightened way. Too, this is one very obvious and thought-provoking reason why your larger muskies are likely to be taken on surface lures of the floating plug type, popping or puddling as the case may be. Also it is a very, very good reason why you should work any sort of surface lure slowly, for these large fish that are "not long for this world" are slow to move, hence are attracted to the bait on the water which seems to be incapacitated. It is easy to get, hence it is taken. That is surely the reason why a live lure that is fished in a still-fishing manner is so readily taken, and why the slow-fished top-water bait is grabbed off. Very simply they are easy to take.

Bullheads always make good live lures for muskies. If it is possible to obtain these in a large size, that is, up to a foot in length, so much the better. Such lengths are not too difficult for muskies to take. For best results, have a pair of old scissors and clip out the spines in the fins. You'll find the lure will be mouthed and taken without the least trouble when it is found that no spine resistance is met with. It might be mentioned as an afterthought that small bullheads up to six inches in length make amazing killers on black bass. Here, too, the spines are clipped out of the fins.

One value in the use of the bullhead or small catfish lure for muskies lies in the fact that the skin of these fishes is tough as shoe-leather and if a hook is seated under the skin it is almost impossible to dislodge it. Usually in musky fishing when a large bullhead is used, two bare treble hooks can be used. These can be 5/0, 7/0 or 8/0 in size according to the size of the bait. Attach the first treble hook by its eye to a snap at the end of a short bead chain no more than 2½ inches in length. By means of a split ring attach the second ganghook, or treble, to the other end of the bead chain to which the line fastens. If you have an assortment of these bead chain devices it will be easy for you to rig up the proper carrier for these two ganghooks. A steel wire or brass leader about six inches in length is a suggestion in that it might be possible for the fish to contact the line and might gash it, thus causing breakage.

In use, the forward treble hook (of the sort used on a spoonhook lure), is seated with one of the hooks of the treble under the skin and out, taking in about a half inch of skin, just forward of the dorsal (back) fin or somewhat down on the side. The second treble goes further back, somewhere in the area toward the back of the dorsal (back) fin. By this hook arrangement there is little harm done to the bait and it can swim around without much effort. Occasionally as one is fishing, the lure can be moved by raising the rod tip. Some fishermen use large size bobbers in this manner of live lure fishing as the result of which the lure can be kept at mid-depth. But if the lure is too large it will submerge the bobber. This is all right of course if the lure can be kept off of the bottom. It is a case of gauging the size of your bobber or float in accordance with the size of your lure, and that can readily be done.

You will note in the above that the trebles are seated on the side or top-of-back of the bullhead or small catfish in such manner that when the musky strikes it is impossible for him not to get hooked. In fact the hooks are in perfect position for accurate and flawless performance in this respect. When a fish does seize the lure, do not attempt to set the hook, or hooks, at once. The practice of the musky in seizing a live lure is to "run" with it, then stop to turn the lure in the mouth preparatory to swallowing it head first. You can make many a miss and get nothing for your trouble if you set the hook too soon, as you are liable to snatch it out of the mouth of the fish. Usually one sets the hook when the line starts feeding out, proof that the swallowing of the lure or the turning of the lure has been accomplished. Then set the hook or hooks sharply, and repeat this setting performance to leave no chance of the hard interior of the mouth of the fish warding off impalement. In this respect let me again call attention to the bony condition of the interior of the musky's mouth. Save for the corners of the mouth and a rounded and tough rim to the jaws you have little to drive the hooks into. However (and note this

carefully) when you use a live lure you get back deep in
the mouth of the fish, as the result of which you can engage with the gullet and vulnerable places around it. Else
your sole place to get your hook in this fish, as stated, is at
the corners of the mouth, and in the tough cartilege of the
rims of the jaws. If you give the fish plenty of time to get
the live lure with its hooks back far enough toward the
gullet your chance of hooking your fish are increased fully
seventy-five per cent.

Another thing should also be carried in mind and never
forgotten, and that is, always keep your hooks needle sharp.
It is interesting in commenting on this that whereas fishermen do keep the single hooks they use fairly sharp, no one
seems to remember that treble hooks also need sharpening
so that when a fish, such as the musky, is hooked, there will
be no blunt points to prevent impalement. Most hooks used
in trebles are of good quality. But it might be in the sense
of a recommendation to obtain, if possible, Mustad hooks,
which are made in Norway. These not only have spear-
pointed tips that hold a keen needle point, but their
tempered condition puts them easily in the forefront among
all hooks.

While I have given the small catfish and the large sized
bullhead the leadership in the array of live fish lures for
muskies, this does not necessarily mean that these are not
equalled by, or even surpassed by other fish lures. In this
respect the certainty exists that the so-called dog-fish, also
called grindle, bowfin, mudfish and lawyer and technically
known as *Amia calva,* has qualifications of greatness as a
musky and pike lure, indeed I sometimes wonder if there
is a better live lure for this greater member of the pike
family. It is certain that it is found in all musky waters that
I know of, and I do know that muskies will seize upon
them as lures, so on that score it can be reckoned as a
choice live lure. So far as great northern pike are concerned,
they take the dogfish apparently in preference to any other
fish lure offered them. To say the least the dogfish is a
durable, long-lived creature and it is probably the most
voracious killer of walleyed pike, bass and other game fish
in the waters than any other predatory species one could
name outside of the ling or burbot. Its asset is durability;

it is just as fresh after hours of use as when first hooked on. Specimens up to two pounds in weight are just about the best for live bait fishing for muskies. I have heard of larger dogfish being used but if you can get one that is a pound and a half or two pounds you have attraction plus in the lure you use. Practically the same treble hook arrangement can be used as I have described in the small catfish and bullhead hook-up. The skin of the dogfish is very tough and will stand lots of abuse before it breaks its hold on the hook.

During spawning time in the spring when these fish come into the streams to spawn one can take them in numbers in all sizes. They can be kept through the summer in ponds and fed on various rough fish chopped up.

I do not doubt but that burbot or ling, found in northern fresh waters, will respond to excellent effect in musky fishing, and I have heard of them being used, but I doubt if the musky has any actual access to them during the regular fishing season save when they come up to spawn which is in late autumn and through the winter, at which time the musky, while not in hibernation, still is none too active in pursuing a four cornered meal. Too, since the burbot through much of the year is in deep to very deep water it is almost impossible to obtain them as lures for live bait use.

Because the sucker was introduced in the taking of the present world's record musky, by Louis Spray, from Lake Chippewa, in Wisconsin, the limelight has been more or less fixed on this fish as *the* lure *par excellence* for muskies. Maybe this is true, and it may also be true that the musky is very familiar with this pucker-mouthed creature as a food item more or less well identified with its year-'round sustenance. Yet other rough fish in this class also should be examined closely as live lure possibilities. The red-horse, a division of the sucker family, becomes important, and it is found very nearly in every water inhabited by the musky. There are many varieties such as the blacktail redhorse, eastern redhorse, golden redhorse, greater redhorse, northern redhorse, Ohio shorthead redhorse, roundfin redhorse and silver redhorse, all of which are useful if obtainable. While there are a number of varieties of the sucker in its proper

division, the common white sucker, which occurs in much
of the range of the musky, is the variety most used.

Rightly taking its place too, in this musky lure line-up,
is the close relative of the sucker, the buffalo fish, which
involves the bigmouth buffalo fish, the black buffalo fish and
the smallmouth buffalo fish. All of these three members of
the sucker family are potential lures, most useful in from
one and one-half to two pound weight. I have never heard
of the carp being used as a live lure for muskies but there
certainly would be no objection to this fish, although of
course it is not always found in the range of the musky.
Here again, if used, the carp should be not over a pound
and a half to a pound and three-quarters in weight.

On the four varieties of fish mentioned you will find the
skin in no manner equal to the toughness of the catfish,
bullhead and dogfish. So the method of arranging the hooks
should be different obviously to prevent breakage of the
skin. You accomplish the arrangement thus: Take a five-inch
long piece of No. 9 steel wire and twist an eye on either
end of it, being sure that enough of the twist of the wire
is made on the main strand so that it is secure. Since the
hook arrangement is along the top of the side of the lure,
and horizontal, cut a slit a fourth inch long in the skin in
front and one about four inches or so in back in line with it.
Run an ice pick under the skin from the one slit in back to
the one in front, to come out at the forward slit and follow
the path of this insertion with the wire. To the forward eye,
as pushed into the open, attach a very strong split ring,
and then turn on the ring a good treble hook three-
fourths inch across the bend from point to treble stem.
If this is a Mustad hook so much the better. To prevent the
hook from sliding back beyond the slit and into the skin,
turn a one-inch piece of wire through the split ring and
make a turn or twist on it to keep it in place and perpendicular. This will act as a block. To the back eye on the
wire turn on another split ring and turn on a second treble
hook. With a very strong snap on the end of your line,
attach the snap to the split ring and your arrangement is
made. The fish can now be let down into the water to move
about at will and at any depth desired. This arrangement

can hardly be equalled, and of course can also be used as desired on any of the other live fish lures mentioned.

One value of having two gangs, one forward of the region of the dorsal fin and the other toward the back is that you are afforded a far greater chance at hooking your fish by this arrangement. Since the musky hits the lure amidships, that is, across the lure, both treble hooks will at once be inside of its mouth. That, in itself, is important. Two other methods avail themselves. One is to have one large treble hook attached to a snap on a gimp wire leader, the hook to be seated in the jaw of the fish thus letting the lure go where it will. There is no gainsaying the fact that this is a good idea. Since the lure is invariably turned to be swallowed head first by the fish, which is an instinctive process, it is obvious that the treble hook, being lodged in the lip of the lure, will make contact deep down, one obvious reason why it is necessary, in this case, to have a leader, especially of metal, else almost certainly will the jaws of the fish come in contact with the line. The second method would be to have one treble hook, a large one on a wire or gimp leader about six inches in length. The hook (that is, one of the hooks of the treble) is seated just back of the dorsal (back) fin of the bait, into some of the flesh and through the skin. By seating the hook into the back part of the roots of the back fin itself, into the tough cartilege at the base of the spines, one will get a more secure hold on the fish and the hook will not easily tear out. It will be found that the lure will swim around much easier with the hook so placed than if it were lodged in the lip of the lure.

Mention of the use of a snap to attach to either plugs or treble hooks as outlined in live lure fishing calls to mind the fact that these snaps are not always to be relied upon. The best ones are what are known as "large" snaps and these have stiff enough wire so that when pressed down to go into the slot as on a safety pin, they really hold to excellent effect. Medium sized snaps should never be used in musky fishing as they are likely to be insecure. The wire is not stiff enough and they are likely to spring out of the slot, something that happens all too often in plug fishing for bass for which the medium snap is mostly used. One of the most interesting recent developments is a typical snap fitted out with a safety snap guard that absolutely prevents the snap pin or arm from jumping out of the slot. This snap, with guard, is called Caldwell's Safety Snap, protected under U. S. Patent No. 2,523,679 and is made by Caldwell of Canton, New York. In light lure casting and in general bait casting, as for bass, a device of this sort is not needed, but in taking large fish, such as muskies and in all sea fishing, it will be found that this strong safety snap is a must as a protection against disaster when probably the largest fish in your fishing career is finally hooked. I cannot too strongly urge that fishermen try out this Caldwell snap as it answers in a most ingenious manner a very great need. These Caldwell snaps are furnished with a 7½ inch metal, twisted leader. Longer leaders in this twisted type, two feet in length, are also to be had, most excellent of course for musky and salt water trolling.

Knowing where to fish with a live lure for muskies is a matter of great importance. One needs to employ a good-sized bobber, round or oval cork. A fisherman who specialized in live lure fishing for muskies told me one time: "It does not matter how large the float is. Invariably the live lure, which is up to two pounds in weight, will pull the bobber or float under anyhow, but that is all right. It will keep the lure well up in the water and away from the bottom and that's the main thing."

It will be found that the lure when moving around and trying to go to the bottom, will pull the float under but when he pauses the float will come up. If the float is large enough its movement up and down can easily be told. As a rule one should keep the lure five or six feet below the surface and some even suggest a depth for the lure of not over four feet down. The reason for this is that the fish operates fairly high up in the water in its feeding operations and is rarely contacted in deep water, something that is well worth knowing. The best places to fish are not difficult to ascertain. Deep water or drop-offs out from points of land are always excellent because there is always good feeding for muskies off of points. Here the fishing can be conducted by the fisherman on land, but a boat or canoe should be handy to jump into when the actual playing of the fish goes into effect. One of the truly choice spots of course is around the mouths of streams large or small entering a lake. This is probably the most excellent fishing ground of all for muskies. Muskies like to haunt the waters around islands, which is another good lead as to where to find them. A deep water channel between islands or between an island and the mainland has points of known merit to its credit. I remember one year when a fisherman took six muskies in one deepwater channel between two islands. There was a spot in it that had a deep basin or pool. The muskies it seemed visited it on their regular rounds.

Another very likely spot is deep water in inset coves, spots that a musky likes to frequent and which is often made a home. By placing the bait in the center of this pool in a cove and keeping well away from the spot, you are likely to have some interesting experiences, and that is especially true if a murderous old pirate of a musky happens to be hanging out in the neighborhood. Poorest place to look for muskies when live lure fishing is along typical monotonous shores. A musky might pass, but you will find that the occurrence is rather rare.

When your musky is found in a stream the chances are dollars to doughnuts that it will be contacted ninety per cent of the time in pools of the stream, hence, if your fishing were concentrated in the same you would miss out on very few chances. Musky fishing in a stream or river is a sort of hit or miss performance anyhow, and I repeat again that many times muskies are taken while one is engaged in fishing for some other kind of fish, as for walleyed pike or bass. A river, unlike a lake, is a mighty big proposition. You can never tell along the main stretches of it where a musky will be hanging out, but you can almost be certain that the pools, great or small, are excellent spots, with a second best spot being where a tributary stream comes in and where a pool is likely to be formed.

Just as musky fishing in any phase of its attraction can be considered in the sense of a gamble, so certainly must live lure fishing be appraised. Live bait fishing for muskies might be given a title, to wit: "The Long Wait." We know a woman who one time was intent on taking a musky off of a boat dock simply because a musky of great weight was said to make trips up and down the shore at times to look the situation over to see if there were any chops and crullers hanging around that needed attention. In fact this fish, which was alleged to be no less than fifty pounds in weight, was one time seen issuing out from under the dock, strange as it may seem. So the lady in question followed my directions and started fishing with a two pound dogfish with a two-treble hook complement saddled down on its back. I think she had that dogfish on the hook doing duty out from the dock for a matter of two weeks. Then one day it happened. A crude flat piece of insulation cork, much perforated, and about six inches across, was used for the floater. It happened on a day in September when the equinoctial storms were brewing. Looking out of the window she detected no cork on the water and at once let out a scream that brought resort inmates coming on the run. How long the fish had been on was doubtful but it seems that four huskies got on the line and pulled the fish in on a beach near the dock. There was no fancy playing of the big fellow, just a heave ho and a movement toward the timber. Yes, the fish was landed: no less than a forty pounder and a perfect specimen!

Mention has been made in the above that the fish in question was taken in the month of September. This calls to mind a condition in musky fishing that should not be lost track of. As is all too well known the bulk of all musky fishing, or nearly so, takes place in the summer. In the month of August, during what is known as the dog-day season, which lasts sometimes for a matter of ten days or two weeks, the muskies are in that ailing condition previously related anent, during which, if they do not actually lose their teeth, they at least have a most aggravating and sore state of the gums. During this period they do not feed overly much, in fact, as stated, they are often almost emaciated from lack of food. This condition lasts, off and on, in a greater or lesser degree of sensitiveness and distress until the weather in September turns cool and the first frosts take place. Then this mouth of sore gum condition clears up; the gums shrink from a puffed-up shape and become hard; the teeth are rigid; and soon all signs of the mouth ailment will have disappeared. When this comes to pass the fish is ready to make up for lost time and actually seems to feed during every hour of the day. At no time in the year is there such demand for food. Because of this, it would seem that no period in the year is more fitted for the use of live lures than in the autumn. The months of September and October are cases in point, and in the early part of November when Indian Summer was present, I have known some of the largest muskies to have been taken. Let us not forget that the world's record muskellunge caught by Louis Spray, weighing 69 pounds, 11 ounces was taken on the 20th day of October, 1949.

If more musky fishermen would fish during the months of September and October their results would be vastly greater than might be experienced in summer fishing. One might say that there is only one lone musky fisherman in the autumn to every hundred in the summer!

XVIII

FISHING IN THE PADS

In previous chapters the taking of the muskellunge by means of plug lures and various spoonhooks has been covered, also the taking of the great grey warrior by means of live lures, which opens up possibilities in this manner of fishing that should be seriously considered. It is to be admitted that comparatively few care much about live lure fishing; but this does not eliminate the fact that these fish cannot be taken on live lures, probably in greater numbers than is possible by the use of artificial lures.

Mention has been made previously that muskellunge are sometimes taken by fishermen who are fishing for walleyed pike with a June-bug spinner to the single hook of which has been applied a live minnow. If only an occasional musky now and then, or in a blue moon were taken on this lure,

then it might be dismissed as one of those accidental oc-
currences that are hardly to be taken seriously. Yet I have
known of hundreds of muskies (not all large, of course, and
some very small) being taken on the famous June-bug
spinner. Knowing this I am prone to consider it as a lure
that can hardly be left out of the picture. It has its place in
the field of musky lures, although I must confess that very
few recomendations have ever been given it in this respect.
It is thought highly of, yes, as a walleyed pike lure and
great northern pike killer but not as the nemesis of a tribe
of marauding muskies.

Just how this lure ever got the name of "June-bug"
spinner defeats the imagination in finding a correct solution
to the puzzle. Surely there is nothing about it that makes
one think of a May or June beetle, so it is passed along
as an expression that is based on neither fact nor fancy.
As a lure it is spoon or spinner operating on a shaft. In its
most simple form it has a long stemmed hook attached to
the shank, and to this hook the live minnow is affixed for
better or worse. Understand, the hook is not just seated
through the two lips of the minnow. Rather it is passed into
the mouth of the lure, and out at the gill. It is then worked
back outside of the minnow and is hooked into the bait
just back of its dorsal (back) fin. By seating the hook
toward the back of the minnow, short-strikers are nipped
in the bud as it were, and are taken where otherwise they
might snap off the minnow and not get caught.

When mention is made that a live minnow be used in
this manner of fishing, i.e., with a June-bug spinner in combination, it should be understood that if the bait is alive
when placed on the hook it dies almost instantly after the
hook is driven into it. Instead of saying "live" minnow it
would be better to call it a fresh minnow, as dead ones
in the bucket have no value. There is little doubt but that
a fresh minnow as used will leave a fresh fish scent trail in
the water that is closely followed by many fish, and it is
altogether possible that the muskellunge, in common with
the walleyed pike does this very thing. The June-bug
spinner can, of course, be trolled through all manner of
vulnerable musky grounds just as you troll with a spoonhook. It can also be cast from a boat toward shores in

tempting places. This would take in those previously stated nooks and coves, off of points of land, between islands and along submerged reefs or flats, always a good place to cast for muskies. Indeed, I would go so far as to state that the possibilities of the June-bug spinner in the musky field has hardly been appreciated.

Still another manner of fishing for the grey warrior must be appraised else the summation of methods and lures used would be lacking. This manner of fishing applies to the taking of the fish in hazardous places, especially among the pads, reeds, rushes and vegetation in general. There is no gainsaying the fact that muskies at times do seek out the vegetation in which to conduct their feeding, in fact it must be admitted that at some time every day of the fishing season, muskies will spend a certain amount of time feeding in the weeds. To say the least this is a difficult place in which to go after them and yet some of the most hard-bitten muskyteers go into these places without the slightest question, and fish those locations as thoroughly as they would clean shores that have little or no obstructions or detriments either to casting the lure or trolling it. It is because fishing the vegetation and hazardous places seems to the rank and file of the fishermen as a losing proposition from the very start that they turn historic thumbs down on any such foolhardy projects. Doing so they indeed lose out on possibilities they might not come face to face with in other places. The inshore waters may have muskies, but again you may be wasting arm-power and doing no good because the fish may not be there. However, where padded areas are met with, and rushes and grasses prevail, there you are likely to find many a musky hanging out, and such places should be cast out thoroughly, with lures that are especially fitted for this manner of hazard fishing.

Into the picture then comes the pork-rind lure with a type of pork-rind spoon that is more or less common on the market. In bass fishing, using the pork-rind, there is one smaller type of pork-rind spoon that is used, being hardly more than three inches in length. While it is true that these bass spoons, with a pork-rind trailer attached to its single hook, will take muskies and have done so many times, nevertheless the rind spoon for muskies should be larger; in other words, "more of a mouthful." Some of these spoons are five inches or more in length. To give you more or less of a concrete idea what is meant by what we would call a pork-rind spoon suitable for musky fishing, one might select the Johnson Silver Minnow spoon, made by the Louis Johnson Company; their spoons with rind attachments having carved for themselves a most unusual fame in the bass field. The larger Johnson spoons come under the name of "musky spoons" as differing from strictly bass spoons. Being large in size, of course, the regulation pork-rind strips, as used in bass fishing, would be too small to apply to them. So the Johnson Company produced musky rinds that are of a size suitable for use with these larger spoons, indeed the balance of the two for size is very nearly perfect. This is not exactly a new idea, but it is a new enough innovation to not have been introduced too freely in the field as yet. Indeed, I would go so far as to state that there are a great number of musky fishermen who have never seen or used this larger musky pork-rind spoon although being in full knowledge of the value of the small rind spoon when used in bass fishing in the pads and obstructions. If the rind spoon as used in bass fishing has action plus, it might be stated that the musky spoon in this rind class, with its musky rind tail is even more impressive in its dished action and is indeed a delight to look upon.

Never confuse the pork-rind spoon with either the regulation spoon (the kind that revolves on the spoon shaft), or the wobbling spoon which wobbles in an erratic, zig-zag manner from side to side in its prescribed way. The pork-rind spoon is meant to be used with pork-rind strips. It rides the water with rounded portion or convex side down in the water, while the scooped or dished side is up. The single hook, which is attached to the dished or concave side, has a weed guard coming up to its point, as the result of which it comes through the pads and weeds with a good rating as a weedless performer. The invention of the pork-rind spoon did one notable thing, it made it possible to fish the pads, sliding over the tops of them with ease, carrying the rippling, undulating, animated pork-rind along with it. Where this spoon is in a musky size and the rind is cut large in what is known now as a "musky rind," it has an appeal to the old grey warrior that cannot be denied. The Johnson Silver Minnow, as this pork-rind spoon is called, is silver plated and should always be kept well polished. Attention might be called to the fact that this Company also puts out this pork-rind spoon, both in bass and musky size, in a black enameled finish, and is remarkable for the fact that it has proved itself a killer both in bass and in musky fishing.

Fishing the pads and vegetated areas is always a gamble both in bass and musky fishing; you may be able to land the fish you have hooked and you may not. If you are in close proximity of open water the fish should be hurried there as quickly as possible to stage the completion of the catch so far as possible in the unobstructed water. Of course this is easier said than done. The best plan in fishing from a boat when casting the pads is to back the boat toward them instead of running the bow in. This is of great importance inasmuch as the man at the oars is then in position to immediately slap oars into the water and move out into weedfree or padless water. If the bow were pointed in, the boat would have to be turned around to point out before any progress out into the lake could be engineered. This takes time and before the boat is going out the fish will, like as not, be lost. But by backing in it is only the matter of a split minute before the boat is moving out. Then, after setting the hook a number of times, very soundly, to allow of no chance of its not being securely lodged, one puts the bend in the rod and puts the line and its pounds test into action. Your success in taking the fish out of the pads depends entirely how deep in the pads it has been hooked and how great an area of pads you'll have to go through before your mission is accomplished—if it is accomplished. I have known of so many muskies lost in the pads that I am extremely skeptical of the average fisherman being able to hustle a big one out of these confines, especially when caught well within the midst of the conglomeration. On the other hand where a musky is hooked only ten or fifteen feet in the pads from out-lying free water the chances of bringing the fish out are increased in due proportion to the limited area through which the fish has to be horsed. And when I say "horsed" I mean just that. In fact you either horse the fish out or you take no fish at all: it is one of the two. One does not stop to do any fancy playing of the fish. The pressure is applied, and this, in conjunction with the boat going out, serves to get the old brute started moving and that is the main thing. I might mention that this sort of playing of the fish can be spectacular for when forced in this manner by main strength, the fish will take fright and will plunge upward in the air, often his full length. This helps, simply because the fish will churn the pads and cause them to part, along with the swashing side to side action of the tail and body. Before you know it the fish will be completely out of the pads. But remember this; once you have a startled and frightened fish out in clear water, he will fight desperately and you need to keep a taut line on him to assure his final capture. How the fish is landed will be told later on. But remember first, last and all the time when fishing the padded or weeded areas, back the boat toward the area to be cast over else you may commit the folly of losing what may be a world's record fish. And don't think our North American waters cannot produce something that will rival seventy pounds!

There is another lure that burst into prominence years ago that cannot be left out of the musky lure picture, especially as regards the fishing of weeded and padded areas. This lure is the Shannon Twin Spinner, originally put out by our good friend of years ago (now passed into the bourne from which no fisherman returns), William "Smiling Bill" Jamison, the man who invented one of the first of the surface lures to be used in bass fishing, the Coaxer. The first Shannon Spinner was used almost solely for bass fishing. However, the fact that musky fishermen began taking muskies on it in the weeds eventually brought about the making of a musky Shannon Spinner which proved an instantaneous success. Its single hook was masked with feathers or bucktail and there were two weed guard wires that went up to protect the hook point from contact with the weeds. On the end of each of these guard wires was a spinner attached to a small swivel. When reeled these spinners twirl and add fascination and a focal point toward which the attention of the fish is riveted. There is little doubt but that among lures with spinners the Shannon Twin Spinner must take an important place, in fact it is a real threat in musky fishing. In using it in the latter division there should be attached to it a strip of musky rind.

One value of the Shannon Twin Spinner lure is that it slides over and around, and in and out among the pads, reeds, rushes and vegetation in general without picking up a weed. With the Johnson pork-rind spoon it remains one of the very few lures that can be used in fishing the pads and vegetation and should be in every musky fisherman's tackle box looking forward to such time as the great fish are likely to be found, not in open water, but right up there in the thick of it where plugs and spoons with exposed, unprotected trebles prove utterly useless.

While muskellunge will be found off and on through the summer in vegetated locations, particularly among the pads, there is one time one is almost certain to find them plunged into such surroundings, feeding or otherwise bent, and that is during the month of September. Nor does this apply to one section of the country where the musky is found, solely, but, in fact, everywhere in the range of the species. A musky fisherman of long standing told me that after the fish have survived the sore mouth or sore gums condition of the dog-day season in August they will come out of deep water and at once go into the pads; in fact it is in the pads, so he claimed, that they would do their first feeding when they were again in trim condition and stripped for action. He claimed that one September he had taken nineteen muskies, every one of them in the pads and had brought out every last one of those he hooked. So fascinated was he with this September fishing in the pads that he made two trips a year into the north, one in the month of June and the other in September. He stated that if he were given a choice of one best time of the year to fish for muskies he would select September as the best of all. And his fishing, so he said, would be concentrated in the pads entirely. Here is a setting for the prospective musky fisherman to direct his attention and even those dyed-in-the-wool fishermen who have religiously avoided fishing the pads believing them null and void as possible producers!

Add another lure to the list of possible musky killers in the pads, weeds, rushes, etc., I am referring to the Sputterfuss, made by the Arbogast Company, a lure not too well known and not too greatly pushed by the company that makes it. My fishing partner of years standing, Hank Werner, uses this Sputterfuss not only in bass fishing but in musky fishing as well. I do not think that he had ever used it on muskies until one year when several outstanding muskies were taken on it. The Sputterfuss is a lure possessing two revolving propeller type spinners and is meant to be reeled across the water at great speed. In fact according to Hank Werner the reeling should start almost instanteneously with the drop of the lure to the water, since if the lure sinks its skittering motion is lost. That a musky is able to hit this lure as it skips across the water is something that seems impossible, but it is a fact that both bass and muskies are able to catch up with it or intercept it "on the run." The Sputterfuss of course carries out the oldtime skittering method which is still in use to some extent in the eastern part of the country where a strip of pork-rind is used on a single bare hook and is propelled across the pads by means of a long canepole. My suggestion for the use of the Sputterfuss is to hurry the lure over the same track several times if possible to catch any fish that may have come up to the path of the lure to see what it was all about. I known musky fishermen who reel the lure over the same path two or three times.

Some years ago there was put out a lure called the Halik Frog, the same being made in a large size with the object in view of using it in bass fishing. At the time I wrote the manufacturer that it was in a bull-frog size and certainly was too large for bass fishing, as the demand for that species would more nearly be a medium size down to a baby size. The company did make these two smaller sizes. In the meantime there was a place found for the large size, one that I would surely call a "musky frog." If the large Halik Frog proved of little value in bass fishing the same cannot be said to be true so far as muskies were concerned for it accounted for a number of husky specimens and in this way established itself as a lure with distinct value in top-water fishing in the pads for muskies. Now as to whether the muskellunge gathers up frogs in the course of its forays in behalf of finding that four-cornered meal or several of them per day is something rather difficult to say. Such frogs at least are far from numerous in any Ontario portion of the range of the muskellunge if they are to be found at all, especially in a large size, let alone a medium size or small size. However, in areas of the United States in this range of the species such large frogs are to be found. The first time I ascertained the value of the large sized Halik Frog as a musky lure was in Minnesota where, one evening, we were watching a stretch of pads in a cove to detect, if possible, the movement of a fish feeding as we knew that a musky was in this general location. It was, at the time, approaching dusk and it was during the normal time for feeding operations on the part of the fish. We did not have long to wait after paddling the canoe into close proximity of the location, for we detected a heave in the pads that certainly betokened the presence of a large fish, and it was accepted as fact that it was a musky.

It was when I looked in my tackle box that I spotted that bullfrog size Halik Frog, and on the instant I picked it up, having, I believed, found a place to use it and a fish to try it on. I would imagine it was no more than a minute or so before I had my lure attached to the snap and had cast it to the approximate location where I had seen the fish make its disturbance.

Now the Halik Frog is not only weedless but it is so organized that its legs move in a most lifelike manner. You can reel it up on the pads, and gently pull it off, and as it lies on the water put a swimming motion into the legs by working the line. I doubt if a more lifelike lure has ever been made.

The spot to which I cast the lure was right in the middle of the pads. However, as I reeled it out of the pads it encountered an open patch in the pads about six feet across. I am quite sure that the fish followed the lure out from the pads and as it entered the free water and I put action in the legs by means of a jiggling action of the rod tip. Suddenly there was a swirl of water and a smashing strike that virtually engulfed the lure. Luckily the lure was deep enough in the mouth of the fish to allow the hook to become seated firmly in the corner of the jaw. This I made certain by setting the hook not just one time but several times in quick succession. In the meantime the guide had backed the canoe out and with a taut line I got the fish started toward the open water. We did tangle with some pads, but the antics of the fish served to keep the line on the move, as a result of which it did not become wrapped around those tenacious stems. Once out in free water we moved into the bay proper and there tired the fish out and eventually landed it on a sand beach. It weighed 32 pounds, not a large musky, but one with a powerful lot of vim and pugnaciousness to him.

Since that time I have come to look upon the Halik Frog in the large size as a musky lure that packs many possibilities. I have not mentioned this lure among the plug lures as detailed in a previous chapter simply because it belongs in a class by itself. Unlike most all of the plugs it is weedless and therefore can be used in the weeds, which is more than can be said for any of the general run of musky plugs in that they have bare gang hooks and can only be used in open water.

I have mentioned in the above how we fished for this musky at dusk and watched the padded area for evidence of a fish on the move. Let me state that there are two times during the day or around the clock when you will be most likely to find the musky in the pads. That would be in the early morning right after sun-up when, for an hour or so, they are present in the weeded and padded places in sufficient number to make things interesting. Of course, as I stated once before in this book, your average fisherman never gets started fishing until about seven or eight in the morning, hence misses a choice fishing time of the day. For that matter few, if any, guides at any musky camps I have ever been in ever start fishing till eight in the morning, at which time the morning feeding interval is over. At the crack of dawn the muskies are up and at them and those padded areas are really things to study and fish with every care.

Then in the evening you'll find the muskies on the move from twilight on into the dark. I have taken them when it was so gloomy with oncoming darkness that it was difficult to see where the lure fell. The musky is different in this evening fishing than the pike. The latter virtually ceases

feeding near to the period of darkness. It may not be truly
dark until nine or nine-thirty in the evening, and yet the
musky can still be taken then. The pike will have ceased
feeding around six o'clock. So much for the differing nature
of these two related members of the pike family.

Some inveterate fishermen fish the pads and do no casting till they see a fish make a movement or heave. This
is something like "fishing the rise" in dry fly fishing, where
the fisherman waits to mark down a rising fish and aims
to take that fish. The musky fisherman claims that one can
ruin these pad-fishing spots by casting blindly into them,
and of course there is a lot to that. However, if I know the
clan of muskyteers, I do know that not one fisherman in
fifty would be willing to sit and wait for a musky to show
his presence. I have done it, but that is not saying that it
is a demand that you must follow. Mainly, get on the waters
in the very early morning for an hour after sun-up and in
the evening and you will be fishing during the best times
around the clock.

XIX

MISCELLANEOUS
CONSIDERATIONS

I once asked a hard-bitten muskellunge fisherman, who
had pursued the brutes for a lifetime, what he thought was
the most important thing to know about muskellunge fishing. It did not take him more than a moment of concentration to arrive at an answer. He said: "The most important
thing to know about musky fishing is how to land the fish
once you have hooked him!" For the life of me I am not
able to find a more fitting answer to the question propounded. Indeed, it is one thing to get the great grey
warrior to sock the living daylights out of your lure and
quite another to bring that fish out of its native element
that it may be hung up in camp for all men to see and to
go forth and do likewise.

It is not strange that some of the most interesting things I have heard in my day is the manner in which many and various muskellunge have been landed. Possibly one of the oddest experiences I have had myself was on one of the trips I made for years in the Lake of the Woods country with my old guide, Howard Thompson. We were returning from a jaunt north of Lake of the Woods and were coming up through Cedar Lake, into Cedar River which comes out of Kakagi (Crow) Lake. Since those days the Fort Frances-Kenora Highway has made its presence felt in the region and it is not quite as wild as it was at the time of which I speak.

Where Cedar River drops out of Crow Lake there was a shoot or spillway. At the foot of it there was a great pool, and in this pool I had always been able to take some excellent fish, not to forget that one spring when I took an eighteen pound lake trout there. We had landed at the portage about fifty feet from the spillway, and while Howard was making the canoe carry across the portage I took my rod, intending to pick up a fish or two in the pool for our noonday snack. I had hardly arrived at the edge of the spillway (I had been in the shadows of the shore trees), when to my great surprise I saw a large muskellunge move in out of the churned water, a beautiful specimen of his kind and one I would imagine some fisherman would cross a continent to set hook into. What happened certainly happened so fast that it was like unto split-second operations. I had a heavy duty musky spoon with a red bucktail masking the treble on the line. Almost in a flash I cast into the white water and reeled the lure into the clear water in front of the fish. When the spoon came out of the white water, the fish glimpsed it. The fish was taken utterly by surprise, and almost instantly glommed the lure, and he was on.

It was probably what happened the next few seconds that was the interesting part of this whole excitable performance. I set the hook and I had the fish out of his native element before he had a flicker of presentiment as to what had happened. What is more I rushed him up on shore, threw the rod down and fell on him just as he came into action. And if I say that "he came into action" I mean just that. There I was down on top of him while he was threshing around in a manner the like of which I had never seen before and have not seen since. He was as slippery as an eel. He was wrapped around in the line. And over all, arose my call to Howard for immediate help. Howard, coming down over the brow of the ridge, got one fantastic glimpse of what was going on and came helter skelter down to the shore to aid me in this most ridiculous of tasks. Between the two of us we man-handled the critter into submission. As I remember it we could not find the scales to weigh him but I would imagine the fish to have gone close to forty-five pounds. We took a picture and later released the fish. In all my lifetime experience fishing for muskies this stands out as one of the oddest ways of landing a muskellunge that could be imagined, and about the most unorthodox. It is a method of landing one of these fish that I would hardly recommend. I certainly landed that big fellow in less minutes I believe than any fish of that species has ever been removed from wet water!

Much humor is brought to bear in muskellunge fishing, both in the fishing and in the landing of the fish. One year three fishermen from Texas had come to Mantrap Lake in the Park Rapids region of Minnesota to take what is called in that region a "tiger" musky. I am quite sure that the stories they had heard of the struggle one of these fish puts up had very nearly unnerved them and made them, at the outset, almost incapable of meeting with the famous fish. But they persevered and one day while trolling on the west shore of the lake a musky was hooked. So far, so good. Three men in a boat, with one musky for them to land. How were they to do this? They had read everything extant on how to hook a musky but never once had anyone said anything concrete as to how to land the fish. It seemed obvious that the fish should be gotten into the boat. There was a sand beach right before them, but it never occurred to them that the fish could be beached. They felt, come what may, that they must perforce get the fish into the boat. The sum total of their deliberations was that it would be impossible to land it off the side of the boat, as they would not be able to get the fish in that way anyhow, in which of course they may have been right. It was decided that all three should stand on one edge of the boat thus bringing the gunwale down sufficient to draw water over the edge, after which the fish, by main strength of the line and manly muscle, could be skidded over the gunwale and so into the boat proper. So far, so good. But when they all stood on the edge something happened and all three fell into the lake. Luckily the water was not deep and the man holding the rod did not let go of it. He did the first thing that entered his mind when he found that he had a footing on the bottom. He held the rod with one hand and the line with the other and made for shore. Once on shore he continued on up into the woods pulling the fish after him. The line didn't snap because it was a thirty-five pound test line. On the return to camp with the fish (which weighed 21 pounds) the three men, well shaken and hardly able to talk and give a coherent description of their experience, had their pictures taken with the fish. I believe that six or eight rolls of film were utilized before they were content with the deed.

There is another story of a fellow who brought a shotgun along in the boat to put the *quietus* to his catch. While the fish was jumping around in the boat the man fired a charge of shot at the head of the fish just as it made a side lunge. The charge missed the fish but blew an aperture in the boat bottom, and very nearly sank the boat. By stuffing his coat or a portion of it in the hole and shouting for help the brave fisherman was rescued from his distressing predicament.

I believe that the beaching of a muskellunge is one of the best ways of landing it. Of course this is possible only where there is a beach or such condition of shoreline as will permit running the fish up on land. Sometimes sandy beaches do not exist, but a rocky shore, especially a flat, rocky shore, will offer a means to landing the fish. In Lake of the Woods, guides so far as possible beach their fish. First, however, the fish is rowed or paddled around for some time to spend it or cut down on its demonstrativeness. When a musky tires he will usually come to the surface, and if almost spent will swim along with back half out of water. In this paddling or rowing around process, open water free from obstructions, is invariably selected. When the fish shows signs of tiring, a place to land it is selected. If there is a sand beach or flat shore rocks, as in Lake of the Woods, the boat or canoe is run in to shore. Keeping the line taut the fisherman steps out of the boat or canoe, as the case may be, backs away from the shore a matter of ten feet steadily reeling. In the meantime the guide has pulled on a pair of white cotton work-gloves. He takes the line, letting it run through his left hand, holding the right hand ready for the seizure of the fish. By bending low he will not alarm the fish. As the left hand comes to a termination point at the lure, the right hand shoots forwards and catches the fish through the gill cover. Then all in one move the fish is hustled to shore. Lake of the Woods guides are very deft in this practice.

Landing fish in the above manner is much carried out because there are an increasing number of fishermen who return their fish to the water. Where fish are not spared but are killed, a guide will often have the fish brought up close to the boat where a weapon that is called the "headache stick" is brought into action. This is something on the order of a young baseball bat. Once the fish is rapped on the head with this he speedily, if not at once, gives up the ghost. For some reason or other, landing practices in some places is certainly open to question. The shooting of a captured fish in the water, the use of a clincher or hook gaff are other practices that are rightfully frowned upon in most fishing circles. Certainly no gaffed fish can ever be let go. Shooting a fish should be made unlawful everywhere, as it is totally unsportsmanlike. If a person or persons cannot land a musky by main strength and ingenuity, then the fish deserves to have its liberty. Therefore, at no time use gaffs of any kind; do not shoot a captured fish and if you want to let a fish go, do not rap it on the head with a bat or club. Beach the fish, and if you aim to let it go, do not permit it to thresh around on shore as this will scar the fish and cause fungus growth. This is certain to occur during the hot weather of summer, but not during the chilly weather of autumn.

Muskellunge fight at their best from 12 to 20 pounds weight. Indeed, some specimens of the above weight put up a most violent battle, a credit to the species, which probably has served to act as a blanket recommendation of the fish as one of the leading scrappers from fresh or salt water. However, it should be remembered that after a musky increases in weight he loses a considerable amount of his fight and aggressiveness, although I have had them leap clear of water in the thirties of pounds, but this is met with less in fish of over forty pounds. The reason for this is that weight is against them; very simply they are unable to throw themselves out of water as avoirdupois acts as a weight holding them down. Muskies, as a rule, never leap out of water save in shallow places, as on top of reefs where they are able to get purchase on the bottom with the tail which gives them the needed spring to project themselves on high. In deep water this is impossible, one of the reasons why you rarely, if ever, see this occur in deep water while wearing down a big fellow that you have taken. As a musky grows old—and heavy—he slows down and is forced to take his food in a leisurely fashion, and such food as is easy to get. This is one reason why, as in Lake of the Woods, muskellunge work up on the flats and reefs where they are able to accumulate no end of dull-witted suckers and mentally deficient bullheads. At the same time it is one reason why top-water lures, worked fairly slowly, are likely to take some of the largest muskies in the swim. Moving not too fast, the top-water, lure, such as the Mud Puppy, the Hula Popper and the Jitterbug are deadly poison to large muskies, especially if they are worked around the pads in the course of the evening feeding session or in coves which some big fellows are likely to call home.

From my observation I would say that most losses of muskies occur from trying to force the fish while he is yet full of fight and fright. Wearing the fish down by rowing or paddling around and around over a great circle will eventually slow him up and bring him to the surface. That is the time when it is possible to do the beaching with every reason to believe that the venture will be successful.

A question often asked by persons going on canoe trips into the wilderness where muskies are to be met with is: "We do not want to keep any muskies as we would not be able to take them out anyhow. Is there a chance of taking these fish out of water and photographing them with a reasonable possibility that they will live after they are returned to water. We do not want to waste these fish."

That is indeed an interesting question and one that has engrossed much attention in various quarters. The answer of course is that it all depends upon the size of the fish and the condition he is in. Muskies running up to twenty pounds have a tremendous amount of vitality, but as they get heavier the effect on the fish physically, of being hooked, played and landed is anything but advantageous to its health. Too, the state of the weather has to be taken into consideration. During the heat of summer if a muskellunge is played and beached the chances are strong that he will die before any pictures have been taken. If a picture can be taken and the fish immediately returned to water there is some chance of its surviving the ordeal. We have had some experience in this inasmuch as most muskies taken have been returned to the water. One time we worked over a large musky for a half hour before it came alive and swam away. To revive the fish you hold it, back up, in the water and you work the jaws up and down, at the same time agitating and sloshing water into the mouth. If the gill covers open and close there is hope. If they do not do so the chances of saving the fish to release it are very slim. If you hold the fish up with your hand under the gill cover, care should be observed that the gills are not touched or harmed in any way. I only want to observe that this is far from easy to do. If the gills are punctured and blood issues from them the fish has little hope of surviving—at least that has been my observation. The heavier the fish, the harder it is to hold it up without using drastic tactics, something that can be done only if the fish is to be kept. In cool to chilly weather in the autumn the fish will last far longer than otherwise. The musky has great recuperative capacities, but even it will succumb to harsh treatment, scars and injuries and certainly to injured gills which are, after all, the lungs of the fish. In applying artificial resuscitation to a musky, do so in water at least three feet deep. In cool to chilly weather muskies come alive very easily.

Many individuals going into the wilderness on canoe trips seek to save the skin of a muskellunge, by putting it in a pickle and bringing it home. There are directions on how this should be done but it would take up valuable space to explain the needed comprehensive details. Anyone interested in any such plan should visit a taxidermist and obtain thorough details on what to do in skinning out the fish and how to take care of it. In this respect I have read many directions anent skinning out fish to be put in a salt pickle to be brought home for mounting, but usually such directions have been set down by writers who do not know what they are writing about. It is far better to get these details direct from an acknowledged, well versed taxidermist and to follow his suggestions implicitly. It is not an easy thing to do, and that is especially true on a canoe trip where the pounds-total of the outfit militates against any manner of additional over-burden. Invariably, I would say, get your directions from a taxidermist before you set out on a trip, that is if you intend bringing the skin of a large specimen back with you.

That something should be said with regard to the watercraft used in muskellunge fishing is a foregone conclusion since a poor boat cannot be used successfully in properly maneuvering the fish to its capture. All too many boats used are flat-bottomed and "skim" over the water with the speed of a water-logged tug boat. In many cases one has to put up with primitive craft of this sort, especially on waters little fished and where one has to depend upon what an old settler has to offer; that is, unless you bring in your own boat which has everything to recommend it. In this respect I am very partial to the use of the typical canvas-covered car-top boat which has a weight hardly more than that of an aluminum canoe and which can be lodged on top of the car and strapped down in a most satisfactory manner. One of the most used models of this car-top boat (the name CARTOP by the way being the trade-mark of the Penn Yan Boat Company, registered in the U. S. Patent Office) is the standard car-top, same having a length of 12 feet, a width at beam of 45 inches and a stern depth of 36 inches. It will take a 5 h.p. outboard motor and has a weight of 67 pounds. It can either be paddled or can be rowed with oars, the latter by far being the more suitable for all-around muskellunge fishing.

In the class of aluminum boats that will carry to excellent

effect on top of a car of regulation length on typical boat carrying devices is the Aluma Craft, which are light, sturdy and well designed. This Aluma boat is practically unsinkable; the flotation chambers under the seats will support the motor and several passengers even when the boat is filled with water. These are round-bottomed boats, 12 to 14 feet in length, ranging in weight from 110 to 150 pounds. Excellent maneuverability and stability is assured in this type craft and they row with comparative ease, something that is a strong point in their favor.

Much in use in the Lake of the Woods country is a type of canvas covered skiff which possess a desirable width, a flat-bottomed construction having stability, not difficult to row or paddle and able to stand much buffeting by waves. Bettering upon these older boats with their vulnerable canvas covering, always prey to gashes and injury, are the 17 and 19 foot aluminum square-enders made by the Grumman Aircraft Engineering Corporation, and also by the same Company an aluminum boat type which is fifteen feet in length. In the square-enders the 17 foot model has a weight of 81 pounds, a width at beam of 37 inches, a depth of 13 inches and a carrying capacity of 1100 pounds. The 19 foot square-ender has a weight of 113 pounds, a depth of 14 inches and a width at beam of 40 inches, and a carrying capacity of 1550 pounds. Usually on canoes the outboard motor is placed on a bracket on the left-hand side near the stern. In these square-enders the motor is lodged on the square end with the result that the propelling possibilities of the motor are greatly enhansed. The 15 foot Grumman aluminum boat has, as stated, a length of 15 feet, a width at beam of 40 inches, a depth amidship of 14 inches, a width at stern of 31 inches, a bow height of 23 inches with a total boat weight of 110 pounds. In company with the Aluma boat this Grumman boat affords the closest one can get to perfection in actual boats made of aluminum.

One reason why canoes have been used greatly in musky fishing in Lake of the Woods is the fact that their lightness makes it possible for the paddler to expend minimum effort. This means something where a big musky has been hooked and you have to get going in split second timing so that the line can be kept strictly taut and so that the hook cannot be thrown. Before the advent of the Grumman aluminum canoe the canvas covered product held the field to its own, as it did not have any competitors. With the advent of the aluminum product the old canvas covered canoe was crossed out by canoe operators in the north. Most outfitters along the Minnesota-Ontario border, in what is known as the "Canoe Country," are outfitted with the aluminum product. As a result the aluminum canoe has practically replaced the canvas covered canoe. The same might also be said for boats, the Grumman and Aluma type aluminum boats being adopted more or less consistently throughout much of the north country. Ideal for canoe trips and for general muskellunge fishing would be the 18 foot Grumman alumi- um canoe which length is known in both canvas-covered and aluminum as the Guide's Model. In the Grumman type there are two models, the light and the standard. The light Guide's Model weighs 60 pounds, has a width at beam of 36 inches and a depth of 13 inches. Its load capacity is 1158 pounds. The standard model 18-footer has a weight of 78 pounds, a width at beam same as the light model and a like depth. It has a load capacity of 1140 pounds. It will handle outboard motors up to 5.5 h.p., same being attached to a side bracket near the stern of the canoe. This is defi- nitely one of the safest canoes made, flotation being assured by air chambers in either end of the canoe. The canoe will never sink even if filled with water. Added to this is the fact that the almost flat bottom of the Grumman canoe makes for stability of a most noteworthy order. This is of the greatest importance in waters where muskellunge fish- ing is conducted inasmuch as they are sometimes extensive waters where wind and waves demand a boat or canoe able to stand abuse. It might be interesting to state that the muskellunge is often caught during windy and wavy condi- tions, in fact some of the largest of the species are then active and on the move.